A LIFE
IN
DARK PLACES

Paul J. Giannone

Torchflame Books
An imprint of Light Messages

Durham, NC

Copyright © 2019 Paul J. Giannone,
Emergency Management Consultant, LLC
A Life in Dark Places
Paul J. Giannone
paulgiannone2@gmail.com
www.paulgiannone.com
Edited by Darrell Laurent

Published 2019, by Torchflame Books
    an Imprint of Light Messages Publishing
www.lightmessages.com
Durham, NC 27713 USA
SAN: 920-9298

Paperback ISBN: 978-1-61153-334-7
E-book ISBN: 978-1-61153-335-4
Library of Congress Control Number: 2018968561

Except as noted, the photographs are by the author.

This book is dedicated to my daughter Kara and my wife Kate who have inspired me and supported my writing. And to my mother Theresa Eaton, my mother-in-law Myrtle Huntley, my three fathers, my natural father Patsy A. Giannone, my stepfather Glenn C. Eaton and the uncle who helped raise me, Anthony "Tony" Fede and my sister-in-law Karen Huntley Romanow. All have departed this earth now, but they all gave me the building blocks to be a good citizen of this world and are not forgotten.

ACKNOWLEDGEMENTS

Now it is not good for the Christian's health,
to hustle the Aryan brown.
For the Christian riles and the Aryan smiles,
and it weareth the Christian down.
And the end of the fight is a tombstone white,
with the name of the late deceased.
And the epitaph drear:
"A fool lies here who tried to hustle the East."[1]
— Rudyard Kipling and Walcott Balestier,
The Naulahka: a Story of East and West

It is said that in every human being there is at least one story. This may be true, but getting that story out and molding it into something readable is another matter entirely.

First, I would like to thank Wally and Betty Turnbull at Torchflame Books in Durham, NC. My words would have never been printed if these wonderful people had not listened to my passion and read my stories and supported me.

Second there is my editor, Darrell Laurant, who over two years of patience, grammar, spelling correction and my internal frustration has managed to patiently fine-tune *A Life in Dark Places* so it is readable. And through all this we remained friends.

And a cordial nod to Susan Amato who volunteered to be a second set of eyes in the editing process.

Sometimes a mention in the dedication of a book is simply not enough, and this is true for my wife, Kate Huntley, and my daughter, Kara Giannone. They stuck with husband and dad through periods

1   This poem was copied from the *Stars and Stripes Pacific* and written and carried in Paul Giannone's notebooks while serving as an advisor in South Vietnam 1969-71. The words symbolized to Paul the ineptness of American policy and rather than "Aryan lies" shows what those in the Third World need to do to survive in this face of inadequate American policies and programs

of depression, writers block and mood swings. They too were my editors and confidantes as my ghosts arose again when revisiting the "Dark Places" in my life.

And a "Semper Fi" to my friend and counsel Robert "Bob" MacPherson for writing the Introduction to this book. Whenever a former army sergeant can get a decorated retired Marine Colonel to be his friend, you know he must be doing something right in this world.

I would like to recognize Marjorie Rosen, who told my story in Biography Magazine[2] and got the ball rolling in the initial phase of this book. Thanks also to Francis X. McCarthy, my friend since my University of Michigan college days, and Bernie Edelman, a friend in Vietnam and forever after for spending time on the book and encouraging my work. And there is the support group of friends from Rochester and Auburn, New York: Carol and David Hampson, Dianne Defurio, Ted and Paige Herrling, Gary and Peg Salvage, Jim and Helen Burns, John and Mary Marcon, Marge and Bill Tracey, John and Bonnie Gleason, and John and Marcia Spoto.

I have received encouragement and support from my friends in Atlanta, Vince and Mabel Jeffs and Paul and Lynn Harren. In North Carolina, I received support from George and Leslie Small, Chuck and Diane Catotti, Barbara Kennedy and Diego Caballero and my numerous friends from my days at Family Health International. Marketing support from Hillsborough friend Sherry Kinlaw and web support from Jim Musson of Digital Computer Services. And then there are the artists, writer, professors; Allan Harmon, Brian Delate, Marge Harmon-Hemans, and George Haddow.

I have to acknowledge that my inspiration and my base comes from a variety of delightful people from all walks of life, cultures, religions and political beliefs with whom I've had the privilege of walking this planet. The officers and enlisted men of the 2nd and 5th platoons of the 29th Civil Affairs Company, especially Hal Smith, Pat Cariseo, Steve Cunnion, Jim Cormier, Neil O'Leary, Richard Galli and Terry Rumph, provided support and counsel as only brothers-in-arms can. A warm remembrance to Dennis Barker, my civilian supervisor in Vietnam; the people of Vietnam and the countless other countries I have worked in during this haj. I thank you for your friendship, coun-

---

2   Rosen, Marjorie. "Paul Giannone, Life Line to the Desperate and War Ravaged." Biography, April 2002.

sel and compassion. You have all taught me how to see through the fog of war and peace and seek the truth no matter where it brings you. I am a better human being because of you all.

My thanks for the U.S. Army, the Near East Foundation, U.S. Catholic Conference, Family Health International, the American Red Cross, CARE and Centers for Disease Control and Prevention for believing in me as a professional and allowing me the privilege of learning, experiencing and working through these great organizations.

I would also like to acknowledge, thank and commend the field work of the UN agencies, including World Health Organization (WHO), United Nations High Commissioner for Refugees (UNHCR), U.N. Office for the Coordination of Humanitarian Affairs (OCHA) and of U.S. Government agencies such as United States Agency for International Development (USAID). I want to make it perfectly clear that these agencies play a vital role in international humanitarian and development assistance and deserve our individual and our governments backing and support. Some of my stories might be perceived by the reader as anti-UN or anti-USAID, but stories such as the "Gypsy Boy" are a reflection of the failings of individuals, not an organization. In my stories about USAID or CORDS, these organizations are implicated but they are the by-product of a broader systemic problem, a 40-year pattern of American international policy failures that I have repeatedly identified in my work and I optimistically hope someday will be corrected.

I had to take certain writer's liberties with this book. I acknowledge that these are my words and mine only. My writings do not represent the views of the agencies I have worked for. My stories date back more than 40 years and my memory may be flawed, but I have well researched all the hard facts and they will stand the test of time. In some cases I had to compress my stories or time sequences in order to make my words readable.

In Chapter 5, "Don't Mean Nothing," I created the three soldiers targeted by the planted explosive charge. I did this because I wanted the reader to understand that those of us who wear the uniform and take the risks are real people. The men in the chapter are symbolic of many of our fallen who had their lives ahead of them when it was so uselessly taken from them. Too often, then and now, we see the names of our fallen heroes as only statistics in a paper or

TV news program. Veterans do not feel this way. When one of us is killed or injured we feel the bite and the pain.

Kara's birth in 1993 gave me the impetus to continue with a book I started in 1982. I wanted my daughter to know about me in case the worst happened, but I also wanted her to know and understand that the world is a beautiful place filled with many wonderful people. But it would be remiss of me not to acknowledge another great motivating force. I believe in the yin and the yang of this world. There is a dark side and it surrounds us all. I wanted Kara to understand the dark side of life, be able to recognize it and to fight against it. In many respects, what drove me to complete these chapters was the fact that I have seen the dark side too many times in this world and fought against it when I could. I have personally witnessed and been targeted by the hate, the prejudice and the threats. The most painful were those I called friends, and helped them in their careers, only to have them turn on me for ego, promotion and power.

My book acknowledges the extremes in this country and our world that are destroying democracy and humanity. It is both the ultra-conservative and ultra-liberal who are leading us down an evil path. They use names such as God, Buddha, Vishnu, or Allah to hurt others. Some distort our US Constitution and Bill of Rights to support their own agenda and greed for power. These individuals have caused me a great deal of anxiety, a feeling of betrayal and too many sleepless nights, but they will never imprison my humanity, soul or sense of humor.

These people are few in number but have caused a disproportionate amount of suffering in relation to their numbers. I acknowledge them for what they are. They have been my great motivators when I was tired and worn out from my work, for I knew if I said nothing I could not look my family or my fellow human beings in the face again.

To Kara and other readers, I will admit that I am not a writer but a witness. My words are the truth as I know it and my opinion and advice is what it is but it is born out of observation, service and hard work and backed up by my own research. My roots are both blue and green collar. I have put into words for the reader a slice of our history that the government cares not to talk about and the media does not fully report. For those who might care to read my words these are solely my opinion and guidance.

INTRODUCTION

As a former career U.S. military officer and now, after almost two decades of working in humanitarian assistance, I have met a number of exceptional people. They are dedicated, talented and courageous men and women. They work in dangerous environments such as Bosnia, Rwanda, Kosovo, Iraq, Afghanistan, Sudan and Syria. They walk into these places without weapons or the force of a military or governmental strength behind them. They enter mayhem with only the protection of a humanitarian mandate to provide assistance and do "the right thing" for all involved. It is hazardous work. They are too often killed, injured or kidnapped by any number of opposing forces. They are not naïve "do-gooders." They have a deep belief in something intangible. For some, it may be a religious or spiritual foundation. However, for the majority, it has nothing to do with faith. It is a belief that in midst of violence, deprivation, inhumanity and mass destruction, someone needs to "step up." They do not go for adventure, adrenaline or thrills. Those people are quickly discarded. It is a calling. It is a deep consciousness he or she may not understand. It is a draw. It comes from a place that tells them what they need to do to assist.

Of all the people, I have met along this path, Paul Giannone may be the most extraordinary. Certainly, it is because of what he has done. His book details places where most people would never consider going. Some of that territory includes his journeys crossing open plains to reach Kabul under the Taliban; Tehran during the revolution; travels in Sierra Leone and Rwanda and living in the landmine-infested swamps of Sudan.

However, there is an unspoken subtlety to Paul Giannone. As outlined in his book, Paul is a veteran of the Vietnam War. For most, this is an interesting theme throughout his writing. He eloquently speaks to emotions, events and feelings. But, for those of us who made that same trip over the fourteen years of US engagement, he is astounding because he "went back." Those of us who returned started building walls around the war. Over the years, we made the walls higher and reinforced the gates with thicker steel. It wasn't from fear or hatred. It was a way of coping and getting on with life.

The author exposed himself to it all, again. For many of us, our trip was a day-to-day battle with an intrepid, dedicated and skillful enemy. They took casualties. We took casualties. It went on until one way or another your number was up. Paul saw the war from a different perspective. He saw the endless streams of blood soaked and screaming wounded, both enemy and friendly, coming into his consciousness every day. It must have looked like an endless conveyor belt of death and misery. He then had to deal with people who came to Vietnam and the war to participate from their compounds or luxury apartments in Saigon and DaNang. That toll alone, should have broken him.

Yet, he persisted. He volunteered to go back during the Boat People crises as a humanitarian and assisted those kids and their parents who were rescued at sea from their floundering unseaworthy boats. He returned again and again to assist with the reconstruction and rebuilding of the nation. He assisted in the development of pandemic flu plans for the Ministries of Health in Vietnam, Laos and Cambodia; at his own personal risk he visited landmine infected provinces in Cambodia and wrote funded projects to have them removed; and he returned to Hanoi, Vietnam and with a team helped develop a Ministry of Health Emergency Operations Center. He put himself outside the memories of a war and embraced the people. He discarded the politics and ventured into the truest components of humanitarianism. I still marvel at his capacity.

If I picked up this book and looked at the Table of Contents, my first thought would be—"no way. No one could have been to all these places and survived." It is all true. I watched Paul come and go from these places for decades. He has experienced all of this and is remains one of the most dedicated humanitarians I have ever met.

When people speak to me of dignity, decency and courage, I think of Paul Giannone.

—Robert Ingles-Séamus Macpherson,
Colonel USMC (ret)

CONTENTS

Dedication iii

Acknowledgements v

Introduction ix

Déjà Vu 2016 1

The Pit 20

The Child 25

Betrayal on the Street Without Joy 36

"Don't Mean Nothin" 49

The Party 55

The Old Man 67

A Small Victory in a Hamlet Called An Duong 76

A Cold Night in Hell 99

Escape From Tehran..126

Land of the Big PX 137

Falwell's Folly..158

The Day the Music Died 178

What Do We Do When They Come for the Children? 188

The Village of Many Widows 200

The Mutilated of Sierra Leone 206

A Chicken Dinner in Kigali 1998..212

Nuns, Clowns and Refugees..219

The Gypsy Boy 234

The Day the Music Started 240

Hoi Binh at Last 256

Epilogue: Tapestry of My Life 276

The Author 283

DÉJÀ VU 2016

"It's Deja vu all over again."
—Yogi Berra

Syrian refugee baby, with binky at a transit center in Serbia.

The two-year-old baby stared at me from her mother's arms, her eyes devoid of expression. Was she staring at me or through me?

It was 10 degrees below zero in the northern refugee transit site in Serbia. I was freezing, despite being triple layered with hat, thermal long johns, winter wool socks and thermal gloves. The baby was shoeless and sockless with no gloves, clad only in a light parka and light pants.

She and her mother were just getting off a bus, preparing to join the refugees who would be crossing the border into Croatia on their circuitous trek to northern Europe. Soon, mother and child would be surrounded by support staff members who would provide warm clothes, food and protection from the elements. In less than 12 hours they, along with hundreds of other refugees, would cross the border frontier into Croatia.

Once again, I had found myself in the middle of the tragic and chaotic movement of displaced people.

It started with an email on December 23, 2015 from the non-government agency SOS in Vienna. A close friend who now had a senior position at SOS had recommended me. SOS was dealing with the refugee crisis in the Balkans and needed someone with experience.

SOS is a worldwide organization that deals with children. They do a wonderful job at establishing "Children's Villages" in over 100 countries and prepare them for adulthood through education and social interaction. Now they were in the refugee business, due to fate, circumstances, and new directions dictated from SOS International Headquarters in Vienna.

I talked on the phone to the Vienna office before Christmas. SOS International wanted me to travel to the Balkans as soon as possible and asked if I could stay and support operations for three months. Although I had incorporated as a consultant, I was enjoying my retirement and listening to friends and family telling me to retire completely. I was 67 years old.

But then again, it was Christmas time, SOS dealt with women and children, whom I could never turn my back on, I was not doing anything at the time and I had the skill sets.

I talked to my wife, Kate, and my 22 year-old daughter, Kara. The three of us had planned a short family vacation to Nashville after the New Year, yet both were supportive. Kate told me "this is what you do and you must accept this." I called SOS in Vienna and made arrangements to go to the Balkans. As a Christmas gift to SOS and the women and children, I reduced my consultancy rate by 75%. This was not an assignment that I wanted to make money on.

Three days after Christmas, I was on a plane bound for Belgrade, Serbia. My arrival was not warmly welcomed, however, because it seemed the SOS international headquarters had not communicated well with the country's office directors about my arrival.

There were two problems. First, many of the country directors were not thrilled with SOS International's decision to add response to emergencies as a new service. SOS' primary function is building their children's village compounds with numerous, well-constructed houses. In those houses are as many as 8-10 children from the community who have been abandoned, were living on the street or have special needs. In each house there is a professionally trained "SOS parent" whose main duty is to form an "SOS family."

A basic element in an SOS family is that the SOS parent has a solid relationship with each individual child. This work entails, among many other things, addressing the child's past and maintaining contact with the biological families when appropriate.

This is a no-nonsense approach to child raising, geared toward education and career development. In the SOS families, discipline, education or training and household chores are part of the child's daily responsibilities. But there is a lot of love and compassion as well. Adoption is not allowed, and these children have a very successful rate of transitioning to functioning adults in their communities.

The other problem was that the main religions in the Balkans are Roman Catholic and Orthodox Christian. This creates two Christmases (December 25th and January 7th) with New Year's in between. So I arrived in the middle of a long traditional family holiday season

The welcome I received fit the sub-zero temperatures. With my experience, I understood about the communication issues between headquarters and country offices. This is a common problem in many non-government organizations (NGOs). Moreover, as a Roman Catholic I was respectful of the religious issues. Nevertheless, refugees in flight are a 24/7 issue 365 days of the year. There are no holidays, long weekends of leisure, family holidays or days off for a refugee. When an organization involves itself with refugees this is a norm that must be accepted by supervisors and staff.

At any rate, the senior regional SOS management did not have the time to meet with me. I thought of the family Christmas holiday and vacation I had just abandoned but shook this off and focused on the massive job before me. I garnered what transportation and logistics support I could get from the local SOS office and went on a situational assessment of the refugee transit sites in Macedonia, Serbia and Croatia.

I did this mostly by road. Fortunately, the major north-south highways in these countries were excellent and, for the most part, two-lane highways. Still, it was winter, and sometimes we were driving in "white out" conditions. The refugees were mostly from Syria, Iraq and Afghanistan but we also saw some from Somalia and Pakistan and a few other African countries. They arrive in the Balkans mostly from Greece or Turkey, and Macedonia was generally the first stop on the trek north to Europe, with Germany their main target.

The situation was chaotic even before I arrived, to an extent I had never before experienced. In a sense it was almost Biblical (or Quranic), like Moses fleeing his oppressors and miraculously crossing the Red Sea. In this case it was Syrians and Iraqis fleeing oppression and crossing the Mediterranean Sea. Alas, there was no miraculous parting of this body of water and many would drown before reaching what they believed to be the Promised Land.

—Ggia - Wikimedia Commons - CC BY-SA 4.0
Overloaded refugee boat in the Mediterranean heading for Greece.

Only drastic moves would stop this flood, but if a governmental barrier was put up, this human tsunami would seek out the lowest point and go around it. They were desperate to survive and the momentum would not be stopped by borders, barriers, walls, laws or policy.

When I arrived and started my three-country assessment I wondered to myself if we had forgotten everything we had learned these past 40 years. The United Nations High Commission for Refugees (UNHCR)[1] was the UN agency in charge of this operation, joining forces with the governments in the Balkans, the International Organization of Migration[2] (IOM), local and international Red Cross and local and international NGOs. Where were the seasoned professionals with years of experience in Asia, Africa and the Middle East? If they were there I could not find them. It was a new crop of responders and the overused phrase "re-inventing the wheel" hit me at every stop.

Actually, it was worse. Forget reinventing the wheel—the theme seemed to be, let's all push these refugees into Northern Europe as fast as possible without using wheels. Did the UN consider safety, security and family reunification—their mandate—part of the equation?

To be fair, I saw many good things during my journey in the Balkans. First and foremost were the peoples of Serbia, Macedonia and Croatia, especially those young courageous staff members who were thrust into the breech to deal with this refugee crisis. These people were compassionate, kind, flexible and innovative in the face of no training and experience, and willing to live and work under incredibly severe conditions. I was proud to work with them, and, yes, to learn from them. My opinion of the peoples of the Balkans took a radical shift in a short time. They went in my mind's eye from a cold, insensitive Eastern communist bloc, a horrible stereotype, to the incredibly compassionate, family orientated, urbanized, trendy and modern people who make up the Balkans.

Some of these good deeds were truly innovative, for it was hard to deliver social services to people on a race to move to the next northern transit point in 10-12 hours. The unwritten strategy for the refugees was to go through government check points at border crossings and as quickly as possible find transportation and head for the next northern border. What could be provided in such a short space of time?

---

1   The primary purpose at UNHCR is to safeguard the rights and well-being of people who have been forced to flee their countries. They provide critical emergency assistance in the form of clean water, sanitation and healthcare, as well as shelter, blankets, household goods and sometimes food. http://www.unhcr.org/en-us/what-we-do.html.

2   IOM is committed to the principle that humane and orderly migration benefits migrants and society. As the leading international organization for migration, IOM acts with its partners in the international community to: Assist in meeting the growing operational challenges of migration management; advance understanding of migration issues; encourage social and economic development through migration and uphold the human dignity and well-being of migrants. https://www.iomint/mission.

While waiting in a transit site in the Balkans
children draw the fear they had during their escape.

SOS, working with Save the Children and UNICEF and other
agencies, developed "mother safe rooms" where woman and children
could have a few hours of peace and quiet before they moved on.
Nursing mothers could nurse their babies in privacy. Children had a
place to sleep and play while their parents rested or did administrative work. Drawing was popular with the children, although most of
the crayon drawings depicted war and escape. It was heart-breaking.

Diapers, baby formula, snack food and water were available
at the mother safe rooms. They were also often heated and secure,
with the ever-present NGO staff members on guard. When I arrived
at one site, the SOS staff were dressed up as clowns or Santa and
gave toys to the delighted children. It was a sight to see—a field of
smiling children fighting to have a picture taken near Santa and a
clown.

Another new innovation I had never seen before was the cre-
ation of free WI-FY space and rooms. The rooms provided free access
to computers and cell phone charging stations. Refugees could use
the computers or recharge their cell phones and contact family in
the country they had fled letting them know they were safe and their
location or contact friends and family resettled in other countries letting them know they were traveling north. Both the safe rooms and

computer access not only provided needed services but a moment of solace to the refugees in the chaos that surrounded them.

As for the refugees, they did their best under very confusing, exhausting circumstances and were generally respectful. Those outsiders who might question their refugee status had either not looked at what the war had done to cities like Aleppo or simply looked on the event with the coldest hearts possible.

SOS volunteers dress up as Santas and clowns to provide some joy, toys, food and warm clothes to refugee children and their families at Presevo transit site.

Were there terrorists among these refugees? Perhaps, but that is not a sufficient reason to stop the flow of the desperate. Were there Mafia among the Italians who migrated to America in the 20th Century? Possibly, but the higher probability was that Italians were drawn to the Mafia because of the prejudices inflicted upon them by the US population and government. This is a lesson we do not seem to learn as our newest Muslim and Hispanic brothers and sisters sought entrance through the "Golden Door." Did these refugees riot and protest at times? Yes, but only because they were constantly fed conflicting information by various organizations, principally the UN and local governments.

When the world seemed to be turning its back on this crisis, the governments of Macedonia, Serbia and Croatia opened their borders and let this tide of unfortunates pass onto northern Europe as quickly as possible. Students of Balkan history know what took place there in the late 20th century, but sometimes a country and people can turn their focus to good rather than evil. And praise should go to these governments for their efforts and kindness.

I talked to and worked with individuals in those governments who were in charge of immigration, border control, police and the military. All seemed eager to help these destitute people. Was there confusion and misinformation? Of course. The situation was out of control, and these government employees were largely unprepared to deal with the massive scale of the refugee movement thrust on them. Still, they managed to provide compassionate service despite restrictive budgets and a shortage of equipment and personnel.

In discussions with senior leadership in each country, I often found them confused and amazed that so much monetary and physical support was going from the United Nations and the European Union to Greece and Turkey and so little going to the Balkans.

On the negative side, UNHCR's planning was inflexible and disorganized. Weekly coordination meetings were held at all sites, led by the national government, but they usually devolved into long useless "report out" sessions rather than drawing future weekly/daily plans or systems problem solving. Short and long range planning and trending analysis were almost non-existent.

At the transit sites along the northern and southern borders of Macedonia and Serbia and the eastern section of Croatia, refugees were registered by the appropriate national government agency, put through a security screening process and released to the NGO's for food, clothing and limited shelter (often not heated or cooled). The Red Cross, Merlin and other NGO's maintained medical stations, and critically ill refugees were referred to local hospitals.

Under these dire conditions, with few heated sleeping accommodations, the transit sites were only capable of handling 200 refugees at most. At the peak of the migration, however, as many as 1,200 arrived daily. The strategy was then to process refugees as quickly as possible to allow them to continue their northern migration. Speed took the place of security, documentation and family reunification.

However, the registration of a refugee family is an important step in providing security for a family and supports for long term family reunification and resettlement. At each of the five transit sites I visited in Serbia and Macedonia, the average interview time was less than 10 minutes.

As the director for Vietnamese boat people registration in Singapore from 1979 to 1981, I had considerable experience with the 25,000 refugees we processed. A quick family interview for my group was 4-5 hours. A well-documented registration included (1) a complete list of immediate family members traveling in the refugee group to include relationship and dates of birth; (2) a complete list of family members who are living in any country in the world , other than the country they were fleeing; (3) a complete list of family members who are living in the country fled; (4) medical history, problems and needs of the refugee group being interviewed; (5) identification of pregnant women and those handicapped; (6) educational and work backgrounds of adults in the refugee family unit.

There are multiple reasons for an accurate and complete registration. A complete family listing of those traveling in family groups allows immigration officers and NGO's at later destinations know if anyone is missing, or even if an entire family has disappeared. There was no way to determine this in the Balkans operation. While currently the UN is critical of the safety of refugees fleeing through the Balkans[34] it was the UNHCR and IOM who set up and agreed to the systems that put these vulnerable people in harm's way.

Accurate information on family members living overseas or the home country aids the resettlement countries in family reunification. If a refugee has a valid claim for a parent or sibling in another country like Denmark, that family grouping should go to that country. If a person arrives in a country fleeing North Africa and claims a refugee family already resettled, the reunification process is fast and easy—just as long as the new refugee's family registration form matches the ones already resettled. If there is not a match on the forms, this is usually a case of immigration fraud and should be dealt with accordingly. This situation occurred numerous times with Vietnamese boat people.

A listing of health or special needs issues is imperative for those assisting the refugees all along the trek and at final resettlement destinations. If a person has diabetes, heart problems or a wound, the care givers must know that in order to provide proper medication and care. Refugees may not be asked this information

3   "No Safety for Refugee Women on the European Route: Report from the Balkans: Women Refugee Commission, 2016 https://reliefweb.int/sites/reliefweb.int/files/resources/Refugee-Women-on-the-European-Route-Balkans.pdf

4   "UNHCR: refugees face police violence, push-back in the Balkans." UN News 13 January 2017; https://news.un.org/en/audio/2017/01/621602

at a transit site or may not divulge it for fear of slowing their trek to Northern Europe. Education, experience and occupation information is helpful for a refugee once resettled in finding employment or continued education options. While in transit, this information is used by refugee camp managers to find useful volunteers in refugee camp administration. A refugee doctor, nurse, teacher or electrician can be very useful in a refugee or transit camp.

There were other problems in the Balkans. Refugees approaching the southern Macedonia border crossing from Greece would be led to a hole cut in the corrugated borderline fence and not the normal border crossing, which was in sight. There would be a preliminary security screening by Macedonian border security, and then these refugees would be required to walk about a quarter mile, on a very rough path, to the Macedonian transit/processing site. Often NGO staff would escort the refugees down this hazardous route. The refugees walking this road were exposed to the elements such as rain, snow and wind. The road was muddy, full of holes and ruts, making injuries a distinct possibility. They were vulnerable to human traffickers and could have easily been abducted, especially at night.

Initially, this nightmare path was not lighted, forcing many refugees to cover uneven ground in the pitch dark. The refugees had to make a choice on this part of the trek—carry their children or help the elderly or carry the blankets, clothes, water and food given them by relief agencies in Greece. This pathway was littered with the discards of what families needed to survive but could not carry. (It should be noted that refugees too elderly or who could not walk were bused through the normal international border crossing).

I feel that at this point UNHCR and IOM forgot or ignored their mandate about refugee protection, since the easy solution would have been for all refugees to go through the international border crossing between Greece and Macedonia, a modern facility requiring little in upgrades to accommodate refugees. Or, UNHCR or IOM could have arranged for buses to be pre-positioned at the hole in the fence to safely move the refugees to the next transit site.

The same pattern was repeated as refugees crossed the frontier between Macedonia and Serbia, but worse—the trek was on a longer, rougher pathway that was three-quarters of a mile.

Once the refugees cleared the transit processing centers with registration and security screening, they were free to travel using any private transportation available to them. This would mean the use of trains, buses and taxis but at the refugee's expense. It was certainly profitable for private transportation companies, as buses and taxis could be seen lined up for miles waiting to take on vulnerable human cargo. In my 40 years of refugee work I have never seen a situation in which refugees must pay for their own transport to escape oppression. The money they were expending on transport was needed to help them resettle once they reach their final asylum country.

To me, this was always IOM's job but a recent review of the IOM website may explain this change. It stated under its Strategic Focus section that IOM was to provide "secure, reliable, flexible and cost-effective services for persons who require international migration assistance.[5]" I am not sure how "cost-effective" worked its way into a primary dictate of IOM refugee migration planning, displacing safety and security.

I know the Serbian and Macedonian governments were actively trying to regulate price gouging by private transportation companies, but price gouging was occurring. The fact they had to pay at all amazes me. For IOM, was this cost effective? Was it cost effective to allow refugees to cross dangerous border areas on foot, exposed to the elements and human traffickers, and then pay for their own escape?

One of the uglier issues that came to me was how the definition of "refugees" was being used and why this northern migration system existed at all. Somewhere the governments of Macedonia and Serbia decided that travelers arriving from Pakistan, Sudan, Nigeria, Iran or other African or Middle Eastern countries were not "refugees" but "economic migrants," and unbelievably UNHCR appeared to agree.

According to UNHCR, refugees are "someone who has been forced to flee his or her country because of persecution, war, or violence. A refugee has a well-founded fear of persecution for reasons of race, religion, nationality, political opinion or membership in a particular social group. Most likely, they cannot return home or are afraid to do so. War and ethnic, tribal and religious violence are leading causes of refugees fleeing their countries[6]."

By contrast, an economic migrant is "someone who goes to a

---

5   Mission Statement IOM—IOM's Strategic Focus section https://www.iom.int/mission
6   https://www.unrefugees.org/refugee-facts/what-is-a-refugee/

new country because living conditions or opportunities for jobs are not good in their own country[7]." Yet unless there is a complete registration and interview process, how could anyone tell if someone was a refugee or economic migrant?

I watched one heart-breaking scene in which seven or eight Pakistanis were being escorted by Macedonian police back through the hole in the fence to Greece. One man had blood running down the side of his face. If an adolescent girl flees Iran because she is being forced into a marriage she does not want, is she a refugee or economic migrant? According to one account, a Pakistani police officer was deported back to Pakistan even though he and his family had been targeted for death because he came from the wrong religious sect. The UN definition emphasizes that "ethnic, tribal and religious violence are leading causes of refugees fleeing their countries."[8]

From what I have witnessed, this abuse or politicization of the definition of refugee is a worldwide phenomenon. It should stop, and UNHCR is the agency that should be the arbitrator. Instead, it has failed in this mission, in the Balkans and elsewhere in recent history.

Within the first two weeks of my initial assessment of the Balkan transit system, I began to question why the system existed at all. Refugees would arrive in Greece from Turkey or continental Africa and the Middle East. They would then be registered and screened at the southern border of Macedonia before being moved to the northern Macedonia transit site on the Serbian border.

Once at the southern Serbian transit site, they would again go through security screening and registration before they were allowed to move onto the northern Serbian transit site and more bureaucratic administration. I assumed this would happen again in Croatia and Slovenia and then again when they entered Northern Europe. None of this information was physically or electronically passed on along the refugee pipeline to support the refugees or other governments or expedite processing. NGOs did what they could to pass on critical health information but I felt this was inconsistent. The question that kept screaming in my head as I observed this steeple chase for three months was "Why?"

---

7   http://www.infomigrants.net/en/post/1837/how-does-the-united-nations-define-a-refugee

8   The US government and the United Nations should take note that refugees fleeing the violence in Latin America are by international definition "refugees" and act accordingly.

Arrows indicate the refugees' route through the Balkans to Northern Europe.

I checked—at the Greek border there was a rail system that could easily have transported the refugees directly into Europe from Greece on trains. The countries in between would have simply been a pass-through. Moreover, the road system that went north was on par with Europe and America, which made bus convoys possible. A system could have been established in which a very accurate security and registration process led by UNHCR would be completed in Greece. Refugees could then be placed on buses or trains with a UN group leader carrying an accurate manifest of those aboard the transport. Each refugee would carry a dossier of the family registration. Agreements could have been made with Austria, Germany or Hungary to be the main temporary target staging area for these refugee caravans. All the documents could have been electronically forwarded as a security check.

Who wanted this system? Certainly not the governments of Macedonia, Serbia, Croatia, and Slovenia. I began to wonder who the UN was working for—the refugees or the European Union (EU). The transit system or pipeline slowed the refugees' movements, squeezed them economically and put them at more risk.

Another safety and security issue in the northern trek was the train stations themselves. The central Belgrade train terminal did have small numbers of refugees arriving there daily (estimated at around 150) but when we assessed the site there were two beleaguered, freezing Red Cross workers on the lookout for them. How they identified refugees was not determined. The refugee processing site was across a busy intersection with little signage in the terminal giving directions. If refugees missed the Red Cross workers and the signage they were at risk from those who prey on the vulnerable.

Reuters
Dangerous boarding of train by Syrian refugees.

Even worse were the train terminals in Southern Macedonia and Serbia. At these sites there were no supervision, monitoring or system for the loading of refugees on the incoming trains. It was merely survival of the fittest—who could force their way onto a train car. If you were disabled, elderly, or a minor you could be shoved out of the way or onto the tracks. Refugees were vulnerable to abduction at these sites. With no monitoring there was no way of knowing if there were injuries or if refugee families became targets of human traffickers.

Finally, this cumbersome system was stopped, the pipeline collapsed, and deals were cut that refugee camps would be established in Turkey and refugees in the Balkans would be returned to that country[9]. This was a great political victory for the UN and EU but weak in humanitarian principles. Those refugees now in limbo at Balkan transit sites began to disappear from these sites trying to find their own way north. The desperate journey out of Africa was slowed but not stopped[10]. For political expedience the refugees who were still fleeing the horrors of war faced Greek and Turkish internment if they were caught. Or, they might be forced to cut deals for northern transport with those criminals that deal in human trafficking.

And where were the Arabic nations in all of this? What were Saudi Arabia, Iran, the United Arab Republic, Egypt and Oman doing to take in the refugees fleeing Iraq, Afghanistan and Syria? I understand the split between Shiite and Sunni, but these were their Muslim brethren.

After all, according to the one Quran (2:273), "Those needy ones who are wholly wrapped up in the cause of Allah, and who are hindered from moving about the earth in search of their livelihood especially deserve help. He who is unaware of their circumstances supposes them to be wealthy because of their dignified bearing, but you will know them by their countenance, although they do not go about begging of people with importunity. And whatever wealth you will spend on helping them, Allah will know of it."

With the exception of Jordan and possibly Egypt, few Muslim refugees have been taken by Arabic countries. For Saudi Arabia, a nation that prides itself on its Islamic tradition and who imports thousands of immigrant workers from around the world, this makes no sense under Islamic code or the labor market economy. The UN, international governments and the media tried to counter this lack of resettlement offers by indicating that Arabic nations have given a great deal of money, but this issue involves not only economics, but social justice, compassion and religious freedoms. I would ask the Islamic leaders how Mohammad would react to this situation.

Halfway through my tour I was able to get SOS to send me Denny Hamilton, whom I had known for over 10 years. Denny is an expert in emergency operations, and provided the wisdom, energy and support for what I knew had to be done. We arranged for two

---

9   "Has the EU Really Resolved Its Refugee Crisis" The Conversation, https://theconversation. com/has-the-eu-really-solved-its-refugee-crisis-80435; July 7, 2017

10   "The Anguish of Refugees Trapped in the Balkans", Equal Times, May 2018, https://www. equaltimes.org/the-anguish-of-refugees-trapped-in?lang=en#.WuHzJ4jwaUk

classes of 20 SOS field workers and headquarters staff from Macedonia and Serbia to be trained in Belgrade at the Park Hotel on the
basics of emergency management. Both Denny and I felt that these
40 trained staff would be the core team for emergency response in
the Balkans and elsewhere in the world for SOS. The training curric-
ulum could be used as a model worldwide for SOS' new venture into
emergency response.

The training was a great deal of work for Denny and me. We
both had training templates on the subject matter but they had to
be customized to fit Balkan culture, language and government regulations. The two classes we had were superb. As a trainer it is hard to
explain the feeling you get from sharp, engaged participants who are
not too shy to challenge your teaching and tell you what will work
and not work in their working environment. I think trainer and participants learned from each other in the two weeks.

This training was at the end of my tour. I left the work in
Denny's capable hands, but came home physically and mentally
exhausted, haunted by children freezing in the snow and frightened
people being deported back to a homeland that would do them
harm. Still, there were some tender moments—a baby hugging a loaf
of bread as big as her; smiling and exhausted SOS workers going the
extra mile to show compassion and support for beleaguered refugees.

A very warm, happy baby with a loaf of bread at Presevo transit site.

Maybe things would be better in the future, and I felt as though I played at least a small part in that.

At home in Marietta, a medical exam proved the time had taken its toll on me. I had lost weight, my blood pressure was high and I was back on an emotional roller coaster ride. I promised myself, my wife, daughter and friends that I would not go back into the field again.

On May 29, I received an e-mail from the person who recommended me for the position. I thought it would be a thank you for the work, but mostly it was a dressing down. In part of the e-mail, the friend who recommended me for this assignment stated: "From what I have been told from regional and national staff (for right or wrong—I am not the judge, but perception in itself is a real thing) your expectations/demands for support, esp. during the first week(s) have been received as going too far." I was there during the Christmas period and I am sorry refugees do not get holidays off. Was asking for a ride to the transit sites "going too far"?

The e-mail went on to state that "I had expected to use the expertise of you and Denny far beyond Eastern Europe but also in the other two regions affected by the crisis. This apparently was not possible."

So I was criticized after I left by the people who did not want me there in the first place and my friend took their explanation, I suppose, for political expediency.

I mention this incident only because it highlights the reluctance of many NGO's and their leaders to acknowledge any sort of dissent to the status quo. The idea seems to be: "We're trying to do good, so therefore we can't be criticized."

It was obvious from the start of my work that local SOS directors did not like their headquarters' decision to become involved in emergency relief. I came along and told them the paradigm had shifted and they had to do more. I became the target of their anger but as always I smiled and did my job. I assumed that is was easier for SOS headquarters to agree with the local SOS Directors—thus the e-mail—but I did not expect this from a friend.

It was, indeed, deja vu—all over again. But I had my own reward for my work in the Balkans—a long planned trip to Vietnam with my wife Kate and daughter Kara in August. Both had been to Vietnam before with me in my Centers for Disease Control assignment in Hanoi, but this time we would take three weeks visiting my old wartime duty stations in Hoi An and Hue.

I wanted my wife and daughter to see those places that were still etched in my memory. I wanted to drive them through the once-ominous but strikingly picturesque Hai Van pass (translated as Ocean Cloud Pass) that connects Da Nang and Hue. But at these sites, what they witnessed was only peace, beauty and prosperity. I wished for some sort of shadowy, mystical veil I could walk them through, a passage back to my time of the gun. But this was just an aging grunt's foolishness, and I could only observe Kara as she told me what her eyes perceived.

On our last morning in Vietnam, Kate and I were sitting at the trendy "RunMan Bistro" having latte and Vietnamese coffee as a recording of Frank Sinatra crooned to an almost all-Vietnamese clientele. I sat there trying to mesh past and present together, but I couldn't. The country had so dramatically and wonderfully evolved since "our" war that it is hard for me to believe it had happened, and I kept asking myself "how could we have gone to war against these people?"

Most evidence of that war has been scrubbed away. One may see an occasional bunker while traveling in Vietnam, but these are cement and probably from the French War; Americans mostly used sand bags which disintegrated over time. The fighter jet protective revetments[11] remain at the Da Nang airport, but they seem out of place.

My trip back to where I wore a uniform and carried a grease gun and experienced the fear and horror of war provided holistic, visual and sensual healing for me. I thought of what Chief Joseph of the Nez Perce said as he surrendered to the US government: "I will fight no more forever." That is how I felt. I was free of it.

I knew the bad dreams would still come, but seeing the reality of Vietnam today, my PTSD would linger in the shadows of my soul and return to me some nights. The development and prosperity that surrounded us all but extinguished all physical signs of the "American war," and it was truly a lifting of a weight off my chest. I felt more veterans should return here if they could come to Vietnam with an open mind and heart.

---

11   A revetment, in military aviation, is a parking area for one or more aircraft that is surrounded by blast walls on three sides. These walls are as much about protecting neighboring aircraft as it is to protect the aircraft within the revetment.

What was most helpful was walking with my wife and daughter along the same streets where I once carried a weapon. Yes I told them of the bad and good experiences I had, but it was more of a history lesson than the transference of the fear and terror of over 40 years ago.

I was most fascinated watching Kara interacting with the Vietnamese people, trying their food and visiting historic sites. I kept thinking "that's my girl"—like her father, unafraid to engage other cultures and open to new experiences. Kate and I were pros in cross-cultural engagement, since we had lived and visited a number of countries, but there was Kara, walking tall and proud. She knew not to be the stereotypical American tourist, taking the time to be respectful, quiet and polite and listening, learning from what the Vietnamese were so happy to give us.

As I sat there at the bistro, I reflected on my 40 years of work, now at an end. No more wars. No more refugees. In a flash of my mind's eye the past seemed to race by in reverse starting with the Balkans and ending with a skinny, naïve young public health advisor during the Vietnam War. In that 40-year span I had done some good things, helped and trained people, created systems. I had gained many friends, colleagues and associates but had also bucked the system when the truth needed to be told and had, in turn, been betrayed by my employers and some who I thought were trusted friends.

As my speeding clock unwound I was back there for a few seconds. I could almost smell the humidity and blood; feel the damp sand in my uniform. I was lying in that pit again at the Hoi An airport, with artillery flares lighting the sky and death surrounding me.

> It is not the critic who counts, not the man who points out how the strong man stumbled, or where the doer of deeds could have done better. The credit belongs to the man who is actually in the arena; whose face is marred by the dust and sweat and blood; who strives valiantly; who errs and comes short again and again; who knows the great enthusiasms, the great devotions and spends himself in a worthy course; who at best knows in the end the triumph of high achievement, and who at worst, if he fails, at least fails while daring greatly; so that his place shall never be with those cold timid souls who know neither victory or defeat.
>
> —Theodore Roosevelt, (Paris, Sorbonne, 1910)

THE PIT

What difference does it makes to the dead, the orphans and the homeless whether the mad destruction is wrought under the name of totalitarianism or the holy name of liberty and democracy?

—Mahatma Gandhi

Normal daytime medivac, Hoi An "International" air strip 1969.

We had been lying in a washed-out sandy trench alongside the Hoi An military runway for what seemed like an eternity.

Peering cautiously above the rim of that hole, I could see the tracer rounds and parachute flares from a nearby battle, but that fighting was someone else's hell. My hell was at the bottom of the pit.

The bright starlit night and the flares overhead only accentuated the horror. Four badly wounded South Vietnamese soldiers were lying just a few meters from my feet, their lower bodies mangled and bleeding uncontrollably despite the best efforts of a South Vietnamese medic.

Based on the damage, I assumed that this patrol had triggered a Bouncing Betty mine, the kind engineered to spring up out of the ground and explode at waist level. At that height, the shrapnel was dispersed enough to disembowel an entire squad rather than just the man who triggered it.

Or maybe this carnage had come from an American-made Claymore mine. It didn't matter—whatever it was, it had done its job well.

As an Army medic, I'd been brought out to the airstrip along with a radioman to assess the situation and call in a U.S. helicopter to evacuate the wounded if needed. Obviously, this time, it would be needed.

Three of the men looked as if their lower bodies had been ripped open with meat cleavers. As hard as the Vietnamese medic worked, the bleeding didn't stop. I gave him what bandages I had and a tourniquet I carried in my medical aid bag and he used them as proficiently as he could.

The other soldier was the worst. He must have been the one who stepped on the mine, because it had taken off both of his legs above the knee. Everyone's eyes, even those of his wounded comrades, fixated on him.

If there had been any mercy that night, the trauma and shock of the wounds would have knocked this man out. Instead, he lay awake, staring up at the stars, the flares and the tracers. I had been in Nam long enough to recognize that glassiness in the human eye—a sign that death is stalking. He had the look, but that night death would not come quickly.

And then the awful motion started. This half-soldier began to lift his stumps in the air and examine them. He did it slowly, purposefully, repetitively, raising and then lowering them. It was horrible. The chatter on the radio began to increase in volume and intensity as the radioman desperately called for the Medivac chopper.

Summoning a Medivac liftoff was usually pretty mechanical. The radioman would call in the location, the security situation, and the number and disposition of the wounded. Most of the time, a helicopter would be circling above you before you knew it. But not this awful night.

Somewhere out there among the tracers and the flares, Americans were wounded and dying, making four Vietnamese casualties a very low priority for Medivac. The radio operator pleaded to the communications center in our compound back in Hoi An, begging for a chopper. Failing at this, he began to curse and threaten. All the while the half-soldier kept raising and lowering his bloodied, bandaged stumps.

I put my hand on my .45 caliber pistol and began thinking the unthinkable for a medic—taking a life, rather than saving one. What were the odds that the half-soldier would make it out of this pit alive? And even if he did, what would his life be like in his country? The ARVN—the South Vietnamese Army—threw out their broken soldiers like garbage. There was a street in Da Nang near my headquarters lined with thousands of these limbless, obsolete soldiers. They sat in groups talking, smoking, arguing, begging, and waiting. But God only knows what they were waiting for, since the street they lived on led to nowhere. There was no future for such half-soldiers in Vietnam.

The radio operator stared at me through the darkness as I nervously played with the flap holding my pistol in place. He knew what I was contemplating—a quick, short blast of mercy. Instead, I moved my hand away, swore at the radioman and begged him to do whatever he could to get these men out. I began to focus on the firefight off in the distance and avoided the carnage in the pit, as if my staring into the darkness could will the chopper to arrive. The brutal Asian heat seemed to freeze time.

At one point, the half-soldier stopped raising his stumps. We all thought he was dead, but soon the heavy lifting started again.

The radioman finally got a reply that help was on the way. Simultaneously I heard the rotor blades of the incoming Medivac. Time accelerated as I picked up a hand-held strobe light and ran to the center of the corrugated, single-strip runway. I held the powerful flashing beam over my head with one hand and cradled my M-3 grease gun with the other, wanting the pilot to see the face of a "friendly" on the ground even though it might expose me to enemy fire.

Fortunately, no shots rang out, and as the chopper was touching down, the radioman and the Vietnamese medic ran to get the wounded out of the pit and inside the helicopter. The last man out of the pit was the man with no legs. The crew chief of the chopper told us to take him off his stretcher and place him on one already bolted into the helicopter. As we hoisted him up, the prop blast from the helicopter blades shook the stretcher, spraying me with his blood. Then the chopper lifted off.

Without remembering how I got there, I found myself climbing down from my truck back at the Hoi An Military Assistance Command/Vietnam (MAC/V[12]) compound. As I passed the radio shack, a radioman came out and told me that the legless man had died on the way to Da Nang. The pilot called it in. The pilot also wanted to know why "*we* had waited so long to evacuate the wounded."

I was numb. I shook my head and walked away from the radio operator wishing that the sky pilot had been sitting in that awful pit with me the last few hours. The sun was just coming up as I went back to my quarters. I sat in my blood-soaked uniform, drank bourbon until the pain went away, and cried until I could cry no more.

My ghosts, especially the half-man from 1969, came to visit me in the night for years. For the most part, I managed to keep them walled up in the dark recesses of my mind, but the dead always seemed to return. And they were waiting for me in Angola.

I went there in 1997 as part of an international effort seeking ways to reduce or eliminate civilian injuries from buried land mines. Twenty years of war in this country in southwestern Africa had sown 10 million land mines buried among 10 million people, creating a country of the limbless. In Angola you can't walk down any city street or visit any village or school without being confronted by the hobbling victims of these mines. My work in Angola made it impossible to forget that long-ago night in Vietnam—and now, I was adding to the horror with new experiences.

I remember the face of a little girl in a refugee camp in Angola's Bie Province. She was about 10 years old, had only one leg, and walked on crutches.

---

12 U.S. Military Assistance Command, Vietnam (MACV) was a joint-service command of the United States Department of Defense. MACV was created on 8 February 1962. MACV was first implemented to assist the Military Assistance Advisory Group (MAAG) Vietnam, controlling every advisory and assistance effort in Vietnam. https://en.wikipedia. org/wiki/Military Assistance_Command,_Vietnam.

I thought of Kara, my own daughter, growing up in America. What would it be like if some awful thing, buried in the ground years ago, had ripped a limb off her? What if she had to lie in a pit for hours waiting for help to arrive?

Still, if anything like that should happen to my daughter, there would at least be hope. The little girl in Angola had none of that, only the prospect of a life of begging on village streets, an empty life on a journey, down a street, that most likely would go nowhere.

Young refugee mine victim, Bie Province, Angola.

THE CHILD

In many ways, the most tragic figures of the war were those Vietnamese who trusted the Americans and believed in their own responsibility.

—Frances FitzGerald,
*Fire in the Lake:
The Vietnamese and the Americans in Vietnam*

All too often, even now, I find myself standing in the doorway of a cramped, damp and unclean space. I know it lingers only as a nightmare, yet I can still see it, still smell it. I can still feel the fear of those who lived the last moments of their lives there.

The center room of what was ironically called a "prison hospital" was roughly 20 feet long by 12 feet wide, about the size of a large living room. The mold-covered walls of stark concrete surrounded a combination waiting area, nurses' station and examination room. As it all comes back to me, I see again an old wooden desk and chair, a glass medicine instrument cabinet and wooden benches.

Hoi An political prison.

The benches ran along the walls on either side, but no one sat on them. This wasn't allowed—a ridiculous prison rule.

The cabinet held no instruments, no medicines. At the far end of this room, a hospital sheet was draped over a single metal wire strung from one wall to another, forming a flimsy barrier for the patient examination area. The sheet itself was splattered with blood, dirt and what appeared to be bits of skin. An equally filthy and dilapidated ob/gyn examination table sat behind the divider.

Usually, the room before me in this dream is the "female ward." According to prison regulations, it was for women and children under the age of 12, with the ward at the opposite end of the building for males 12 and older. The entire building was permeated with the sour smell of unclean human beings living in close proximity to each other, a smell much worse than that of any refugee camp I have ever visited. This mixed odor of vomit, perspiration and feces oozed out of the doorway openings, mingling with something more bestial and primordial—the aura of fear.

As I stare, the dirty floor of the female ward seems to be alive and moving, and I see that it is covered with bodies. There are no beds. The patients lay on dirty mats on the bare floor. You could hardly put a foot down without stepping on a limb or torso.

Barbed wire covered the barred windows and stretched over the ceiling. This barricade ensured that no one could escape, but its openings also created a perfect nesting ground for the birds whose droppings covered the walls. Along with the obvious signs of rat infestation, this added an animal smell that mixed with that of human misery.

When I return there in my mind or in my dreams, I am rarely alone for long. Almost always, the smiling face of Mr. Quang—the prison commandant—appears at my side. Like most Vietnamese, he was short in stature, with jet-black hair and eyes. His very round face and dark skin made him look more Filipino than Vietnamese and he had a cruel smile and the rough hands of a peasant. This was the man in charge of interrogations.

As a U.S. Army public health adviser, I was assigned to conduct inspections of this facility and bring what medical aid I could to help the prisoners. On my first trip there, I asked Mr. Quang about the capacity of the prison. He hesitated, anticipating my next question, and then replied, "About 400 prisoners."

"How many are in here?" I asked, incredulously.

Smiling again, he informed me that the prison now held approximately 1,400 men, women and children. I would later learn that the figure was closer to 1,600. Mr. Quang shrugged his shoulders and suggested I inspect the holding centers.

It was common knowledge among American troops that every major city and town had at least one political prison—a facility supported by the U.S. government that served to detain political prisoners and gather intelligence about the communist political infrastructure.

Why not? We were at war, weren't we?

At each cell block, hands were thrust out between the iron bars, faces pressed against them. Occasionally I would glimpse a pair of eyes. As I passed close to one of the cells, a little girl reached out and tightly grasped my hand. I knew only a few words of Vietnamese, but it did not take much to understand that this wretched child was in pain and pleading for help.

In the old Errol Flynn movies I constantly watched as a boy, the hero always escaped from the dungeon. At Hoi An Prison, the only possible route to escape appeared to be death.

After just a few minutes, Mr. Quang quickly moved me along to the male section. He did not want me to see any more women and children.

The silent guards unlocked the door, and we walked into a concrete room that could not have measured any more than 10 feet by 10 feet, full of prisoners squatting from shoulder to shoulder. Their ages ranged from about 12 to over 70. So many bodies were crammed into that space that squatting was their only option. There was no room to lie down or even to sit.

As we crossed the threshold of the cell, the prisoners immediately jumped to attention. Several obviously did this with a great deal of pain but they also moved quickly. Fear and torture are great motivators. I asked how many times a day these men were allowed to leave the cell to exercise, bathe, eat and relieve themselves. The response was an abrupt "twice a day for fifteen minutes and a bath once a week." I dared not ask what happened to a man once he could no longer squat.

The next stop was the kitchen, the primary reason for my health inspection. A complaint had gotten to province headquarters, and rumor had it that there were actually queries about the prison coming from Washington.

Among other things, there had been outbreaks of scurvy and beriberi. Both are ancient afflictions with simple cures that have been known for centuries. Scurvy could be corrected by introducing fresh fruit to the diet; beriberi with more grain, yeast or meat. Neither should ever have occurred in a country as lush with vegetation and fowl as Vietnam. When the task was assigned to me, the implication was that this story might make the press if something was not done.

My first glance at the kitchen turned my stomach. It was filthy. The food was thin rice gruel, re-cooked so many times it was difficult to distinguish as rice. The grain offered no vitamin benefit. Looking through the large cooking pots I could see only a few bits and pieces of a substance that might have been fish or meat. An occasional strand of green leafy vegetable floated in the brew. It looked more like vomit than food.

The flies and rats got their portion of the meal long before the prisoners did, so it was no surprise that gastrointestinal problems were rampant in the prison.

Returning to the dispensary, I passed a two-room concrete structure that was entirely surrounded by barbed wire. It looked like an evil birthday cake created in hell. This was where prisoners were tortured.

Some were tortured for information. Many were tortured for the sake of being tortured. There was no significant information or enemy secrets to be had from most of the prisoners, but they still became the victims in an escalating spiral of violence. We seemed to have forgotten that many of these people were the ones we came to protect.

This building did not discriminate. Men, women and children all spent time in the interrogation center.

Back in the dispensary, I set about preparing to see patients. My first was a girl, about sixteen or seventeen. She lay on her back in a corner of the women's ward, her head pressed tightly against one wall and her face towards the other. Her arms and legs flailed about frantically, as if she were in the throes of an epileptic fit. As I approached, she made the most ungodly sound—a combination of pain and horror that came from deep within her small frame and made me shiver as I neared her.

Then I saw that the girl was pregnant—very pregnant, by the look of her. My inexperienced eyes guessed she was already about seven or eight months along. I grabbed her flailing arms and looked at her face. Her eyes were glassy. Drool came out of the side of her mouth. She was unaware of my presence.

Luckily on this trip, a U.S. Navy doctor had accompanied me to the prison and was now in the same ward. I yelled for him, and as he began his examination, I backed away to give him room.

Meanwhile, a male inmate had somehow had made his way to the doorway of the women's ward. He beckoned to me and I walked over. The man was in his late thirties or early forties. He stood bent over, as if looking at his feet, and told me through the use of Pidgin English and Vietnamese that he was in great pain. He kept repeating the Vietnamese term "dau," meaning pain. His head and stomach hurt, he said, and he could not sleep at night.

I examined him and found a long lateral bruise running six inches on either side of his navel. There were several swollen welts on his head. He had obviously been a recent guest at the prison interrogation center.

I was not allowed to supply any medicine, and with none in the dispensary there was little we could do. I could only dispense what I carried in our B-1 unit, the Army term for a combat aid kit. I gently took his arm and gave him as many aspirin as I could, and told him in Vietnamese how to take them. I thought to myself "I would not be able to sleep at night, either, if I were being tortured," but there was nothing more I could do, nothing more I could say.

The doctor called me back to the girl. He sat on his haunches with his stethoscope dangling from his neck. I wanted to see a happy glow on his face, indicative of the fact that we had discovered new life in this place of suffering, yet the smile was not there. He slowly pulled off his stethoscope, handed it to me, and told me to listen to the girl's abdomen.

My untrained ears heard nothing. I looked at him questioningly. What was I supposed to hear? He took his thumb and middle finger and thumped it against the girl's stomach. She screamed and I heard an echo sound. He put his hand on my shoulder and told me that the girl was not pregnant. He calmly explained in layman's terms that the girl had been through some sort of trauma that caused her to literally gasp in large amounts of air. The air was being forced into her stomach, then released only very slowly and very painfully. Consequently her stomach had blown up like an enormous balloon. This was causing a tremendous amount of pain. It also accounted for the eerie noise she was emitting.

We questioned the dispensary matron. She said in Vietnamese/American slang that the girl was "*dinky dau*," meaning crazy. We discreetly questioned some of the patients and learned the truth.

She had been brought to the interrogation center and tortured repeatedly for several days. Her captors had inserted live electrical wires into her vagina. Sometimes they would attach these wires to her ear lobes and electrify her brain. Other times they would drop water on her to intensify the electric current.

Sadly, this was not my first exposure to torture.

Once, at a short-term holding center for POW's near my compound, I saw an elderly woman who broke into uncontrollable spasms whenever she was touched. The senior medic who had accompanied me understood immediately. He shook his head, swore under his breath, and muttered "Electric shock." This old woman had been tortured with electric current, and her "interrogators" were not just Vietnamese. Some were Americans.

I returned to Mr. Quang's prison for periodic inspections over the next six months. Twice, I saw girls under the age of 16 who had been tortured to insanity by electric shock. The interrogators had discovered that women did not stand up to electric shock torture as well as men, and so that became the method of choice for them.

The men got a combination of electric shock, beatings, sexual mutilation and a torture known as "waterboarding." The latter was performed by holding the subject down with a towel over his mouth. Hot soapy water would be forced into his mouth through the towel. The soap would clog up the towel causing the victim to drown or suffocate.

Another method of water torture was to force water up the victim's rectum with a high-powered water hose. The internal organs usually ruptured, causing a slow death by infection or internal bleeding.

It was a Vietnamese version of the Salem witch trials. If an individual was labeled a Viet Cong suspect, he or she was arrested without warrant and made a political prisoner and was then tortured. The torture continued until a confession was wrung out or until the prisoner died. Those who wanted the slightest chance of survival confessed to being a Communist. Often those who confessed were not VC but simply people who wanted to live, and they were unable to provide information on troop and weapons locations, so this, of course, prompted more torture.

In those days it was in vogue in America to display car bumper stickers that read, "POWS NEVER HAVE A NICE DAY." I did not condone the treatment of our POWs by the North Vietnamese, but as a soldier you have to be prepared to be captured. In a combat situation, torture is expected. Here, though, the South Vietnamese and their American counterparts were torturing civilians–a classic case of guilty until proven innocent.

I had heard the counter-arguments before: "But the communists use torture." Of course, they did. But unlike the Americans, the Communists never professed the ideals of human rights and democracy.

Consider the girl whom I mistook for being pregnant in the Hoi An Prison. I personally pursued an answer to that question, and found out that her father had been a member of the political party that opposed the ruling Thieu regime in the 1968 elections. Campaigning at the village level, he was not a Communist but a democratic political opponent, trying to put an end to the rule of the corrupt regime that controlled South Vietnam.

The girl's father boycotted the elections in protest, along with many other Vietnamese. As part of the voting process, each person who voted had his or her ID card stamped. This was done supposedly to prevent people from voting twice. It also identified those who did not vote. To no one's surprise, President Thieu and Vice President Ky won the election in a landslide. One of their first acts to consolidate power was to declare that all the political opposition were Communist, and opposition leaders were immediately arrested.

Phase two was to eliminate the grassroots support of the opposition parties. From that point on, any Vietnamese citizens stopped by security patrols and at government checkpoints were subject to arrest if their ID cards indicated they had not voted. Some were just shot on the spot.

As for the girl's father, he was arrested. So were all his family, a common practice in cases such as this. His daughter was separated from the rest of the family and taken to Hoi An Prison.

When I had learned the full story of the girl's arrest, I approached Commandant Quang. I realized she could not be released by any of my efforts, but I demanded that this girl no longer be tortured. What information could they possibly get from her? For the first time in my career as an adviser, I raised my voice to a Vietnamese. I felt the cards were in my favor, since they so urgently needed my presence to counter any negative press stories on the care of the people at this site. To my amazement, the commandant consented without argument. It was a victory but as it turned out it was a short-lived one. The commandant and I were about to become adversaries in an even more direct way.

The girl was returned to a cell. As best as I could determine she no longer was harmed. I would see her from time to time. Her condition seemed to be improving. I was coming to the prison about two or three times a week now, bringing whatever food or medicines I could. The commandant still would not allow me to stock the prison with supplies because, as he said, "Prisoners are not to live better than war refugees." Soon the girl was transferred to what I was told was a better facility.

Then a woman with a young baby showed up at the dispensary. I discovered them as I entered for an early morning visit. The woman was sitting on the floor with her back against the wall, staring off into space. I estimated her age to be about thirty, and she was terribly thin. Her skin was pale and rubbery like leather, and there were dark circles under her eyes. Her baby lay cradled in her arms, wrapped in filthy rags that obscured any view of the child.

By now, I had arranged for a prison inmate to act as an interpreter. He was a boy in his late teens who most likely had learned his English from U.S. Marines. Every sentence of his started and ended with a colorful expletive. I did not know his name or anything about him. I did not want to know. The less I knew about him the better, because his future was not a bright one.

Through this interpreter, I told the woman not to be afraid, that I needed to look at her baby. The woman did not respond. She did not move. I gently rolled back the soiled cloths. I wasn't surprised this time. I expected what I saw before me.

It was a baby boy, but he looked more like some wounded animal. He was small enough to almost fit in the palm of my hand and he was in a severe state of malnutrition. His skin was stretched over his face and his eyes bulged out. There was little movement or response to touch.

I tested to see if the child would grab my finger if I put it into his hand. I got no response. There was no reaction, either, as I rubbed a pen along the soles of his tiny feet.

My guess was that the baby had been born prematurely, but this was well beyond my medical skills, so I left the prison and returned with another Navy doctor. He confirmed that something had to be done immediately. The best thing would be to transfer the infant to a hospital. He needed to be moved somewhere clean and protected. The horrendous conditions at the prison made this imperative.

I raced to the commandant's office and walked in without waiting to be announced. The commandant said he knew of the woman and child in question, but flatly denied my request to move them. He told me the woman was suspected of being the wife of a prominent Communist party member. There would be no release for her or her child.

I knew what I was facing in trying to move this child out of prison. He and his mother were the by-products of Operation Phoenix, a U.S. government-sponsored endeavor supported heavily by the CIA and intended to identify and eliminate Communist political party cadres in villages and hamlets. It was another program highly praised by American officials for its successes. And it did succeed in eliminating a large portion of the Communist infrastructure. The problem was, it also eliminated many other villagers.

The program became a license to kill, arrest or torture anyone labeled as a communist suspect, and gave an already corrupt Thieu regime carte blanche to remove any of its opposition.

Foolishly, I thought I could rationalize with Quang. How could a baby this young be considered a Communist? How far could the mother and child get in their weakened states if they did try to escape? How did we know this woman was indeed the wife of the person claimed? I never got beyond his malevolent smile.

So urgent was this case that I decided to go over the commandant's head. For the next few days, I went from one office to another at Province Headquarters. Neither the U.S. Province Senior Advisor (PSA) nor the Vietnamese Province Chief would see me, but I'm sure they were aware of my quest. Finally, my CO cautioned me to back off. American public health advisers had no business interfering with the internal affairs of the South Vietnamese government.

In desperation, I returned to the prison and begged Quang to release the child into my custody. I would take full responsibility. I would find a person to care for the child. The mother could stay secured at the prison. The answer was still no.

When I returned to my quarters that evening I was told by my CO that I had been ordered to report to company headquarters in Da Nang to clear up some "administrative matters." I was to leave immediately on the next available helicopter or Air America flight, and plan to be gone about three days.

This was too much of a coincidence. I protested, to no avail. The next morning I was on the early morning Air America flight to Da Nang. The "administrative matters" were negligible, but they kept me in Da Nang for four days.

When I returned to Hoi An, I grabbed my weapon and medical kit and headed for the prison. I drove like a wild man. When I arrived at the prison I checked my weapon according to regulations and ran to the dispensary. I bolted through the main entrance and cut to my left toward the women's ward. The mother and child were gone. I turned and saw the matron. She refused to look me in the eye. I ran to the commandant's office.

Quang was standing behind his desk pouring tea. He was pouring two cups as if I was expected, and before I could say a word he mused, "You know, at times, even I don't like this job."

He continued, "If I didn't do as ordered, like you, I would find myself in a place worse than this."

A pause.

"The baby is dead. It started the night you left. The fever got worse and it went into a coma. I was under strict orders to do nothing. My superiors hoped that, if the father heard of the situation, he might give himself up. He did not. The baby died. The mother has been transferred to Da Nang for security purposes."

I turned on my heel and walked out of that prison, then told my platoon commander that he would have to court-martial me or put me in a combat outfit before I would go back. The illusion that brought me to Vietnam—to help in the fight against our enemies, the Communists—was quickly dissolving. Instead, I had discovered that we were often the enemy.

My first tour there was drawing to a close. I could work in a stateside army hospital until my discharge. I had the opportunity to sign up for a second tour if I wanted and could decide where I wanted to work. There was no reason to stay and many reasons to leave. My life literally depended on it. And yet, I could not leave a place that had so thoroughly defeated me, body and soul, without some personal victory, no matter how small.

I once met a wise old Austrian doctor who had been working for the World Health Organization. He told me that as a public health adviser, my responsibility was exactly that, the health of the public. If I could save one life, make one person's living situation more bearable, then I had fulfilled my duty. I would have accomplished a victory. It was so simple and so positive.

I had some power as a public health adviser in Vietnam. I could use that power to help the people in Vietnam, not necessarily the government of Vietnam. In return, I hoped, the strength and courage of these people might save me a little as well.

My first big threshold in life had been volunteering for the Army, the medical corps and Vietnam. I didn't realize it, but I was standing on an even bigger threshold.

I heard there was an active Vietnamese public health organization in Thua Thien Province. I could work for them if I signed up for a second tour. I decided to stay in Vietnam. The next year would bring me to the heights of what an individual and groups of people could accomplish when working together. It would give me my lifelong career and my own philosophy of what public health and international development meant. I would develop lifelong friendships and learn a great deal about my profession and myself.

Yet all of this came at a cost. The price of my admission to the world of international development was a realization of the depth our own government would stoop to in order to forward its undemocratic agenda, and how ego and the need for power could easily supersede the need to protect the lives of the vulnerable.

I would learn that America was on the verge of losing its first war—and in the process, a pattern was developing that would reap a terrible cost in lives and our national pride for years to come.

BETRAYAL ON
THE STREET WITHOUT JOY

A funeral procession makes its way through the (refugee) camp—two women carrying the covered body of a child on a makeshift stretcher. The other villagers hardly look up to watch it pass." The children die so quickly here," says one woman. "But perhaps it is a better way."

—Frances FitzGerald,
Fire in the Lake:
The Vietnamese and the Americans in Vietnam

The heat seemed alive, as suffocating as a python's coils. The world appeared to us as if we were standing drugged behind a shimmering veil. Uniforms stuck to our bodies. There was no getting used to it.

For the new guys, the heat was a killer. Even before the morning sun came up they began to melt, like popsicles dropped back home on asphalt in August. Along that sandy strip of coast the air shimmered and waved like gas fumes.

Mike O'Neal and I were helping move refugees from their camp back to their original homes in Quang Dien District. A continuous parade of five- and ten-ton military trucks rumbled by our vehicle, heading north, hauling refugees and whatever meager possessions they could carry. The people inside these vehicles reminded me of the aged dairy cattle I used to see being trucked down a country lane in Cayuga County, New York, heading for the slaughterhouse.

I tried to shake off the thought. The Hoi An Prison had been an excellent teacher, and I had learned to know when to pick my fights and when to salute and back off. This operation had the support of the bigwigs in Washington, senior officials in Saigon, Colonel

Chism, the Province Senior Advisor (PSA)[13] and the District Senior Advisor (DSA). No matter how wrong or unethical this game of cards might be, it was four senior aces against two E-5 junior Non-Commissioned Officer (NCO) jokers. The game was fixed. We were going to lose.

SP/5 Paul Giannone holding refugee child in refugee camp
Quang Nam Province 1970.

Still, if I *had* paid attention to all the implications of what was happening that stifling summer day on that isolated sandy strip, I would have lost my sanity. Refugees were becoming my business, and I had no choice but to keep working.

War hates civilians, because civilians get in the way. They take bullets that should be spent on enemies, and then must be rationalized away as "collateral damage." They often question or protest the validity of the war. Refugees form camps and need to be cared for, wasting material, time and manpower. If there were no civilians, wars would be cleaner, easier, less cluttered.

We had tried to eliminate civilians in Vietnam's war zones by creating "free fire zones"— designated areas in which any living thing

---

13   Province Senior Advisor—The PSA was the senior most American advisor in Vietnam at the province level. He/She (who could be military or civilian) coordinated with the senior Vietnamese provincial official on military operations and pacification/social development programs.

was considered an enemy combatant. As viewed through gunsights, rabbits, water buffalo and human beings were all the same. If a soldier saw movement in these zones of death, the orders were "shoot to kill."

Free-fire zones essentially eliminated the villages within their boundaries. The "good" civilians living in these areas had to be moved in order to be "saved," and, more importantly, to allow the army to get at the enemy. Once homes and villages were eliminated, civilians became refugees (or, in military jargon, "Internally Displaced Populations").

Those Vietnamese who refused to move were often killed. The logic of the day was, *if you stayed in these zones, you must be the enemy.* In Quang Nam, the province to the south where I had previously served, this philosophy had created between 60,000 and 80,000 refugees in a single province.

Despite those numbers, however, the Americans and our Vietnamese counterparts blatantly ignored the refugees they created. I had seen the glossy reports on the positive impact of American aid, but I had also witnessed the reality behind these reports. The refugee camps were often horrific places—places of disease, starvation and death.

Indeed, this was one of the great contradictions of the war—avoiding civilian death was America's rationale for free-fire zones and refugee camps, yet both actually killed civilians. In my work, the thought kept rattling in my head: "Weren't these the people we came to save?"

Of course, having large numbers of refugees in every province in Vietnam meant that the enemy controlled the land outside the major cities. One indicator of a war being lost is the inability to control territory, and by 1970 our government was fighting a deteriorating battle in Southeast Asia.

And because the Pentagon was trying (and sometimes succeeding) to convince Congress and the American people that the U.S. was actually winning the conflict. the refugee camps were rarely mentioned. In fact, the medical and food aid designated for these people and written up in glowing reports was often sold on the black market by corrupt South Vietnamese officials. This material often ended up in the hands of our enemy.

Working in refugee camps in Quang Nam Province, I had

struggled against the misappropriation of relief supplies, to no avail. At the time, I was a young, naive army corporal. What could I do? The chain of command for the distribution of refugee assistance involved players too big and too powerful. There were careers and money at stake for all involved, from the U.S. Military Assistant Command/ Vietnam (MAC/V)[14] District Commanders to the PSA, to the big bosses in Saigon.

The passing trucks provided us with a temporary reprieve from the futile fight for survival in which we were engaged. We were trying to save lives, and we were losing.

These trucks had been transporting refugees almost nonstop for more than three weeks, and deep ruts had formed in the clay road from the weight of their cargo. The truck wheels would get lodged in the ruts, and the vehicles could not be detoured from their northern direction, like a train held to its tracks. The drivers had learned to pull the manual throttle on the dashboard out far enough that the trucks would move along on automatic pilot, allowing the driver to sit on the window sill of the driver's seat to catch whatever breeze he could.

From my vantage point in a three-quarter ton truck a few meters off the roadway, I could easily look up at the men in those trucks. They were not so different from soldiers in any war— young men who followed orders and tried to stay alive. If they died, they hoped their sacrifice would mean something. Seeing these young men pass me, I felt old. I was only 22 but my 12 months in-country had accelerated my aging process.

Music blared from one of the trucks. I recognized "People Are Strange" by the Doors, a song that described what a typical GI experienced in Vietnam on a daily basis. "*People are strange, when you're a stranger. Faces look ugly when you're alone. Women seem wicked when you're unwanted. Streets are uneven when you're down.*" [15]

That song had become part of the soundtrack for the war, the lyrics reflecting our feelings. We were rocking to the Doors while the government was marching to John Philip Sousa.

---

14   MAC/V, as the U.S. Military Assistance Command/Vietnam was known, had advisory compounds in each provincial capital in Vietnam with sub-offices at district level. MAC/V fought the "other" war for the hearts and minds of the population. MAC/V advisors worked with the South Vietnamese military, as well as with local police, health, education, agriculture, and public works government agencies.

15   "People Are Strange"; The Doors written by Jim Morrison and Robby Krieger, 1967 Strange Days album

The song receded as the last truck carrying its human cargo passed by. I got up from where I lay on the front seat of my truck, grabbed "Butch" (my M-3 burp gun), and prepared to resume the internal battle.

It had all seemed so easy and logical at first. I was to assist Mike in relocating 8,000 refugees back to their homes using transportation support from Camp Evans, an artillery fire base about ten miles to the west. We were taking these refugees back to villages and farms they had fled seven years before, due to their fear of the Viet Cong and their attempt to escape the free fire zones. Taking people home looked good in print.

Mike and I were billeted with the MAC/V District Team at Quang Dien. A district MAC/V team is responsible for a wide range of activities in its jurisdictional area, including training local defense forces and patrolling the area looking for VC and NVA (North Vietnamese Army regulars). The teams also engaged in "civic action" activities—agricultural projects, health care, refugee assistance, water and sanitation, and education.

Both Mike and I were on attached duty from the 5th Platoon of the 29th Civil Affairs Company based in Hue City, the provincial capital. Though we took our orders from the Commanding Officer (CO) of the MAC/V Quang Dien District team, we were not MAC/V soldiers. From the start of the assignment, Mike and the District MAC/V CO butted heads.

Mike was assigned to work on district-level development projects with special emphasis on refugee assistance. As a medic/public health advisor, I was to assist the South Vietnam District Public Health Service improve the medical programs in the district. I focused on augmenting the local delivery of health care and improving lines of communication and supply between district health clinics and provincial public health headquarters in Hue City. As I had extended for a second tour of duty to work in provincial public health, this was an interim two-month assignment designed to get me district-level experience.

Mike had blond hair, intense blue eyes and a bouncy stride. He emphasized points by increasing the volume of his voice and nodding his head, much like a professor lecturing a student. This pedantic style annoyed me at first, but I soon came to understand that Mike cared intensely for people.

That passion was his greatest strength, but in Vietnam, caring could also prove to be an Achilles' heel. Mike tended to look at things morally instead of militarily, logically instead of politically. Except for this, he was well-suited for his work. He was college-educated, had two years of Peace Corps experience, and was fluent in Vietnamese.

As our supervisor, the District MAC/V CO was the immediate outlet for Mike's indignation. Our commander saw the war as a chance to improve his career, and he saw Mike as a nuisance. Our CO had no sympathy for the Vietnamese and had few abilities or skills in command or military strategy. The men on the 14-man Quang Dien District MAC/V team hated him.

The CO was extremely short and thin. When he wore his helmet all you seemed to see were the helmet and boots, much like a cartoon caricature. He wore a standard-issue military haircut. The only distinguishable things about him were those highly shined and bloused airborne boots. Normally, you did not wear airborne boots like this unless you earned them by jumping out of a plane, but in a war zone people could get away with things like that. The team members called him "Boots" behind his back.

The first time I met Boots I made a mental note to never stand next to him if under enemy attack. In Vietnam, inept leaders like Boots often got killed by "friendly fire." An accidental, or not-so-accidental, M-16 round from someone he had abused could quickly end his tour of duty.

The main conflict between Mike and Boots centered on the relocation of refugees. Mike wanted to keep the refugees where they were for safety reasons. Boots had orders from above to move them to their original home sites. All else aside, I doubted whether Boots cared if we kept the refugees where they were or resettled them on quicksand. But he had his orders.

About two weeks into our assignment, I saw Mike and Boots standing close together near Boots' jeep, engaged in a heated dispute. It was a rare sight, because Boots hardly ever ventured outside the protection of the MAC/V compound. A born coward.

Boots was almost standing on his tiptoes, yelling in Mike's face. Veins were popping out on his shaved head. Spittle burst from his mouth. He was screaming, "Move them! Move these fucking bastards up that goddamned road! You're behind schedule and the

PSA has been on my ass. I don't want any more arguments. And I don't want you going to province headquarters to try and go over my head!"

I saw Mike bite back a smile. Obviously, at 5'3," it wouldn't be hard to go over Boots' head.

Boots kept shouting, "I just want these people moved to the north like the PSA ordered! If you can't do it, I'll replace you. You might just find your educated ass with the grunts in a real war at Dong Ha!"

Although it would be difficult to replace Mike, the threat was real. We both knew that Dong Ha was a "hot" area, under fire day and night. In those days, if you didn't do what the Army brass wanted, they had the power to "disappear" you. Dong Ha had become a graveyard for troublemakers or those who did not conform.

Mike was brave, but he was nobody's fool. No one wanted to die for the corrupt Thieu regime in Saigon, and a dead Mike would do these refugees no good.

In reality, Boots had the power on his side. The threat came from the PSA, the senior American military and civilian advisor for Thua Thien Province. The PSA worked with and advised the senior Vietnamese military and civilian leader for the province—the province chief. Colonel Chism, the PSA for this province, was career military, cast in a John Wayne mold and out to make a name for himself.

He was, therefore, in the perfect position to be made a fool of by his sly and smarter Vietnamese counterparts.

Based on our orders, Mike and I were involved in "winning the hearts and minds" of the Vietnamese people, encouraging the civilian population to support the South Vietnamese government and thus turn against the Communists. It was the "other war," and the flawed, highly political logic behind the refugee movement in Quang Dien District. According to the strategic thinking, the best way to show that the Thieu regime was in control of the countryside was to show that people could live safely and return to their home villages. And so that became our job.

At the tactical or field level, however, it was obvious that the South Vietnamese military was not truly in control of the relocation "home" sites, making them extremely dangerous. The VC owned the land at night, and anyone there after dark who did not support Ho Chi Minh would pay an extreme price.

This was Mike's nightmare. On the surface, it would look very good for Colonel Chism and Boots. In reality, some 8,000 Vietnamese were going to suffer in a very gruesome way.

During the First Indochina War against the Viet Minh, the French colonialists had called the area where the refugees were to be repatriated "*la rue sans joie*," (the street without joy). During that period it had been the operational area of the Viet Minh army's Communist Regiment 95. In his book, "Street Without Joy," Bernard Fall described the "street" as, "...a string of heavily fortified villages along a line of sand dunes and salt marshes stretching from Hue to Quang Tri." It was on this road that during the French War the French military convoy Mobile Group No. 4 was massacred by the Viet-Minh.

The reputation of that desolate swath of land had not dimmed over the years. Local citizens told tales of seeing ghost convoys in the night and of hearing the cries and death screams of long since departed French troops. Now, the Viet Cong occupied the same bunkers and underground storage areas dug nearly two decades earlier.

After his argument with Boots, Mike came back to the truck angrily muttering and pointing to the trucks passing by loaded with refugees.

"Pablo," (he called me Pablo), he asserted, "We're killing these people, you know that, don't you? We may not be pulling the trigger but we are sure as hell killing these people. Look at that, these trucks are filled with women and children, those too old or sick to do anything."

"May God have mercy on them," he said, "and may He damn the ones who got us into this fucking war. Those people don't deserve this. Hell, they're anti-communists! It was these people who came to us for help."

With his bush hat, Mike wiped away the sweat that was running down his face onto an already wet uniform. His blue eyes seemed to cut through me as he continued, almost pleadingly, "Pablo, it doesn't matter who does the killing. The blood is on our hands as well and it will be there forever."

What could I say to him? He was right. The blood was not only on our hands; it permeated our souls.

Still, I replied "It don't mean nothing," which translated into "there's nothing you can do" in the standard GI jargon of the day. "The idea is for us not to get killed in Vietnam. You've done everything you could. Forget it, or it will kill you. Or the Army will kill you. Boots would love to have the excuse to send a wise-ass college kid like you to Dong Ha. If you become fertilizer you are going to do no one any good."

It wasn't that I had no compassion for Mike or these people, but I had been through even worse these past 12 months. I had my ghosts—too many of them, rooms full of them—and like it or not, I was collecting more.

How many refugees had I seen starve to death? I remembered counting five babies dead of malnutrition in one morning in a refugee camp outside of Da Nang. Those babies looked more like rats than humans, and they had died in the shadow of mountains of food supplies.

That food was stored in huge warehouses in Da Nang, pallets wrapped in the familiar red, white and blue packages embossed with the words "Donated by the People of America to the People of Vietnam." The familiar two hands clasping in friendship was also stenciled on the packages.

God, how I hated that symbol! In those days I was much like Mike — angry, frustrated and indignant. The food and medicines in those symbolic wrappings could have saved so many lives. Instead, it was all too often given to corrupt Vietnamese officials who, in turn, sold it on the black market. Rumors even surfaced that it was being sold to the Viet Cong.

It was then that I began to understand the true picture. Yet in response to my official protests, I too was threatened with combat duty. I, too, realized that I could be "disappeared." And, of course, there were always the nightmares of Hoi An Prison to deal with every night.

I looked at Mike again. The trucks and their bewildered occupants kept rolling toward the north in clouds of dust. The procedure for sending them back to their land was simple; it was a plan developed by Mike himself before he understood the implications. The area in Quang Dien District in which the refugee camps were located was in a section of the village of Quang Phuoc. The refugees had been placed in several camps in this region, about a 20-minute ride over a rough road by four-wheel drive military vehicles.

We used vehicles from a transport company at Camp Evans. Our day began at 7:00 A.M. when the trucks would rendezvous in front of our little district MAC/V compound. With our own truck in the lead we would head northeast up a dirt road, crossing a rickety one-lane plank bridge near the hamlet of Cho Ngu Xa. From there we followed an increasingly deteriorating dirt road, crossing terrain that alternated from dune to swamp and back to dune. Our primary assembly point was near the hamlet of Xom Phuoc Lam, located by a huge inland bay. The bay itself was a physical barrier that separated Quang Dien District and the narrow strip of land that formed Huong Dien District and the Gulf of Tonkin. From this point on we moved north along Road 597, which paralleled the bay.

The refugees were to be dropped off along this road near their old home sites. The logistics of the move had been simplified by Mike. He had divided each of the refugee camps into sections. Each section was to amount to one day's work. At the end of each working day Mike informed the village elders and designated section chiefs as to which section would be focused on the next day. It was expected that the designated section would be ready to move when we arrived at 8:00 A.M. Personal items were to be packed and huts disassembled. The trucks would make as many trips a day as necessary to move an entire section. But it was understood that we would have to be back in our compounds before dusk. After dusk we no longer controlled the area.

The question of security was always on our minds. There were Viet Cong units operating in the area and there was always potential for ambush. The threat of hitting a land mine was also extremely high. Road 597 was a road in name only: most of its surface was rutted sand and thick mud. Yet this was the only route.

We had no mine-sweeping equipment. Even if we did, we had no time for such a tedious job. The terrain gave ample protection for anyone who might want to bury a mine on the trail on any night.

The only protection we had from mines was to sit on our flak jackets and pray that if we drove over one, the explosion would not remove our most precious organs. I began having nightmares of my body parts floating by my face after such an explosion, and I often reminded Mike that the flak jacket routine was only a psychological device.

I had seen a ten-ton truck hit a land mine. The rescue party was only able to find a piece of the driver's skull. We were driving a three-quarter-ton truck.

We did take the normal precautions against ambush and sniper fire. All of us carried weapons, bandoleers of extra ammunition and grenades. We wore flak jackets whenever we were not sitting on them. We looked the part of soldiers, but we weren't. Not really. If we were ambushed, it would be by professionals, and most likely they would outnumber us ten to one. The chance for survival would be nil.

Whenever I made my joke about the flak jackets Mike would look at me and tell me to "look mean." How could I look mean? I was too scared to look mean.

Eyeing the terrain as we drove along, Mike and I would pick out the points we thought excellent for an ambush, but the Viet Cong were cleverer than we imagined. The ambush was never sprung. Mines were never laid. We should have foreseen what that meant. There were clear signs of what was to come even on the very first day of resettling refugees. The Vietnamese officials from the provincial and district governments were great ones for taking credit. But they were conspicuously absent from the scene during the official opening ceremonies for the refugee move.

The villagers refused at first to start packing, or packed haphazardly. Their reluctance and foot-dragging on being returned to their "real" homes ought to have been another warning to us, along with the cold, angry stares that greeted us each morning. I began to feel that I was a member of an army of occupation that was imposing its will on the people, rather than a force that had come to a country to offer its citizens freedom from Communist rule.

Today was no different than any of the others. We would arrive at the pick-up points to find the refugees had done little to prepare for the move. Every step we made seemed to be held up by intentional delays that quickly escalated into open hostility. While opposed to the move, Mike had followed orders and done everything in his power to complete the move on time, even if that meant yelling at the villagers and forcibly loading their possessions onto the trucks. Mike acted as a good soldier, but the seemingly cruel manner in which he had to behave was ripping him apart.

Up to that point, I felt my main function was to provide medical assistance to the refugees as well as to back up Mike in case of an ambush. I now had a new responsibility — guarding his back in case the refugees turned on him. We, not the Viet Cong, had become the enemy. Each day it took an increasing amount of coercion and force to get the people to pack up and move out. As each day passed with no sign of the usual officious Vietnamese district bureaucrats, the bad taste in our mouths worsened.

Mike and I couldn't blame these people—hell, we couldn't blame them if they did turn on us. We were moving them into a region that we admittedly could not control. We were forcing them back to their enemy, the enemy they had fled. Moreover, the move was occurring at the worst possible time of the year.

For years, these people had cultivated the land near their refugee camps. The rice fields near these camps needed to be constantly tended and irrigated, and now we were moving them away from their food source. Who would feed them now? The South Vietnamese government? Experience told me that this would never happen. The Communists? Not a chance. We were moving these people into an area where they faced ether a quick death at the hands of the Viet Cong or a slow death from starvation.

To add salt to the wound, I heard rumors that the absentee landlords of the lands the refugees had fled expected seven years' back rent from them. The refugees also were still paying rent for the land they tilled at the refugee sites. The line between liberator and enemy became increasingly muddy.

About a week after we deposited the first refugees at the relocation site, the Viet Cong began skillfully applying the pressure. Every few evenings, sometimes late into the night, they dropped mortar rounds in or near the relocated villages. I heard of no deaths or wounded. But killing was not necessary. The crack of the mortar shells hitting the ground was enough. Like the howl of a beast breaking the silence of the deadly night, each explosion said to these people, "We are out here, waiting."

The villagers asked a local Army of the Republic of Vietnam (ARVN) unit for help. The ARVN did nothing. It was certain that, after we completed the move, the Viet Cong would move into the village. The village leaders would likely be tortured and killed. The villagers made the mistake of choosing the wrong side to protect them. In the end, the people who had chosen democracy over communism would be forced to capitulate to their new masters.

Mike had anticipated the situation. On his days off, he drove back to Hue City to try and stop the insanity. He discussed, pleaded and begged—all to no avail. Boots wanted it. Colonel Chism wanted it. And President Nixon and our government wanted it. And so the move was completed.

On September 20, 1970 *Stars and Stripes Pacific* ran a two-page photo story on the refugee move in northern Thua Thien Province. The title was "New Security Brings Life to Street Without Joy."

Conspicuously missing from this glowing, apocryphal article were the facts—the suffering, the terror, the likely cost in human lives.

The "Street Without Joy" was a part of my informal education in U.S. foreign policy. It reminded me that our government too often operates on lies. I continued to work with Mike until he was discharged from the service. He was never the same. That operation had taken some of the intensity from his blue eyes. He no longer walked with a bounce and urgency to his step.

I had learned to distance myself, but the relocation of those villagers changed me too. It brought me more ghosts. My nightmares worsened. It took more alcohol and more pills to get to sleep at night. I prayed to God that this would not follow me home, knowing full well that it would.

If the political prison in Hoi An was my hell, the refugee move up the "Street Without Joy" was my purgatory. It was part of the harsh learning experience in my war. I finished my time in Quang Dien District and reported for duty at the offices of Thua Thien Provincial Health Services. Dr. Do Van Minh, the Provincial Health Medical Chief, and Dennis Barker, a public health advisor for CORDS (Civilian Operation for Rural Development Support) became my supervisors, my mentors and my friends. They would be instrumental in the positive work I would ultimately do in Vietnam.

"DON'T MEAN NOTHIN"[16]

What stories can do, I guess, is make things present.

—Tim O'Brien,
The Things They Carried

The bump of the C-130 hitting turbulence jarred me out of a disturbed sleep. Eyes closed, I wriggled in the webbed paratrooper seats, vainly seeking a comfortable position. There was none. When I finally glanced up, trying to take in my surroundings, I found myself eye level with a duck.

Ducks were low on the priority list for those trying to hop a free ride on military flights, but they occasionally made it. U.S. officers had top priority, followed by U.S. enlisted men, then Vietnamese officers and enlisted men and finally Vietnamese civilians. The civilians were allowed to hand-carry almost anything on board, which meant not only personal effects but, yes, chickens, pigs, and ducks.

This duck was not in a particularly good mood and took a snap at me from time to time. I tried to befriend the beast and engaged it in small talk.

"Who do you think will win the World Series? Do you really think the Beatles are splitting up?"

It didn't work. He wasn't very sociable. The owner of this foul fowl wasn't following the conversation either, but had the good nature to laugh at my attempts to communicate.

I didn't mind the duck. Down the row, another GI was sitting next to a piglet with diarrhea.

At 3:30 in the afternoon the cargo plane began its circle above Tan Son Nhut Airfield. Soon it would be making its steep military-style

---

16   Author's note: The incident to be described in this chapter actually happened, but I heard about it second-hand and was unable to find a newspaper account containing the details. Therefore, all of the participants have been given fictitious names. The story is included in this book because, to me, it epitomized how individuals on both sides were victimized by the war. I also wanted to put a face to the dead; all too often we are just numbers in a newspaper.

descent toward the runway in an attempt to avoid enemy gunfire. On the ground at that same moment, Sgt. Larry Hunter, Spec/4 Ivan Stanbushski, and PFC Wilbur Smith were climbing out of their Military Police (MP) jeep. They were from the 516th MP Battalion and had been patrolling inner city Saigon. They had parked by an open-air noodle vendor to take a break over a couple of Cokes and some Pho[17].

Hunter stood 6 feet 3 inches. He wore his blond hair long, in complete disregard for military regulations, and topped it with a worn bush hat instead of the usual helmet issued to military police. The hat was decorated with grenade pins, buttons with cartoon-strip characters and peace signs. Despite his size, Hunter was "short," meaning he had only a short time left in Vietnam: 19 days and a "wake-up" and he would leave Vietnam and the U.S. Army forever.

Ivan Stanbushski was a physically short and stocky 20-year-old who had left his folks' cattle ranch in Wyoming to go off and fight the communists. Early on, his comrades began calling him "The Polish Cowboy."

Like so many others, Ivan had come to Asia with patriotic zeal and a sense of adventure. After just seven months "in-country," however, his disillusionment with the war was already complete.

Will Smith was the new guy. He had been in-country only three weeks and had not yet experienced any hostile action. He would bear the label of "cherry," or virgin, until he did. "Cherries" were razzed by senior men and Smith was no exception.

Smith had the build of an athlete. He was tall and skinny, with ebony skin and perfectly defined muscles. Although his arms and legs seemed almost too big for his torso, he had sensitive hands that moved gently and expressively when he spoke. Not only a good athlete, Will was a gifted student and had done well in high school, but his family did not have the money to send him to college. He might have received an athletic or academic scholarship, but he hadn't pursued one.

He was very patriotic. His father had served in Korea and his uncles in World War II.

"Don't you know," he told other soldiers on more than one occasion, "one of the first medals awarded in WWII was a Navy Cross during the battle of Pearl Harbor. It was awarded to a black man, a

---

17   Pho [pronounced fuh] is the Vietnamese national dish; an aromatic, nutritious^ and delicious rice noodle soup served with a side plate of fresh herbs to add as you please. https://www.phocafe.co.uk/our-food/what-is-pho/

brother by the name of Miller on the battleship West Virginia[18]."

Ivan and Hunter both felt a medal to be a poor substitute for life. Ivan gently put a hand on Will's shoulder and told him not to try and get one of those "glory medals" here.

"Go home with no medals but go home alive," he said. "Besides, Ivan and I are too 'short' for you to do something brave and stupid."

Hunter interjected, "Hell, brother, I'm so 'short' I can sit on a curb and dangle my feet." And with that the three of them broke into laughter.

Once they got settled at their post, the two senior men automatically surveyed the street scene before them. They had parked the jeep within easy view of where they sat and kept a vigilant eye out for any suspicious activity. This position also gave them quick access to the M-60 machine gun mounted on the rear of the jeep. Ivan cradled his M-16 in his lap. Hunter put his M-16 down next to him but adjusted the .45 caliber pistol resting in the holster around his hip. Will held onto his weapon, looking anxious and ill at ease.

The noodle shop was on a small side street several blocks from the main thoroughfare, Tu Do Street. The buildings pressing in on the sidewalks were mainly two-story cement structures of French colonial architecture. The ground floor of each generally housed a family-owned business, the second floors reserved as living quarters. Many of the businesses were small import/export companies. These were enclosed and shuttered. Mixed in, however, were several grocery and spice shops that sat wide open to the passing traffic. Normally, the street was bustling with activity, but at 3:30 in the afternoon, siesta time was well under way. There were few people or cars to be seen.

The building in which the soldiers sat was a street noodle shack, illegally erected in an empty lot. The building that had formerly occupied the site had been hit by a misguided U.S. airstrike during the Tet Offensive in 1968, and the owners had never rebuilt.

The shack had three walls made of scavenged wood and stolen sheets of metal. The dirt floor was strewn with litter. The ceiling was thatch, supported by irregularly shaped wooden tree limbs thrust up

18 Doris "Dorie" Miller (October 12, 1919—November 24, 1943) was an American Messman Third Class in the United States Navy. During the attack on Pearl Harbor on December 7, 1941 Miller manned anti-aircraft guns, (despite having no formal training in their use), and attended to the wounded. For his actions, he was recognized by the Navy and given several medals. He was the first African-American to be awarded the Navy Cross.

irrationally from the floor. The interior contained a small refrigerator and four plastic tables with iron-framed chairs. Electricity was supplied by a single frayed electric cord that drifted off to God knows where. The chairs were small, as if from a children's play set, and the MPs overflowed them. Food came from somewhere behind the structure. A bare light bulb hung from the ceiling. The smell of cigarette and cooking smoke competed with the odor of a Vietnamese fermented fish sauce called *nuoc-mam*.

Hunter and Ivan loved the local atmosphere. Will was jumpy. He could not see what these crazy white dudes saw in this dump or its food.

Watching the MPs savor their Cokes and pho was 17-year-old Tran Van Duong, who stood placidly in the street behind a rickety noodle cart. Carts such as his could be found plying all the back alleys and city streets of Vietnam. For many travelers familiar with the region, the spicy smell of soup cart noodles is synonymous with Asia. Tran was not an industrious noodle merchant, however, and his cart was not what most travelers would have been familiar with. Rather, it carried captured American C-4 plastic explosives.

Tran was a VC-trained sapper. He was the worst kind of enemy, because he did not kill for his country, but for revenge. His need for retribution was fueled by the kind of hate that can only be forged by personal, total and unjust loss.

Tran was the son of an apolitical village farmer in the northernmost province of South Vietnam, Quang Tri. In 1965 his father had been rounded up with a number of other farmers by a South Vietnamese National Police Field Forces cordon-and-search operation and shot "trying to escape."

Later, Tran would learn that his father's arrest had more to do with economics than with politics. The police captain who had ordered the arrests soon purchased the land of each of the accused villagers and Tran, his mother and younger sister were forced into a refugee camp.

In 1967, during an American offensive against suspected VC strongholds, American artillery hit the camp. Tran's mother was killed, his sister maimed. It did not take long for Tran to join the VC not caring if he lived or died. That alone made him a most deadly enemy.

Tran casually rolled his noodle cart into the street and headed in the general direction of the food stall. The young sapper played his part well, calling out the fictitious wares he had for sale in the sing-song fashion of other noodle merchants. He walked slowly, projecting the impression that he couldn't care less whether he ever got to the end of the street.

The MPs sat in the right front corner of the stall, the corner nearest him. As he sized up the situation, he decided it was perfect. He was a noodle vendor heading for a noodle shack, so the GIs would most likely assume he was coming to get re-supplied. He steered the cart by the American jeep and parked it along the right front side wall, just a few feet from where the GIs sat talking.

Tran nonchalantly reached over and activated the C-4 explosive device. Then he turned and walked down the street in a direction that was out of the Americans' line of sight.

Inside the shack, Hunter had his back up against the front right wall. Ivan sat to his right facing the street, hunched over the table. Will sat more at ease now, tilting back on his chair. His hands were propped behind his head. The men were laughing at Hunter's description of the "el grand decor" of their surroundings and its gourmet cuisine.

Pleased with his joke, Hunter turned his head to signal for another round. At that moment the C-4 blew. Frozen for eternity in Will's eyes would be the image of Hunter's body disintegrating before him. Caught in an orange ball of flame and bright red blood with his index finger pointing toward the sky and a cocky smile on his face, Hunter's body came apart.

In slow motion, Will saw the details of the explosion clearly. First his hands and arms came off, then his head. His legs rocketed past Will's own body. Ivan was torn completely in two. He would be found under the rubble, looking like a tattered doll that had been abandoned by children, internal organs splayed across the dirt floor.

Both Ivan and Hunter died instantaneously. Will was blown across the room, through the plywood wall. He lost both legs and his right arm.

In a war, people react quickly to disaster. Military ambulances appeared as if out of nowhere to put what was left of Hunter and Ivan into body bags. Will was carefully placed on a stretcher, and because of the excellent work of an American medical team—and possibly an uncaring God—he would live for the rest of his life remembering his three weeks in Vietnam.

From his safe vantage point down the street, Tran watched the blast and its aftermath. For the first time in a very long time, a hint of a smile crossed his face. He turned and walked a few blocks to his own favorite noodle stand, sat down and treated himself to a Coke and a hot bowl of pho.

About the time the medics were putting Ivan's remains in a body bag I was making my way by taxi to a hotel near where the explosion had occurred. I was alone, having already bid my adieu to Ong (Mr.) Duck. I located the hotel easily enough and argued with the taxi driver for a suitable amount of time so as not to appear a tourist.

Dennis Barker, my supervisor from Hue, was waiting for me in the lobby. He had taken a flight down a few days earlier and had arranged a hotel room for me.

THE PARTY

It was a white man's war being fought by blacks, a rich man's war being fought by the poor, an old man's war being fought by the young.

—Frances FitzGerald,
Fire in the Lake:
The Vietnamese and the Americans in Vietnam

What Dennis Barker lacked in formal education, he more than made up for in experience and an extremely practical approach to problem solving.

Moreover, Dennis was the sort of person everyone liked. He had bright blue eyes and a William Holden smile. The Vietnamese in Hue trusted his judgment and his word—a rare combination in advisory work in those days. Yet like my friend Mike O'Neal from Quang Dien, this often put Dennis into direct conflict with his superiors.

Shortly after the refugee move up the "Street Without Joy," I was reassigned to work at the offices of the South Vietnamese Provincial Health Service in Hue City. At this office I was considered to be on attached duty to CORDS (U.S. Civilian Operations for Rural Development)[19] and because I was in a civilian office, I could wear civilian clothes when on duty. If I wore a uniform, I was not to wear any rank identification. This was because I was advising Vietnamese who were of higher rank than me. In order for me to function in this very status-conscious society, it was best that I not be seen as a mere U.S. Army E-5 "Specialist."

Dennis, a retired U.S. military health specialist with 28 years of service, became my civilian boss. He gave me the benefit of his many years of experience, and I gave him my total support. In the

---

19   The CORDS program was the brainchild of Robert Komer, President Lyndon Johnson's special assistant for pacification in Vietnam. In that position, Komer was responsible for the government's non-military efforts to "pacify" Viet Cong-controlled areas and return them to South Vietnamese government control.

process, a comradeship developed between us that has lasted until Dennis's death in 1991.

Part of my formal training involved attending seminars: this was the reason I was in Saigon. Dennis had arranged for me to join him at a U.S. government presentation on combating dengue hemorrhagic fever[20], a disease that was on the increase all over South Vietnam.

I jumped at the chance to attend this seminar, not only for what I could learn but also for the opportunity to see Saigon for the first time. Plus, attending this seminar would give me the luxury of being alone. Since I had been inducted into the Army I had been sharing bed and board with as many as 50 other men. After two years of group living I craved some time to myself.

Still, I felt a twinge of guilt as I entered the hotel lobby. Why should I have the privilege of three days in Saigon when the other men in the platoon were back in Hue sleeping in our overcrowded hooch[21]? I actually felt a bit relieved when Dennis met me and apologetically told me we would have to share a room.

The afternoon was hot and Dennis and I found ourselves feeling worn out. After a beer in the lobby bar we decided that a late afternoon nap was in order. A shower and a couple hours of sleep would prepare the body and soul for the kick-off party that evening for the seminar participants at the apartment of a USAID official. We went upstairs to our air-conditioned room and washed off the day's dust and sweat. As we settled on the two single beds Dennis politely informed me that before my shower I'd smelled like a barnyard animal. I laughed and told him my story of my traveling companion, Ong Duck.

The nap did not take. My sleep was restless and brief, and I woke up before my snoring roommate. Not wanting to disturb him, I lay there in the dark room listening to its ancient air conditioner generator kick on and off. Deciding that some music would serve to pass the time, I found the radio on the night stand between the beds and adjusted the volume so that it was just loud enough for my ears.

---

20 Dengue hemorrhagic fever (DHF): A syndrome due to the dengue virus that tends to affect children under 10, causing abdominal pain, hemorrhage (bleeding) and circulatory collapse (shock). DHF starts abruptly with high continuous fever and headache plus respiratory and intestinal symptoms with sore throat, cough, nausea, vomiting, and abdominal pain. http://www.medicinenet.com/script/main/art.asp?articlekey=6627

21 Vietnam War slang for a thatched hut or improvised living space. It could be any type of living quarters like a barracks but usually above the level of a tent

The news was coming on as I found the station for the Armed Forces radio. It was more of the same misinformation. The newscaster was reporting that the war was winding down and that little ground action was being reported. I wondered if the intelligence people really believed that the light was glowing bright at the end of the tunnel and that the end was actually in sight. According to my Vietnamese friends in Hue, the enemy was regrouping and rearming just as it had before the bloody Tet Offensive in 1968.

Over the past few months I was getting more frequent warnings from Vietnamese who knew me, advising against going into a specific district because of an increase in VC activity. Even the maid for my hooch knew about the VC preparations to attack. If my maid knew about it, it was hard for me to assume that General Abrams and the intelligence boys knew nothing. Even more outrageous was the idea that they were probably keeping VC preparations quiet for political reasons.

It was common knowledge that the U.S. government was too nervous to admit that large numbers of NVA regulars were infiltrating across the border, despite our best efforts to stop them. Still, combat officers depended on intelligence reports to give them an idea of what they faced in the field. Withholding that information could have deadly effects. Under-reporting what they could expect was criminal; it amounted to setting up an ambush on our own men. My God, I thought, are we really capable of that? Could we be killing our own men by keeping information from them just because that information could be politically embarrassing back home[22]?

The end of the news broadcast told how three MPs had been the victims of an explosion that day in the city. The name of the district was given, and I recognized it as being near my hotel. The report went on to say that an explosive charge had been placed against the wall of a noodle stand in which the MPs had been sitting. It also reported that two of the men had died while the third was critically wounded. The newscaster warned other GIs in Saigon to be on the alert for such attacks.

I suppose this is what the military meant when it declared

---

22   This would later be known as the infamous "Pentagon Papers." The Pentagon Papers, officially titled Report of the Office of the Secretary of Defense Vietnam Task Force, a historical record and analysis of the Vietnam War. A 1996 article in The New York Times said that the Pentagon Papers had demonstrated, among other things, that the Johnson Administration "systematically lied, not only to the public but also to Congress."

that that the war was winding down—GIs had the opportunity to get killed and maimed in incidents such as this, instead of in large combat operations. I was overwhelmed by feelings of guilt. There were two dead soldiers lying in body bags in a morgue somewhere in Saigon. Another was lying in a hospital, experiencing who knows what kind of agony. They were all probably around my own age. And yet, life, death and maiming in a combat zone are a matter of luck, of timing, of inches. Here I was in a clean comfortable hotel room getting ready to go to a party while they were being prepared for their final journey home.

My thoughts were disturbed by Dennis stirring. I could just make out his outline as he swung out of bed. He sat there for a minute, getting his senses, then fumbled for the bedside light. I was sitting on my bed with my knees drawn up against my chest. My arms circled my legs, giving me a feeling of security. My head rested on my knees.

Dennis looked at me with those all-knowing blue eyes. Experience had taught him when it was best to say nothing, and for that I was grateful.

He slowly began to get dressed, but I stayed where I was. A smile appeared on his face. It was that shit-eating grin of his that would warm an iceberg.

"Well," he said, "Specialist 5th Class Giannone, are we ready to make drunken fools of ourselves in front of the big shots of Saigon?"

I was more than ready. Humor, sleep and alcohol were the only releases.

We left the hotel and fought for a cab in the overcrowded street. Dennis gave the driver instructions and we were off, the cabbie driving like a maniac. It was always a mistake to pay attention to the way Saigon taxi drivers maneuvered their vehicles, because navigation for them was more a matter of aiming than driving.

Nevertheless, the sights, sounds and smells of this Asian metropolis excited my senses. American rock-n-roll music blended with the aromas of incense and spices. The mass of cars, motorcycles, tri-shaws and street hawkers created a Saigon collage. As we sped down the streets of this Asian "City of Lights," I watched the street activity as Dennis talked. He was trying to put me in good spirits before we got to the party, and he was succeeding.

Among other things, Dennis told me of a previous visit he had made to Saigon. Walking down the street one evening, he came upon a block where a firefight had broken out between the National Police and the VC. Dennis ducked into a building that he claimed turned out to be a combination bar and bordello. The fighting forced him to spend the night, but he had a particularly difficult time explaining to his superiors just why he was forced to spend a second and third night there.

Unable to resist Dennis' stories, my spirits did lift, and before long we found ourselves safely at our destination. The party was being held in an apartment in a three-story complex. Security was tight. The perimeter of the complex was surrounded by a high chain-link fence topped with barbed wire. For added protection, rolled barbed wire surrounded the fence at its base. Bunkers and guard towers were strategically placed around the area. I noticed that there was even a foot patrol keeping guard. The security forces were Vietnamese with American military supervisors—most likely private guards who were highly paid and trained.

As we entered the apartment my face must have looked like that of a poor child visiting the home of a rich uncle for the first time. I couldn't believe the luxury. I turned to Dennis and asked how many lived in the apartment. He smiled and responded, "One, plus female companions."

The living room alone was the size of the hooch I shared with 10 other men. Beyond the entrance room and living room lay a spacious dining room, a fully equipped kitchen, three beautifully furnished bedrooms and two baths. Later, as we stood on the expansive balcony, someone pointed out the owner's new 1969 pastel green Mercury Cougar with sunroof and top-of-the-line racing tires.

Dennis noticed some old CORDS friends and drifted off to say hello while I circled the crowded, noisy room observing the other partygoers. They wore a mix of civilian and military attire, and many were already in a state of intoxication. I noted many Americans, but also Koreans, Australians, Vietnamese and an assortment of Europeans.

What interested me the most were the Vietnamese women, not only because I was a young testosterone-driven soldier but because they were so beautiful and so exquisitely dressed. These ladies were the girlfriends of the men at the party, and they were young.

Indeed, the gentlemen in attendance had chosen not so much women as girls. In their high-fashion clothes, they looked like any American teenagers might look going to their first high school prom, except it was as if they had come to this prom with their fathers or grandfathers instead of their boyfriends.

I located the bar, my primary objective in my sweep of the room. As I had expected, the host had a bar as impressive as the rest of the decor. It was 25 feet long, made of teak, and would have made any public drinking establishment proud. The bartender was an elderly Sino-Vietnamese who wore a Mao jacket.

"My word," I said half-aloud as I approached the bar, "We're capturing the Communists and turning them into bartenders. Is this okay with the Geneva Convention?"

The solemn looking MAC/V major next to me turned, smiled and replied, "No, but he makes a pretty good drink. Just don't ask for a Black or White Russian."

In keeping with the atmosphere, I ordered a rum and coke. I am a beer drinker but it seemed fitting with the colonial surroundings and atmosphere. I was starting to feel much better. Hell, I could get used to this. There was nothing wrong with enjoying oneself in a war, was there? Giving my name and rank, I introduced myself to the major. I was in civilian clothes and this was common military protocol and a courtesy.

His name was Major Green, and he was working in military logistics. He was wearing a brown summer dress uniform that made him look entirely brown when combined with his hazel eyes, deeply tanned skin and short-cropped sandy hair. We made small talk. He had an unending supply of stories about the corruption of the Thieu regime. Among other things, he told of large quantities of U.S. military supplies "disappearing" after being given to his Vietnamese counterparts—food, medicine, clothing, ammunition, weapons, and even trucks[23]! They were even missing a soft ice cream machine and an X-ray machine.

Major Green vented about how frustrating this was for him. He could not inventory supplies an hour after he had given them to

---

23   FitzGerald, Frances. "Chapter 10 Bad Puppets." In *Fire in the Lake: The Vietnamese and the Americans in Vietnam*. New York, NY: Little, Brown, 1972. General Dan Van Quang, the Fourth Army Commander, ran a brisk trade in rice and opium; General Vinh Loc of the Second Corps and General Hoang Xuan Lam of the First Corps. Dealt in military preferment's and American commodities; Minister of Defense General Nguyen Huu Co held extensive real estate concerns (rented to the Americans).

the Vietnamese. There were stories of VC being captured carrying new M-16s that, upon checking the serial numbers, were found to have arrived in country only a few weeks before. Some South Vietnamese units in the field would run out of ammunition and be overrun by the VC when it was known that a huge number of supplies had been signed over to their divisional commanders a short time before.

The major complained that South Vietnamese officials were buying beautiful villas in Europe and the U.S. There were rumors of huge transfers of "personal" funds from Vietnam to Swiss and American banks. All this was reported to his superiors but nothing was done. Whenever the Vietnamese reported they needed more material, the U.S. would grant the requests.

"The communists are getting their hands on our goods and money," Major Green said, "Instead of getting weaker they are getting stronger. They are using our own supplies and weapons to beat us. They are using American weapons to kill American boys."

Then, realizing he had said too much, the major withdrew into another Scotch on the rocks.

As I leaned against the bar surveying the crowd, I noticed a fat, boisterous man making his rounds through the guests. I assumed by his manner that he was our host.

The man resembled an aging, overstuffed Tubby Tuba from the comic strip Nancy. He looked like the kind of person who had been teased by other children as a child and who, as a young man, had spent most Saturday nights without a date. Maybe underneath all the fat was a noble and brilliant mind, but listening to him rant at the bar, there seemed to be nothing noble or brilliant about him. It was, rather, through a miracle in the Foreign Service selection process that he had been able to attain his current level of undeserved authority and power.

He no longer had to worry about being ignored when walking into a crowded room. As a senior American Foreign Service officer, Tubby Tuba could bed teenage girls and bully an entire nation.

I estimated Mr. Tuba to be in his early fifties. The saggy skin of his face was the sort of bright red that comes from too much red meat, drink and smoke. His hands were puffy but well-manicured. A pinky ring sparkled amid the fat of his right hand. He wore an unpleasant cocky grin as he smoked a thick Havana cigar, and his arm was draped over the shoulder of a slender Vietnamese girl who looked to be about 17 years old.

Arriving at my end of the bar he introduced himself and his girlfriend. I said hello to him in English and thanked him for the party. Then I said hello, in Vietnamese, to the girl. Similar to my introduction with Major Green, I gave not only my name but also my rank. I then explained that I was in town from Hue City with Dennis Barker. He said he knew Dennis.

We talked about the war. He was curious as to what I was going to do after my military service, having correctly gauged me as a non-career military type. With the alcohol warming my insides, I felt no harm in telling him my grand plan. I said that I wanted a career in international public health and felt I had not only a sensitivity toward helping people but possessed the ability to get things done. My plan was to go to college, study for a public health degree, and return some day to Vietnam as a civilian to help the Vietnamese people.

Tubby leaned back on his heels to assess what I had said. A twinkle came to his eyes. He took a long draw on his cigar and smirked. He pointed at my chest with his little finger and said, "Well, son, when you do go back to the States, the Land of the Great PX, I want you to do me a favor."

He took a dramatic pause to take a few short puffs on the Havana. I waited, wondering why people like him always needed to create a stage.

"You know all those college kids demonstrating against the war?" he asked finally, "Well, when you go back to college I want you to demonstrate *for* the war, because I can't afford to leave."

Then he broke into laughter, pointed at his luxurious apartment, and gave his girlfriend a pat on the behind. Still laughing, he pivoted around on the girl's waist and proceeded on the circuit of his domain. I wanted to put his cigar out for him—in his eye.

I leaned against the bar and thought about what he said, about not being able to afford leaving this war. To submerge yourself in the spoils of war, while young men were still spilling their blood just down the street, was a crime, I thought. To hope war continues for the profit and power you stand to gain was sick and perverse.

In a way, I was grateful to Mr. Tuba. As morally revolting as his statement was to me, his joke was the first bit of honesty I had heard in a long time. He had distilled the reason of why we were in

Vietnam to its essence. It was not to fight communism and promote democracy. Rather, American blood was being spilled for ego, power, greed and profit.

The party suddenly seemed the last place I wanted to be. I walked over to Dennis and told him I'd had enough alcohol and that I would meet him later at the hotel. I got a taxi but when I arrived at the hotel I did not go in. I turned and walked down the street amidst the hustle and bustle of the city.

Saigon was quite a place in 1970. You could almost smell the corruption, radiating up from the sidewalks and drifting from dark alleys. I passed a four-man Vietnamese National Police Field Forces (NPFF) foot patrol wearing light-brown camouflage uniforms and helmets. They carried M-16s on their hips and swaggered arrogantly past me. The last one to pass was smoking pot. These were the troops we told the population to look up to and go to if they needed help.

I found a local bar, fended off a couple of bar hostesses, drank a few beers and then headed back to the hotel. Ever since the party I couldn't get Tubby Tuba out of my head. I kept getting flashes of two MPs lying in a morgue, of teenage girls being tortured by Americans and a Vietnamese soldier lifting the wounded stumps that used to be his legs. By the time Dennis returned I was once more on my bed, sitting upright with my legs pulled against my chest. I did not look at him as he walked in and got ready for bed.

Dennis looked at me with concern, and I began to talk.

"You know, there is something wrong here that goes deeper than this war," I told him. "In order to fight communism, we've aligned ourselves with gangsters, murderers, drug pushers, and thieves. We've betrayed the Vietnamese people, our people, our Constitution and ourselves. But there is even more. I'm afraid it won't end with this war, will it?"

Dennis knew I wasn't through and let me vent. I told him about my conversations with Major Green and our fat host and about the newscast I'd heard about the dead MPs. I continued, not knowing whether I was talking to Dennis or myself.

"Dennis, both you and I come from blue collar stock. There are a few unwritten rules that you learn from your family when you're born with little money. First is a belief in God; second is support of the family; and third, but not last by any means, is an allegiance to your country. You're told to do whatever you can to assist your country because that allows you to support your family and worship God. For the poor and middle class this means voting in elections, paying taxes and sending sons to fight in wars.

"There's also the unwritten rule that you don't question your elected officials. You assume they're acting on our behalf. It's people like Major Green and the fat man who Americans depend on to tell us the truth and support our cause overseas, and they lie, distort or leave out the truth. The major knows the truth but hopes someone else will tell it so he can protect his career. And our fat Foreign Service friend lies not only for his career but for the money and power he gets from those lies.

"These bastards are going to perpetuate the lies, aren't they? And the people in America are going to believe them. Hell, I would've believed them if I hadn't seen how low we could stoop with my own eyes. They'll go back to America, stand in front of the flag and talk of democracy and freedom in Vietnam to Rotary Clubs, Boy Scouts and church groups. They'll talk as if they really believe in it and support it. And when we get kicked out of this country, and you know we will, they'll try to blame our loss on circumstances. Or worse yet they'll blame it on 'evil' liberals. Generations from now children are going to read those lies in their history books and they'll believe them.

"I think this road show is going to continue after Vietnam—as long as no one doubts or questions what they're told—as long as we let them write history their way. The people in power will use our poverty, religion, family values and patriotism as their base to corrupt and intimidate other small nations. The only question is where? Will the Thais let us in after Vietnam? There's great potential in Africa and South America. Hell, there are ex-Nazis hiding out in South America. They were anti-communist, weren't they? The way I feel right, now the only difference between them and us is that their 'final solution' was on a grander scale than ours.

"What's the quote, 'Every man's death diminishes me'?

I knew my monologue was inspired partly from too much alcohol, but it was also too much everything. What I was saying had been growing inside of me like a volcano these past months. The party was the spark that set it off.

Dennis knew this, too. He began talking calmly about what could be done as opposed to what couldn't be done. Basically, it was the same type of speech I had given Mike on the "Street Without

Joy." Dennis pointed out that my duty was to try and save lives. A simple statement, but in Vietnam he had realized long ago that this was going against the grain. No one cared about saving Vietnamese lives because no one cared about the Vietnamese, and that included the Vietnamese government. Dennis' years of experience had given him a strong sense of reality and he urged me to concentrate on what was possible.

As he turned off the light he looked at me sadly and said, "When you go back to the States no one will care what you saw and no one will want to change things. America is beyond that type of change. Believe me, I've tried."

There was not much sleep for me that night. I would not— could not—accept Dennis' last statement. My mind kept drifting back to the party and to the dead MPs. Thinking of those two dead soldiers I wondered about their parents, their brothers and sisters, their girlfriends. I tried to picture what they looked like. I imagined the reaction of their loved ones to the news. I wondered what explanation would be given to their parents. How do you explain a loss as great as this? In my mind, I constructed an explanation of the truth:

Dear Mr. and Mrs. John Doe,

"Your son was killed today on the streets of Saigon. He died without living to his full capacity, without knowing what it is like to fully love and be loved by a woman, without knowing the joys of his own children. He died in what he perceived as a defense of his country and its beliefs. But his country lied to him. You must understand that there are people in America and Vietnam who don't care about you, your son or about our country. They see this war as a career opportunity, a way to gain prestige and money. To them your son was an expendable commodity. He shed his blood protecting their investments, so that the few could prosper over the sufferings of the many."

As I climbed aboard the C-130 at Tan Son Nhut at the end of my stay in Saigon, I knew the final sentence in my fictional letter could be written for anyone who died in Vietnam and maybe for those who would die in wars yet to come. My visit to Saigon had helped clarify who my enemies were. Of course, the VC and the NVA were trying to kill me, but that was their job. It was the ones who sent us to the rice fields, the ones who made us enemies of the North Vietnamese, who were more dangerous. After all, it was their war, and they were forcing us to play in it.

We were the tools for the war, like clay ducks in a carnival shooting gallery. For the ducks, it might seem that the guy paying to take three shots at them was the enemy. But it is the owner who controls the game, sets the rules and even provides rifles to those who want to shoot at an easy target. Whether the ducks are hit or not makes little difference. The owner always wins. Replacing a target was cheap and they could be replaced often as the profit margin was already built into this never-ending game.

Who were the owners of this Asian shooting gallery? Who were my enemies? I started counting them as the C-130 hummed north toward Da Nang: the U.S. State Department, The Department of Defense, the American Foreign Service, USAID/CORDS, Military Assistance MAC/V, the CIA, the South Vietnamese government and those patriotic arms manufacturers.

I looked out the window of my plane as it flew north and saw the beautiful country known as Vietnam. I knew that down there under the scenic foliage the ducks were being hunted. I wondered how many of them had figured out who the real enemy was. How many were getting blasted right now? How many more would be taking their place? How many would return to the United States? How many, in 20 or 30 years, with their memories dimmed by time and circumstance, would allow their own sons and daughters to become sitting ducks in a U.S. created foreign shooting gallery?

THE OLD MAN

The technological irrelevancy of CORDS/USAID personnel, their inept managerial efforts and the inappropriateness of their programs are bad enough, but the most glaring weakness is their refusal to go where they are most needed—among the people.

—William R. Corson,
The Betrayal

A movement caught my eye as I drove along the sandy path toward the ferry that would take me and my interpreter to the mainland. I analyzed the situation and decided that this man slowly climbing out of a rice field did not appear to be a threat. My guard dropped, although just a bit.

Elderly Vietnamese farmer.

I don't know why, but something compelled me to stop. There was nothing unique about this man, who seemed no different from thousands of other rice farmers I had passed since my arrival in Vietnam. Maybe it was the sunset that made me stop. Spread out before me was one of those picturesque twilights you see in travel brochures, splashed in a golden hue.

Still, I was well aware of the danger the setting sun heralded. It was the time of day when the control of the land shifted. During the day, I was somewhat safe. At night, anyone wearing a U.S. Army uniform would be hunted.

Maybe I stopped because I felt both emotionally and physically drained. I needed to connect with something or someone outside of my world.

In the past, I had always found a great deal of solace and good honest information in talking with the Vietnamese. It was such a pity that our government had forgotten that these people were the reason we were fighting in this country. Instead, they had become incidental in our grand scheme to fight communism on "smaller" Third World battlefields. The Vietnamese got in the way of what had become "our" war.

I told my interpreter, Truong, that I was stopping. Actually, it was more a question than a command. My reason for stopping was implied and it was through Truong that I would talk to the old man on the side of the road. Truong, always patient, always friendly, smiled at me as if he had known I would want to stop. He was just a few years younger than me. He was tall for a Vietnamese, about 5 feet 9 inches," smart and good-looking, and he had been able to avoid military service because of his gift for languages.

Truong had been a medical student, which led him to learn French, German and English. I had a trust in him that only two people working closely together could develop. I knew that he translated for me as accurately as possible, which was rare. Often, interpreters had a tendency to edit the flow of conversation for political or cultural purposes. Truong would not do this, though he often gave me very good advice on how to say things and a strategy in dealing with people.

As we approached the man, he turned to face us. He was old, probably in his late sixties, but still very muscular. His face was dry, etched with wrinkles that seemed to reflect the history of the harsh land. His eyes were dark and piercing. He had a warm, compassionate smile that seemed to reflect the glow of the setting sun. As was customary for men his age he wore a long, stringy goatee. Facial hair is a sign of age and wisdom among the Vietnamese. (One reason I wore a moustache was to cover up my youth).

On the farmer's head was a rice hat for protection from the glare of the sun. The hat was of the type Americans generally associate with women, but almost everyone in Vietnam wore them when working in the rice fields.

He cocked his head a bit to get a better look at us, just as we were analyzing him. I said hello to him in Vietnamese, then bowed slightly, taking his hand in both of mine. This was the customary way of greeting in Vietnam. The Vietnamese are warm, affectionate people who demonstrate that warmth through touch. I could remember a village chief in Quang Nam Province who gently held my hand for an entire hour-long conversation.

In a way, I was testing this old farmer. My prolonged handshake was a sign of respect and friendliness. Was he friend or foe? He did not retract his hand, nor did he change his expression. Since the Vietnamese always seemed to be smiling and sometimes used this visage as a defense mechanism, you had to become an expert in interpreting the language of the smile: happy smiles, angry smiles, hostile smiles, cunning smiles. It was all part of understanding and respecting a culture.

This man's smile remained warm and radiant and something inside of me told me I could trust him. I relaxed a bit more.

Our conversation was light at first. We talked of the weather and of the problems and hardships of being a rice farmer in South Vietnam. The old man seemed impressed when I told him that my stepfather had worked most of his life on a farm, finally quitting when it became too difficult for him physically and he realized he could make more money working in a factory.

This statement stirred several questions from the old gentleman. Don't all farmers in America own large farms and have big houses? Is it true they all now ride in air-conditioned tractors? Does the government tax the farmers on the crops they grow? Do the local police and government officials make the farmers pay money to them in order to drive their products to market? Can the government come into a village and take the farmers' produce to feed the army and not pay any money? Were farmers treated with respect in America? Were they proud to be farmers?

I answered each question as carefully as I could with my limited knowledge of American farming. While I talked, I held the old man's eyes in mine while Truong interpreted our words. I told him that America was a blessed country, that God had given us plenty of water and good land. American farmers were more prosperous than Vietnamese farmers on average but not everyone had their own land or house. And though a few farmers rode around in air-conditioned tractors, most did not.

His face took on a look of disbelief as I told him that there were places in America, like Appalachia, where the poverty rivaled that of Vietnam. I explained that farmers had to pay taxes, as did all citizens, but there was no system of local bribes as in his country. No, I said, the U.S. government does not take produce from the farmers without paying. In fact, the government actually pays some farmers not to grow crops on certain lands.

At this statement, the old man laughed out loud. He could not possibly imagine that someone would pay him not to work in his field. He asked where he could apply for this program, and at that all three of us broke into laughter. I told my new friend that farming in America was a tradition that had its roots in our early beginnings as a nation, that there were many in America, including my step-father, who were proud to be men of the soil. I said that in some sense Americans held farmers in high esteem but, sadly, that view was eroding as we modernized. More and more, as in Vietnam, it was hard to encourage sons to follow in their father's footsteps.

We stood there on the side of the rice paddy engrossed in conversation, observing the change in the spectrum of light as the sun sank deeper in the west. I noticed that Truong was becoming nervous. The longer we stayed on the road at this time of day, the greater our chances of being ambushed. But I felt relaxed, watching the world go by with this old man. I wished that I could walk back to his village, drink tea and sit and talk to him all night in front of an open fire.

Of course there was no time for this, but there was something else I wanted to ask. It had popped into my mind during a delay in Truong's interpretation. It was the million-dollar question of the war and potentially a dangerous question for the farmer, because his answer could be considered treasonous. Political questions were avoided at all costs. But there was something about the mood of the evening and the tone of our conversation that told me to proceed.

It was a simple question, really, and I presented it as such. Still looking at him, I asked, "Who do you want to win the war?"

Truong gave me a worried glance but translated my question. The old man paused and absorbed it.

"God," I thought to myself, "The Asians really know the power of the pause." His answer was as simply put as my question. He said, "I don't care. We farmers have always had mandarins over us."

He paused but I suspected there was more.

"Let me ask you, my young friend," he went on, "Why it is your government has allowed those men in Saigon to have more power over us than any mandarins in our history?"

Even as I formulated the answer in my mind, it seemed more like the typical weak official jargon heard on the news. I talked about the Vietnamese tradition of village democracy and of the need to stem the communists. My friend's smile changed. It became patient and compassionate, like the smile a father might give to a son learning to ride a bike, or a professor to a student struggling over a difficult question.

"Your government constantly talks about the idea of 'the big picture' as if communism was some type of mythical dragon that had to be slain with a magic sword," he said. "With such a broad philosophy, your government has totally ignored the individual. Our real needs and thoughts are not considered. Defeat for America is not marching on the shoulders of the communists. This revolution is not an explosion. It is an implosion.

"Your officials believe that the only way to defeat communism is with violence and terror. They use the magical sword. But communism is not some mystical beast. Communism is a weed that grows and flourishes on violence and terror. Swords just get tangled in weeds. That is why the more you do, the stronger they get."

"And, of course, the communists use the sword. They too believe in violence and terror. But they are better at it than you. They are not hypocritical. They are decisive and extremely selective in the use of that power. Americans, because you are novices, tend to use violence randomly and haphazardly. You hurt the wrong people, and every time you do more citizens turn against you.

"Yes," he continued, "We do have a tradition of village democracy, but ironically these traditions have been smashed by Saigon and your government. The tyranny has gone beyond anything that we can remember, and our history goes back thousands of years, not hundreds. The people no longer have any real options. They are being forced to accept the lesser of two evils—and believe me, they understand what this might mean for them. But soon no one will accept that government in Saigon."

I began to interject but the old man uncharacteristically held up his hand and continued. "I know what you are thinking before you say anything, my young friend. You're wondering how an old man such as me knows such facts. You wonder if I might be a communist political cadre. Your government has always underestimated the knowledge of local people[24]. To them we are just poor, uneducated rice farmers. But for us knowledge is survival. We read and listen to any news available in order to survive."

"To answer you before you ask, I am no communist nor will I ever be one. I have lost sons, brothers, relatives, friends and neighbors in this war. They have died wearing the uniforms from Saigon and Hanoi. The killing has been too much for many of us in Vietnam. My original answer still holds. I no longer care who wins the war. I just care that it ends."

I felt a strong sense of compassion for this man. He had taken a great risk in speaking so frankly. If I were a Phoenix operative[25] I could have had him put in jail—or worse. I knew that a warm spirit dwelled in him and I felt close to it. We looked intently at each other knowing that there was no more to be said. Once again, I shook his hand and bowed to him. As I bowed I thanked him for his wisdom and honesty. Accepting my words, he stood patiently watching us as we drove away.

Both of us said little on the trip home. Truong was worrying about the possibility of a burst from an AK-47 assault rifle crashing through the window into our foreheads. I was thinking about the old

---

24   Author's note: In my 40 years of work in international public health, I've learned this constant about our foreign policy—its inability to work, engage, understand and appreciate the knowledge of people at local village and district levels, even though most of our development work and funding seems to target these people.

25   The Phoenix Program was a program designed, coordinated, and executed by the United States Central Intelligence Agency (CIA), United States special operations forces, and U.S. Army intelligence collection units from MACV. The program was designed to identify and "neutralize" (via infiltration, capture, counter-terrorism, interrogation, and assassination) the infrastructure of the National Liberation Front of South Vietnam (NLF or Viet Cong).

man and how thankful I was for his kindness, frankness and warmth. How I had come to love and respect the Vietnamese people during my time in this country.

I had learned to combat cynicism and defeat by concentrating on saving lives, one at a time. This course of action drove me farther away from the American mission and closer to the Vietnamese people. As I dropped my inhibitions and learned more about their culture, I found that the Vietnamese openly embraced me. In my entire life, I had never felt so welcome, so needed and so useful.

Driving my truck back to our compound I knew that my next experience after the war and the army would be my college education. I was excited about that. I knew what I wanted to be and was mapping out in my mind how to get there. I also realized that one of my life's greatest educational experiences would be my two tours in the villages and rice fields of Vietnam. People like this old farmer, Dr. Minh, Dennis Barker, my hooch maid, the villagers I encountered and the men in my platoon were my real-life professors. I learned a great deal from them.

This train of thought was derailed by a sudden burst of gunfire. My insides twisted for a moment, but I quickly realized that it was coming from the barrel of an American-made .50 caliber machine gun somewhere off the road. From the slapping noise after each shot, I figured that a friendly ARVN was test-firing his weapon into water, most likely a river, canal or pond. No cause for alarm, I told Truong. But my hopeful mood had been shattered.

Many who served in Vietnam didn't care much for the Vietnamese. How could they? The soldiers were isolated from the "real" Vietnamese except when on patrol, and during patrols the Vietnamese were looked on with suspicion. "People are strange."

When off duty, the soldiers' only associations with the people were with the "camp followers" and riffraff that hung around the fire bases: hustlers, pimps, prostitutes, drug dealers and salesmen. Unfortunately, these people were the face of Vietnam to most troops. There were camp followers around every military base in the world and there was not much to like about them. GIs had a poor opinion of Vietnamese because they did not understand or really know them.

To me, the Vietnamese I associated with were a different breed. I worked in their offices, visited their villages, went to their homes, ate meals and drank tea with them. To me, they were the ultimate survivors. Generation after generation had known almost continuous warfare, yet they remained loyal to their families. They showed respect for their elders and ancestors, an all-consuming love for their children, and a compassion for strangers such as myself.

Their friendship changed me. That was possibly the greatest gift I received in Vietnam, although it was a double-edged sword. Getting to know the Vietnamese also made it possible for me to see the war and the events surrounding it through their eyes. The picture wasn't pretty.

More and more, I had a difficult time dealing with most Americans inside Vietnam. I felt isolated from my own countrymen and their inability to care for the people whom I had grown to love. Riding in that truck with Truong I now understood that for the rest of my life I would have the gift and the curse of seeing my country through foreign eyes.

An arc of red tracer bullets fired from a machine gun in an ARVN base camp drifted toward the stars as if to underscore my thoughts. I was nearing my compound.

I was proud of the person I had become. I thought of home, family and friends. Would they understand me when I returned? I had stopped writing home my last year in Vietnam. It was easier to distance myself. My mother actually sent me a letter she had written to herself for me to sign and send back to her.

As I joked to my platoon mates, what would I say to her or any of them? "Having a great time, wish you were here?" Or "Just love the bunkers and barbed wire." Had my transformation changed me so much that I could never really go home again or communicate with my mother and friends?

How strange it was for me to be an American in that time and that place. There would always be a chasm between us, the American soldiers of the Vietnam era, and our counterparts from World War II and Korea. The World War II soldier fought to protect our democracy, stop the advance of fascism in Europe and Asia. The modern American soldier, especially the Vietnam vet, unknowingly fought to support a regime that censured democracy. We were more than soldiers. We were witnesses. We had seen the open and festering wound that had become our foreign policy during the Cold War. We participated in its failure.

I wondered what could be done to change the direction we

were heading in as a nation. I was still an American and I loved my country. Strangely, after all I had experienced, I not only wanted to help the Vietnamese but I wanted to serve my country as well.

A chilling thought came over me as we approached the outskirts of the MAC/V compound in Hue. I saw my own reflection on the wet windscreen, and it seemed I was looking at the face of all the ghosts I would take back home with me to America. No matter what I did or where I went they would be with me. A part of me would always belong to Vietnam. I knew in my heart that the communists were going to win. I desperately hoped I could leave before that happened.

I had dropped Truong off at his home, and as I pulled into my compound a weird thought popped in my brain. I wondered what side I would be fighting on if I had been born Vietnamese. In Auburn, New York, I grew up in a world of good guys and bad guys defined in part by my education, books I had read, the movies and TV I watched. Our history texts were filled with good Americans winning over evil oppressors.

Here in Vietnam, reality reversed itself. Both sides were brutal to the innocent. No one wore a white hat or a black hat. The war was all shades of grey. I thought about the old man and the others I had met, and as I parked my truck and cleared my weapon, I silently thanked my "professors" for the education they had given me. What I did not know as I walked toward the MP guard post at the entrance to the compound was that I was on the eve of my greatest education in Vietnam. It would happen in a quiet fishing village called An Duong.

A SMALL VICTORY
IN A HAMLET CALLED AN DUONG

I've become involved with the people here; it's become a personal war for me. I've come to rely on them as much or more than they rely on me. If I don't extend again I will return to Texas and go to college and return to Vietnam to help rebuild this war-torn country. (Sgt. Michael Flynn, April 6, 1967).

—William R. Corson,
The Betrayal

The orders came down from on high, from a congressman in Washington to MAC/V headquarters in Saigon, then to 24th Corps Headquarters in Da Nang, then to the MAC/V Province Senior Advisor in Thua Thien Province, then to the Deputy Province Senior Advisor, who passed them along to the captain in charge of the 5th Civil Affairs Platoon. From there, they migrated to the captain's Executive Officer (a lieutenant), and finally to me, an E-5 enlisted man who was designated as the platoon Public Health Advisor.

From the highest to the lowest, the assignment stopped at my door. There was no one else to pass it along too.

Oddly enough, I was excited. I saw opportunity in the project. The tortured souls in the Hoi An prison and the forced move of refugees up the "Street Without Joy" were behind me. I had learned a great deal in just over a year. I had been mentored by the former Peace Corps platoon members, by my civilian supervisor Dennis Barker, by my Vietnamese counterparts, especially Dr. Do Van Minh Province Chief for Thua Thien Public Health, and by the Vietnamese themselves. I now knew the basics of what made for a good civil affairs development project, and I thought I could make something out of this. It might become a part of my redemption, even a way to appease the ghosts.

SP/5 Paul Giannone US Army 29th Civil Affairs, E-4 Tom Burch US Navy
MILPHAP[26], interpreter and village committee member
An Duong village, Thua Thien Province 1970.

The assignment stemmed from a congressional investigation into a medical dispensary in the village of An Duong. Money had been donated by a couple in Pennsylvania whose Marine son had been killed in combat near An Duong, and they wanted a medical facility built in his memory.

The project had been initiated more than two years before by the Navy Seabees. Construction had begun, some medical equipment had been purchased, but the facility never got beyond the initial stage. There were rumors that the villagers had stolen the construction supplies and medical equipment, causing the frustrated Seabees to stop working on the project. But the couple in Pennsylvania, who had the ear of a congressman, were demanding to see a picture of their son's medical dispensary.

The obvious solution would have been to take a picture of any dispensary and send it on to Washington as another Vietnam "success story." Instead, the project fell into my lap.

The first and most important step in any development project

---

26   MILPHAP—Military Provincial Hospital Augmentation Program designed to augment the civilian medical services in 1965

is assessment. Later in life, I would become skilled in the assessment tools of my profession, but then I was a novice. My assessment was rather simple. I wanted to know whether a dispensary was needed in the area. I also needed to know if the villagers wanted the project and if the Provincial Health Service, for which I was working, could support it with staff and equipment. It would do no good to put up a building if Provincial Health did not have the staff, medicines or equipment to run the facility.

Dr. Do Van Minh, the Thua Thien Provincial Public Health Chief, was plagued by well-intentioned U.S. military "public health civic action construction" projects. On too many occasions, Dr. Minh had been presented with the keys to a dispensary, newly completed by the U.S. military, without the project ever having been first discussed with the Provincial Health Service. It was then up to Provincial Health to staff and supply these clinics, which often became a burden because of limited budgets.

Sometimes the buildings did not meet provincial public health construction guidelines. Some were so small that stretchers could not fit through the door. Dr. Minh jokingly referred to these edifices as "Lilliputian" dispensaries. In one notorious example, two U.S. military civic-action teams had built two very large hospitals within several hundred yards of each other, separated only by a hedgerow. So much for U.S. government coordination and integration plans.

I knew I needed to follow Vietnamese procedures and protocols. It was a time of "Vietnamization"—the U.S. government's attempts to hand the war back to the Saigon regime—so I would need to notify the Province Chief about this project and go through Vietnamese channels for construction supplies and material. Fortunately for me, the Province Chief, a very sharp ARVN colonel with a "ranger" patch on his shoulder, was well aware of the project and its political implications. He also knew that the construction material I needed would be readily supplied by the U.S. government.

In addition, I would make a formal visit to the District Chief and the American district MAC/V team leader to ask permission of the local authority to work in his district. During the life of the project I would make periodic visits to this District Chief to report on its progress. He would then send his report up the chain of command to the Province Chief.

One bright morning, after getting the green light from both

provincial and district headquarters, I climbed into my 1953 U.S. Army three-quarter-ton truck with my medical aid bag in one hand and "Butch," my M-3 grease gun, in the other, and set out for my first visit to An Duong. I was accompanied by Tom Birch, a Navy corpsman, my partner in this project. Mr. Truong, one of the platoon's interpreters, accompanied us.

I'd checked with J-2 military intelligence to get an idea about where I was going and what enemy activity we might be facing. According to my operations map, we would be on hard-surfaced road most of the way. First, we'd drive southeast to the port of Tam My. From there we would take a U.S. Navy ferry to the barrier island on which An Duong was located. Although the island was only a few hundred yards off the coast, there was no bridge. The only way on and off the island was via Navy ferry.

An Duong was about an hour's drive, if all went well. The "choke point" was the ferry crossing. I learned to start out early and give myself plenty of time, for there was always a line of civilian and military vehicles, people and, sometimes, their animals waiting to board the ferry. Loading and unloading was tedious, especially under the sweltering sun. The ferry was an old WWII landing craft that could hold four to six vehicles depending on their size. They were loaded with two vehicles side-by- side and three deep, a logistical challenge for both driver and naval personnel.

So steep was the ramp onto the landing craft that I would literally be looking up into the blue sky, relying on the loaders' hand signals and skills to park my vehicle within inches of another vehicle. Parking was so tight that once aboard, I would often have to shimmy out the driver's window, if I wanted to be out of the vehicle during the crossing. After all the vehicles were loaded, those on foot—U.S. and Vietnamese military, civilians and animals—jostled for the limited space between and in front of and behind the vehicles. The routine was, of course, repeated later to disembark.

Once off the ferry, we drove south, passing a small U.S. military base. This was a Rest and Recreation (R&R) Center set up by the 101st Airborne Division, the Screaming Eagles. After months in combat, soldiers would come in for a break. It was a place to swim, play volleyball, have a few beers, and enjoy some hot meals. The base was heavily fortified and guarded.

From that point on, Tom, Truong and I were on our own. We

were then in what was called "Indian country," where the chance for enemy ambush was all too real.

Because the road was no longer paved, we bumped along over loose sand. Intelligence reports indicated small Viet Cong platoons or squad-size units were active in this area. We knew we were extremely vulnerable along this, the only road to An Duong. Once we went down the roadway the enemy knew we had to come back the same way. They could easily set up an ambush or plant a land mine in the sandy soil. We carried no radios and only a few clips of ammunition. As a precaution, one of us would often stand in the back of the truck with Butch. It gave the person back there a better field of fire if we were ambushed. If we hit a land mine, we thought the one in back might have a bit more protection from the blast. Probably not true, but psychologically it made us feel better.

The trip to the village was only about three miles but felt much longer, especially on extremely hot days. We would catch glimpses of postcard views of the ocean, palm trees and white sand beaches. In contrast, the thought never left my mind that an ambush could be waiting just ahead. The road was deeply rutted. In some places, I could take my hands off the steering wheel and the truck carried on as if on rails. The ruts kept the truck on track. It was a 4-wheel drive all the way and I perfected my off-road driving skills on this road.

Our first trip to An Duong was an eye-opener. As Tom and I disembarked with our interpreter, we were immediately surrounded by the curious—and, of course, kids. As cultural protocol dictated, I approached the nearest villager and asked through my interpreter, Mr. Truong, if I might have a moment of the village chief's time.

A man stepped out of the crowd and was introduced to us as the village leader. He was younger that I expected, in his mid-30s. He invited us for tea in his hut. As we moved, the crowd moved with us. We walked to a small abode, entered and squatted Vietnamese-style on the dirt floor. The villagers circled the hut, discussing our presence, while the kids peeked through windows and gaps in the siding to laugh, smile and try to get the attention of the strange white men with big noses.

I knew from experience that it was impolite to start talking business immediately. In Vietnam, pleasantries were exchanged first. As we waited with the village chief, a few other village elders arrived and I introduced myself, Tom and Mr. Truong and explained that we worked for the Thua Thien Provincial Health Service. I then began to inquire about the village. How was the fishing? I had noticed pig pens as we had driven into the village. I asked about them and the farming activities of An Duong, The village elders seemed to relax when I told them that my stepfather had worked on a pig farm and that my ancestors had been sailors.

As the wife of the village chief brought us tea, a warmth and connectivity filled the room that would be difficult to describe to anyone who has not done this type of work. Here we were, a group of men from different cultures, drinking tea and talking about life and families. As we sat there and talked, wariness dissolved and trust began to develop. The war and the suffering seemed to be someplace else. These types of encounters, wherever I would go in the world, would be the most precious, productive times I would spend on this earth.

As the conversation continued, I sensed an opening that would allow me to broach the subject of the dispensary. I asked how many children were in the village and if they went to school. You cannot talk about raising children without coming to the subjects of health and education. I asked about the children's health and where they went when they got sick. The village elder told me that the only health care facility available to them was across the inlet. They had to use the government ferry.

This meant an all-day undertaking and, because they were civilians, they were a low priority for passage on the ferry. They could use their own boats but that would mean no fishing that day and loss of precious income and food. During the rainy season, the mainland clinic could be cut off to them for days when the sea turned rough. Occasionally a government doctor would come through but that was sporadic, and the doctors rarely carried enough medicine. In my mind, there really was no further need for a needs assessment. My journey getting to the village was proof enough that the place was isolated and needed some form of rudimentary health care.

Casually, I indicated that I had heard that Americans had started the construction of a clinic somewhere in the village. I watched the village chief and his companions closely. The smiles stayed on their faces but their body language changed. They shifted their weight and eye contact was lost for a moment as they looked toward invisible safe spots on the earthen floor.

I assured them in my most polite, soft tones that I was not an investigator but someone interested in the health care of children. I asked if I could see the construction site and the group agreed.

We then exited the hut and walked a short distance down the main road of the village. The children and the rest of the village paraded behind us. After a short walk, there it was. I laughed to myself, shaking my head. The "building" was just the frame, and it was huge. I leaned over to Tom and said, "What we have here is a bowling alley." This was a nickname that would stick.

What we had before us represented typical American thinking that "bigger was better." The construction consisted of four cement walls with empty openings for doors and windows. There were no floors or interior walls; some of the external walls were incomplete or broken. There was no roof or roof supports. I truly did not know what to say looking at this shell of a structure. After the donated "Lilliputian" dispensaries I had inspected with Dr. Minh, I had not anticipated an edifice this large.

We walked the building site. Tom, Mr. Truong and I then again squatted in a circle with the village chief and his elders inside the shell of the would-be clinic. As politely as possible I asked the obvious question, "What happened?"

Again, I was answered by smiles and glances to the ground. To the village leaders it may have been a painful story to tell but I had heard similar stories too often over the past few months.

The Americans, it seemed, had appeared out of nowhere. They swooped into the village in helicopters and drove in on military vehicles. A plot of land had been given to them by the former district chief. Little contact had been made with the village chief. He was told only that the Americans were "giving" the village of An Duong a medical dispensary. No rationale for site selection was given nor did the Americans ask for any help or advice from the villagers. The project was obviously an "American" project and there was no need for any consultation with the village elders or people in the village.

As the walls rose from the sandy soil, problems rose with the bricks and mortar. The Seabees would work when they could and then simply leave the village, sometimes for days. When they came, they brought their own food, water and communications. There was no need to mingle with the locals. They would leave behind stacks of precious construction material—cement, rebar, timber and piping.

And this material soon began to "disappear" from the site.

I thought to myself. What if I were in a small, poverty-stricken town in the U.S. and some wealthy foreigners showed up one day? With no discussion with anyone in the town, what if these foreigners started constructing a large, un-asked-for building on prime land in the center of the town? No advice, support or discussion is held with the locals. Each night the foreigners disappear, leaving behind large quantities of materials that could be used by the townspeople for survival. There is no request for security or accountability from village leadership, putting that leadership in an awkward position. What do you think would happen?

This was the saga that the village chief outlined for me in An Duong. Similar stories were repeated in many civic-action projects in villages throughout Vietnam. The chief knew that his villagers were taking the construction material, but with no link between village leadership and the Americans, there could be no accountability. To the villagers the Americans appeared to be so wealthy that they could leave behind a smorgasbord of material every night and not feel the loss.

We walked back to the village chief's hut for more tea and sat there in silence for what seemed a long time. Sometimes silence can be beneficial, allowing for time to think and accentuating the potential consequences of an action. At the right moment, I broke the silence. I slowly removed a fly that had decided to drown itself in my tea and took a sip. I smiled at the village chief and, looking deeply into his eyes asked, "Does the village want a medical dispensary?"

If he said no, I was prepared to walk away or offer him options such as a school or community center. He conferred with the elders sitting nearby. After a moment, he responded, stating that his village is often cut off from help during bad weather and time of war. Yes, he said, they would like a dispensary.

This was the moment of truth. I told them that from this moment on the An Duong project would belong to them. I repeated this a second time for emphasis. What I could do for them was to act as an advisor. I would be the person at both district and provincial headquarters who would ensure that the paperwork was approved and construction supplies delivered. I would provide whatever help I could in logistics, procurement and planning.

I thought this project out and explained to the village chief what I considered to be the ground rules. I first told him that I had faith and trust in him and his people. I indicated that a prerequisite for starting the project was that the village would select a construction committee. The construction committee would be responsible for completing all phases of the project. The committee would have to use the villagers' skills to complete the work.

I would bring in a Vietnamese engineer to develop plans for the completion of the building. We would also estimate exactly what material would be needed. The list would include cement, rebar, wood framing, piping, wiring, and roofing. I told the chief that if the plans called for 100 bags of cement, and any bags turned up missing, they would get no more. I told him that since the material would be coming from Provincial Headquarters, his village would have to answer for any loss to the Province Chief, not to me. I put total responsibility for the success or failure of the project on the villagers and its leadership. They were going to own that building.

Yet this would come with responsibilities, as well. Besides being their representative at both provincial and district headquarters, I would also ensure that when the project was completed the dispensary would be staffed and equipped from the Thua Thien Provincial Public Health Service. I would be available as much as they needed me. I would use my truck for light hauling of material and arrange military transport for the heavier construction material. I made no promises but I assured the elders that Tom or I would be there until the project was completed.

I had one request, and made it as forcefully as one can in the Vietnamese culture. I said I hoped that once the dispensary was completed it would be seen as a neutral and safe place for anyone who needed medical attention. I asked that whoever came to the dispensary for aid would be given that aid no matter what uniform they wore, no matter their political, religious or cultural beliefs. I told them I believed that health care should not be politicized. My experience in the prisons and refugee camps had sickened me. Too often civilians, political prisoners and POWs were mistreated. I had seen too much of that in this war.

There was one more administrative task that they had to do. Official forms had to be completed by them, and then routed through the Vietnamese bureaucracy in order to get the project approved. I left the forms, which were in Vietnamese, with the village chief and said I would be back in two days to collect them. This was a test of sorts, to see how much the village really wanted this dispensary. I made no offer to help complete the forms. I simply gave the chief the multi-page forms, shook hands with him and the elders, and we got into our truck and departed.

Three days later I returned to An Duong not knowing what to expect. Had the village elders rethought their decision? Had they decided the project would be too much for them? Would they feel that the labor required would detract from the already full-time jobs of harvesting fish, raising animals and growing vegetables? As Tom and I approached the village chief, he pulled out the neatly completed forms and handed them to me with the biggest smile he could muster. A marvelous bond formed instantaneously between us and that village as we accepted the forms and shook hands.

A great deal was accomplished over the next few weeks. As the village chief formed his construction committee, I left the completed forms off at District Headquarters and followed them up the chain of command at Provincial Headquarters. Through the Vietnamese Provincial Public Health Service and the U.S. Civilian Operation for Rural Development Support (CORDS) I arranged for an engineer to visit the site to draw up blueprints and estimate material needs. I made sure both the Vietnamese and U.S. overseers at the provincial level knew this was the project that had U.S. congressional oversight. I continued visiting the village and district headquarters to give them updates on the status of the approval process.

As the project evolved so did Tom and I. I'm not sure if we adopted this village or the village adopted us, but what happened to me would alter my way of thinking, being and acting for the rest of my life. The person I was just two short years earlier no longer existed. The transformation was dramatic. I cared, therefore, I was. As I look back, I realize this altered state had started before An Duong. But An Duong became the catalyst.

A number of the men in my platoon were former Peace Corps volunteers. They took the time to teach me how to look across cultures and see the world through new eyes. I learned to keep my mouth shut and not be judgmental. I learned the answer was not to have an "American" solution for every problem. I learned to observe the people with whom I was working, to ask for their opinion, and then act.

I learned from others, as well. Dr. Do Van Minh taught me patience and timing. Americans are often too quick to act, and our "can-do" attitude is not always an asset. His example also taught me to be optimistic in the face of adversity and impressed upon me the value of politeness, compassion and respect.

Dennis Barker, my civilian CORDS boss, was the icing on the cake in this educational process. He taught me how to be a good advisor. Effective advisors stay in the background; we work behind the scenes, providing advice and our connections to get things done. Our local counterparts would get the credit for all success and we would take the blame for failures. For media events, newspaper interviews and speaking engagements we took the back seat and stayed out of the limelight.

For me and the men in my platoon, what we experienced every day was not isolated or artificial. This was in-your-face development work.

As the An Duong dispensary began taking shape, so did my own moral foundation. Seeing the war through Vietnamese eyes altered the reality. Myths, prejudices and stereotypes dissolved with the sound of cement being mixed and poured and nails driven into supporting timbers and tin roofing.

In the faces of the residents of An Duong, I began to see the uncle who had raised me; in the smiles of the women I saw the patience and caring of my mother and my aunts; in the hands of the construction crew I saw the strong work ethic of my father, my uncles and my step-father. I had seen the evil that man could do but I also saw the good that could be accomplished when different cultures and beliefs come together for a common cause.

The construction project at An Duong would become part of my own development model that I would employ for the rest of my career. I realized that I wanted and needed to work in a field that put me in meaningful contact with my fellow human beings.

I was quite busy during my last tour of duty. Besides the construction of the clinic, I was coordinating a project with another colleague, Steve Cunnion—a similar dispensary south of Hue City at the village of Tui Aui near the 101st airborne base at Phu Bai. At the request of the Province Chief, Steve, Tom and I were also collaborating on the construction of a social disease clinic in Hue City to deal with a huge increase in sexually transmitted diseases (STDs).

On top of all that, I was also coordinating logistics and security for a group providing medical support to Montagnard refugees and for Dr. Minh's monthly missions to some of the most remote and dangerous areas of the province to serve those populations. At one point, I became involved in an overnight trip on river assault boats to provide aid to a village that had a measles epidemic.

But An Duong became my special project and the people of the village became an extended family to me. Tom and I tried to spend as much time as we could there.

The first thing that had to be accomplished was to get most of the construction material to the village.

It was wartime. Operation Lam Son 719, the ARVN "incursion" into Laos to cut the Ho Chi Minh Trail, was about to begin and transportation assets and fuel were at a premium. Even if I could get five-ton trucks from a military unit, the choke point at the Tam My ferry crossing would pose a major problem. The answer came from the U.S. Navy in the form of River Assault Group 32. RAG-32 was based in Hue City, part of the "Brown Water Navy" that used converted World War II landing craft to patrol the Perfume River and its tributaries and canal systems.

Their primary mission was to keep the Viet Cong and North Vietnamese Army from resupplying their troops over the waterways, but RAG-32[27] was always willing to help civil affairs ventures and they gladly agreed to move the needed bulky cement, rebar and wood to An Duong. Moreover, the warehouse was conveniently located on the Perfume River just down from RAG-32's base.

The predetermined date to move these vital supplies dawned cold and rainy, and the Perfume River was very choppy. The construction material was heavy and the flat-bottom armored landing craft dragged deep in the water.

We already knew that the landing craft would not be able to pull right up to the village to unload the construction supplies. The water was too shallow in front of the village. Instead, the plan called for the assault boat to anchor about a quarter mile off the island. Once in position I would fire three shots in the air with an M-16 to let the villagers know we had arrived. They would come in their fishing boats to pick up the materials.

After a long, wet, cold ride the sailors positioned the craft

---

27   RAG—US Navy River Assault Group.

off the village as planned. I fired the three shots in the air. Looking through field glasses I saw no sign of activity in the village. I waited a few minutes then fired another three shots. No fishing boats. I was uneasy. What I had gone through to get precious cement and rebar had been a herculean effort, and I did not want to return it. It would certainly "disappear" quickly in the provincial warehouses.

I worried that there might be VC in the village, but I knew I had to get there and see what had happened. Fortunately, we were able to flag down a passing fishing boat to take me to the village. If there were VC in the village, I was going to die. Taking a weapon with me would make little difference. What if I returned fire and hit children? I handed Butch to a sailor and took my camera instead. Maybe I could get one last photo of the VC who killed me.

As the fishing boat landed on the sandy beach, I winced. Would I feel the burst that hit me? Would I die fast or slow—or worse, be captured and tortured?

But I was not going to die that day. As I trudged toward the village I saw a crowd around the village chief's hut. There were no VC there. I found a high school boy who knew enough English to act as a translator, and it turned out that the impending invasion of Laos was not only eating up construction supplies but local fuel supplies as well.

The fishermen were concerned about using precious fuel on the numerous boat trips that would be required to get the construction supplies from the assault boat. As one of our platoon's best scroungers, I assured the fisherman that within three days I would have replacement fuel for their fishing boats.

It took only a few hours before the supplies were signed for, inventoried and stored in several homes in the village. Four or five bags of cement were wet and damaged; the village chief would not sign for those, and I told him I would gladly replace them. I was very proud of his professionalism concerning the receipt of material.

There were smiles all around. We bowed. We shook hands. I got back to the assault boat for the long, wet, choppy ride home, arriving at Hooch #19 on the Doezema MAC/V[28] compound just after dark. I was sopping wet. I took off my poncho and my medical aid bag and hung Butch on a chair next to my bed, then sat on the

---

28   The MAC/V compound was named after SP./4 Frank Doezema, from MAC/V Advisory Team 3 who was killed in action while manning a guard tower during the attack on this compound during the 1968 Tet Offensive on January 13, 1968

edge of my bunk and opened up a bottle of Mateus wine I had been saving for a special occasion. Not being shot this day seemed like a good occasion.

Two days later, Tom and I drove into the village with four 55-gallon drums of fuel for the An Duong fishing fleet. It is amazing what can be done at a U.S. Army supply depot if you are polite, explain to the supply sergeant the humanitarian mission you are working on — and bring along a bottle of very good Scotch whiskey.

We handed over the fuel drums to the village chief and he handed me my next logistics problem. The sand that surrounded the village was not good for mixing cement. Its salt content was too high. There was good sand about two miles north of the village back down the road we drove in on every day. Could we use our truck to move that sand to the village? We decided we would come to the village daily for the next few weeks. The village would supply laborers to shovel the sand, and we would run as many rotations as we could in daylight.

The building of An Duong.

The more I became involved with the project, the more barriers, myths and prejudices dissolved. The more power I gave up, the more power I seemed to gain. It was not only seeing the empowerment of people who had lost so much to continuous warfare, but a feeling that the success of this project had very little to do with me and everything to do with the people in the village. To me, this was a powerful statement on the human capacity to do good, and what organization and cooperation were capable of accomplishing.

There was a rhythm to the village and a freshness that took me out of the world of war and put me back in a life I used to know. As the villagers saw more of me, I was invited into their homes—and into their hearts. The fact that I brought them construction material and fuel during a time of great scarcity solidified me as a friend they could count on. The fact that I would take the time to sit with them and drink tea and share food made me human in their eyes. People regularly offered me tea and smiles of recognition. One man ran out to my truck one night as I was leaving and gave me a string of freshly caught land crabs. A boy gave me one of his hand-made lizard traps. Tom and I were invited to village events where we sat at the head table with the elders. The significance of this could not be minimized. I was a young man in a culture that paid homage to older men. It was a huge cultural "thank you" to be treated as I was. I was able to do some other good deeds as well.

In my trips to the village, I would occasionally spy a particular boy. He was like a ghost. I never caught a direct glimpse of him. He seemed always to be in the shadows, hobbling on a hand-made crutch. His right leg was missing below the knee. I never saw him playing with any of the other children.

Through inquiries with the village chief, I learned that the village had been caught in a firefight: a grenade from either a U.S. or VC weapon had taken the boy's leg. Back at CORDS headquarters, I made inquiries about what could be done. I was told a Quaker medical group to the south in Quang Ngai Province was fitting prosthetic limbs to the countless civilian victims of this war. It took a bit of doing but I was able to contact this group and, after some haggling, they agreed to help.

On my first visit to the village after talking to the Quakers, I asked to meet with the boy and his parents. I told the mother about my plan but made no promises. I asked if she wanted help for her son's missing limb. If so, I told the mother it would require that she and the boy travel to another province for a few weeks. I asked the boy to pose for a picture to send to the people who would help him. I was surprised at how animated he was while I photographed him. He readily raised his severed limb so the doctors would know the type of damage and the type of prosthesis required. Of course, there was paperwork to be filled out and parental consent to be signed, which we did on the spot. I sent the paperwork and pictures by courier to the Quakers. In short order, we received a green light to send the boy.

I am still amazed that I pulled this off. We had to get the boy and his mom from rural An Duong in Thua Thien Province to the Quaker rehabilitation center in Quang Ngai Province, several hundred miles to the south. Flying them down would be the best and safest way. I approached Air America, the CIA-run air service. Without bribes or arguments, they agreed to take the boy and his mom on one of their regular runs to Quang Ngai. Dates were confirmed. I ensured that the boy and his mom had some money even though they would be staying at the rehab center. We got them to the small Air America airstrip inside the Citadel in Hue City and arranged for someone to pick them up when they landed in Quang Ngai.

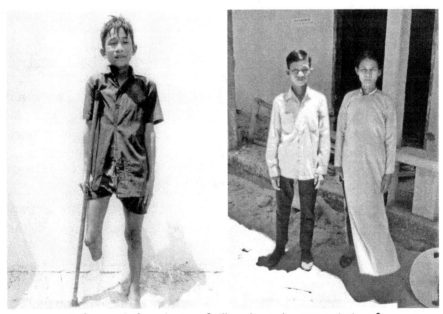

Before and after photos of village boy who was a victim of battle between US Marines and Viet Cong.

In less than a month the boy returned to the village and could now walk upright on two limbs instead of hobbling on one. A few weeks later, I was driving out of the village when a man ran out of a hut and stopped my vehicle. It was the boy's father. He was beaming with pride and joy. He shook my hand and hugged me and gave me a bottle of his best nuoc mam, a fermented fish sauce the Vietnamese put on everything. He also bestowed on me a string of live land crabs.

I took both, not wanting to insult this man's generosity but on the way home I had to stop my vehicle fast to avoid hitting a child and the bottle of An Duong's best nuoc mam fell and exploded into fragments in my truck. For the next month, no matter how many times I washed that cab, nor how many bottles of Mennen aftershave I poured into the cab, my truck smelled like a dead beached whale. It also became a heavenly destination for every fly in the province.

Our projects were moving along. Steve, Tom and I were gaining a reputation—not only among our villages, but at MAC/V and provincial headquarters—as three advisors who got things done under difficult conditions. Granted, we were a bit unorthodox in our planning and acquisition methods. At 22 years of age, I was feeling pretty cocky, but I also had a wonderful career-altering realization. Because I obviously excelled at getting things done in adverse cross-cultural situations, I was a born planner and coordinator and I would be a fool not to pursue a career that utilized these abilities.

Before long, my problem-solving ability was tested again. I was visited by representatives from the hamlet just north of An Duong and just south of the 101st R&R center. The hamlet elders were very distressed. It seemed the U.S. Military R&R center had been dumping raw sewage and garbage on the beach in front of this hamlet. There was no attempt to cover it up: it just lay there on the sand, rotting.

I went with the elders to visit the site. Although the beach once would have been the envy of any Club Med development, its pristine white sand was now littered with beer cans, leftover food such as rotting meat, and other bits and pieces of human and military waste.

Approaching the dump you could not fail to notice the smell. The 90-plus degree heat was "cooking" the leftovers. As I got closer to the site, the cab of my truck filled with what seemed like millions of flies. I had been in refugee camps where there had been masses of flies but this was off the scale. It became uncomfortable to sit there.

You did not have to look long at the garbage to see the rats. Normally these vermin are nocturnal but with such fine pickings they had started a day shift to get at all the good U.S. Army grub. And with a great deal of standing water, I assumed the site would be endowed with numerous mosquitoes at night. This brought the specter of malaria and dengue fever. I pulled out of the site as quickly as I could.

After dropping the hamlet elders off at their homes, I stopped at the R&R center and found the administrative offices. The place was fairly laid back—I could see men on the beach surfing, playing volleyball and sunning themselves. I went into the administrative hooch and asked to see the Commanding Officer. I introduced myself and explained that I was working on a public health project south of the compound and needed to talk to the CO about some public health issues. I was asked to wait and wait I did. About an hour later I was told to go into his office.

The CO's space was decorated with plaques, military insignia, flags, and war souvenirs that reflected on highly polished floors. The CO was a spit-and-polish major, in incredible shape. Through his uniform, you could see muscles trying to rip through the fabric of his starched fatigues, as if the cloth itself were its enemy. He had piercing blue eyes and hair cut so short it was hard to tell what color it was.

I introduced myself, gave my rank and unit, and told him what my mission was in his "Area of Responsibility"—or AOR. Airborne officers generally love military jargon. I then brought up the complaint shared with me by the elders in the hamlet. What happened in those next few moments brought the war surging back to me. It was a microcosm of why we were failing in our mission. The major smiled and then laughed and went into a lecture on, "What I did not understand about the Vietnamese."

"Specialist," he said, "Don't you understand that the Vietnamese get food from the garbage? That the children like to play in the dump?"

And the piece de résistance was his statement that the Vietnamese reacted differently to disease and germs "than we did."

My jaw must have hit the floor. Obviously the 101st had its own "germ theory." The fact that this hamlet was a food-producing entity and did not need garbage to survive did not seem to dawn on the major. Children might be playing in the dump but their parents might see this as dangerous. The fact that this complaint was not coming from me but from the hamlet elders, the major's neighbors, did not faze him. It was easy to dump garbage on the Vietnamese, and that is what he was going to do.

My time in Vietnam and in the military told me when to, "hold 'em and when to fold 'em." I politely saluted the major and bid him adieu. Still, I was frustrated, mad and overwhelmed. The R&R center stood as a shining example of all the prejudices, misguided direction and lack of cultural understanding that plagued our efforts in Vietnam.

But I had an ace in the hole. I had made friends with a U.S. Marine colonel who worked at the CORDS compound on psychological operations. It was his difficult job broadcasting messages over radio and loudspeakers to communicate to the people of Vietnam that we were the right side to be on in the war and that the Americans were the friends of the Vietnamese. Although he knew he was trying to sell support for a corrupt Thieu regime he was also a compassionate man with a great deal of cultural sensitivity. He was not helped by well-publicized civilian massacres, civilians being killed in our air/artillery strikes, and the fact that we routinely arrested, jailed and tortured innocent civilians. When I went to see him, and told him my story of the garbage dump, it must have hit a chord. Still, I saw no anger on his face. He simply said he would take care of it.

It was a few days before I went back to the village. On passing the hamlet with the garbage problem, I saw activity along the beach. Trucks and bulldozers were cleaning up the garbage. Vietnamese workers with spray canisters were spraying insecticide to kill the flies and mosquitoes. In no time the garbage was gone. The hamlet was happy. I prayed that the airborne major's next assignment might be building all-weather latrines in Alaska.

As the work on the An Duong dispensary continued, Tom and I were needed less and less. Occasionally we would scrounge construction materials for items that were left out of the original estimate, things like paint, hinges and rubber piping. We would forage at the nearby U.S. Army base in Phu Bai and sometimes down in Da Nang.

We didn't always need to bring whiskey. More often than not, when Tom and I explained what we were doing, supply officers and sergeants agreed to do what they could to help.

There was always the uneasy concern about VC in the area. One afternoon as we traveled to An Duong, we heard a couple of grenades explode nearby. There were no U.S. or South Vietnamese troops in the area. Tom and I did not know what to make of this so we just kept driving. We were always acutely aware of the potential danger but we tried to balance our security with the need to get our work done.

It was known to everyone in the area that I would gladly pick up hitchhikers along that sandy strip if my vehicle was not loaded down with supplies. I could take no passengers if I was carrying supplies as I felt the axles of my old truck could not take all the weight in the sandy soil, but often my truck looked more like an overloaded Third World bus, with people and animals filling and hanging off the back.

One afternoon as I was heading to An Duong with an interpreter, two young men appeared near the side of the road and flagged me down for a ride. I thought this odd since this was a very desolate strip of terrain. No one had ever shown up here before. The Vietnamese interpreter sat next to me. Tom had other business that day and no one was in the back of the cab with Butch. In fact, Butch was at my feet and not easily reachable. I usually kept Butch in my lap but I had been too casual with my weapon this day.

As the two men climbed in the back of the truck and positioned themselves directly behind me, I noticed that they wore some very large pistols in holsters. They then drew the pistols from the holsters. There they stood, casually dangling what looked like cannons right behind my head. Beads of sweat began to pour down my face. This was it; it was going to be a quick bullet to the skull and there was nothing I could do.

I thought about trying to grab Butch, open the door, swing out and get a burst of fire at them, but there was no way I could be that quick. So I drove on, clenching the steering wheel, waiting for the pistols to erupt. As we approached another desolated spot, one of the young men tapped me on the shoulder with his gun barrel, telling me to "dung lai" (stop). I stopped the truck, certain now that they were going to kill me and my interpreter. But the two men jumped over the back tailgate, smiled at us, waved and slowly walked off over a sand dune.

As I put the truck in gear, I looked at the interpreter. He was slumped back sweating in his seat. I never knew what to make of the incident, and I never cared to inquire more.

The war went on, and the building at An Duong went on.

I was getting "short" — military jargon for nearing the time of my departure from Vietnam and from the army. I was stepping onto one of the most exciting thresholds of my life. I had been accepted at the State University of New York at Brockport, and in less than a month, I would be discharged from the Army. I would never have to carry an automatic weapon again. I would see no more suffering. I would be involved in no more wars. I would get my college degrees and return to Asia, hopefully to Vietnam, and work in public health development.

More importantly, I truly believed that "young Turks," like me, would return home and use the knowledge of what we had witnessed to help change American policy for the better. America would never get involved in another winless war. We would stop trying to create democracy from the barrel of a gun and never again support worthless, corrupt dictatorships. We would no longer be the sole policeman for democracy in the world. We would work in coalitions with other nations.

Such are the thoughts of a war-weary, optimistic, somewhat cocky 22-year-old Army public health advisor. But I was not only about to start my academic education. I was also about to become educated in the realities of power, greed, ego and preserving the status quo. In the weeks before I left, the Province Public Health Service awarded me the South Vietnamese Public Health Medal.

My platoon commander put me in for the Bronze Star and the Army Commendation Medal for meritorious service. He also wrote a very glowing account of my service, including my work at An Duong. However, the military decided to scrap the wording for a boilerplate commendation, as if my work at An Duong and countless other public health projects were not worth mentioning. During the award ceremony at the CORDS compound I was told that the Bronze Star award had been held up and I would be mailed the documentation for the medal and I could "purchase" my Bronze Star medal at an Army-Navy store when I got back to the United States.

The dispensaries at An Duong and Tu Aui were nearing completion, and Dr. Do Van Minh wanted to have an opening ceremony for both dispensaries at the same time. There would be representatives from Provincial Headquarters, MAC/V and CORDS. Dignitaries would be coming from Da Nang. By then the dispensary would be fully equipped and staffed.

But this would not happen before my date of departure. I knew I was leaving the project in the good hands of Tom, Steve and Dennis. They would see it through. My new life was calling me somewhere on the other side of the Pacific and I was eager to go home. I did feel some sadness to be leaving An Duong and my friends.

The day before my departure, I was in my hooch, wearing cutoff jeans and no shirt and packing what I saw fit to take home with me. My Class "A" dress uniform and shoes, never worn, had gone green with mold in the bottom of my foot locker. I had one pair of boots, a couple of uniforms, my prized bush hat and some civilian clothes that I planned to change into the second I was discharged from the army. The rest of my clothes, and anything else in my foot locker, I would give to anyone who wanted it. Butch, my burp gun, would go to Dennis.

In the middle of this I got a call on the hooch phone. I was to go to the CORDS offices on the double.

I swore to myself. What last minute military "Bravo Sierra" had some clerk thought of to ruin, or worse, delay my departure? I was taking the early morning Air America flight down to Da Nang. I was not going to trust my final trip to an ambush along Highway 1 at the Hai Van pass. Once I cleared my headquarters in Da Nang, it would be a "Freedom Bird" flight to "The World" and civilian hood.

I shrugged off my annoyance, put on my uniform, and walked the few blocks to the CORDS offices.

Once at CORDS, I was directed into one of the main meeting rooms. As I opened the door, my heart skipped a beat. Standing there in their best clothes were the An Duong village chief and senior members of the construction committee. I could not believe they were there. It was a long and dangerous trek from the village to Hue. If I were a crying man I would have broken down on the spot. They explained through an interpreter that they had come to say goodbye to their friend.

They presented three gifts wrapped in fine paper for me. The first was a mother-of-pearl painting, a tranquil, peaceful scene of the Vietnamese countryside. In the painting, several deer drank from a running stream in a forest at the foot of hills and under a radiant sun. In the right-hand corner of the painting was the inscription "An Duong Hamlet Souvenir Friend American." The second gift was a wonderfully carved wooden dragon—a strong figure in Vietnamese mythology representing the universe, life, existence and growth.

The final gift was a conical Vietnamese rice hat for my mother. In Vietnam, there are often hidden messages everywhere. So, too, with this rice hat. Inverting the hat and holding it up to the light, I could see, hidden in the weave, symbols for peace and prosperity. That these men thought enough of me to come to say good-bye went beyond any medal someone would pin on my chest. I told them I would always remember them. We shook hands in the Vietnamese two-handed style. We hugged and said our final good-byes. I had won a small victory in Vietnam. It was time for me to go home and move on.

I often think of those men and others whom I had met in Vietnam. I always wondered if they ever knew how much they gave me and taught me; how I felt I owed them not only my life and career, but also my philosophy of life.

The painting and the carving remain some of my most-prized possessions. To me, the painting represents peace and tranquility, my wish for Vietnam. The carved dragon represents the power when humans work together with mutual understanding and respect for a common good. The rice hat represents the importance of family and culture. The symbolism of those gifts became my foundation. Ironically, they also represent what is missing in our domestic and foreign policy.

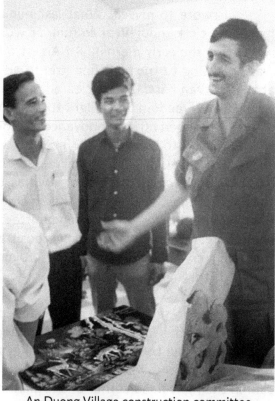

An Duong Village construction committee
presents me with going away gifts
at MAC/V Headquarters the day I left Hue City.

A COLD NIGHT IN HELL

The Shah is an island of stability in a turbulent corner of the world.

—Jimmy Carter

There is no cold like all-night cold. It seeps into the body, invading and stiffening muscles and bones, stinging fingers and toes, twisting emotions.

All-night cold demands wakefulness, leaving only time to think.

I was posted to Iran as an administrator/coordinator for a schistosomiasis[29] research team from the University of Tehran, based along the Iraq border in the mountainous southwestern Iranian province of Khuzestan. It was my first international assignment since I had left Vietnam seven years before.

Our families were back in the city of Ahwaz, and I worried about Kate, my wife of less than three months. Kate is a strong and independent woman and I trusted her judgment, but this was her first overseas experience. Moreover, I had already escaped one very close brush with death in these mountains the night before.

She was in Iran because of me, but who could have anticipated that the situation in this country would have deteriorated so quickly? The Shah's "Peacock Throne"[30] was sinking fast. Had I known how fast, I would never have left Kate behind that morning.

I tried to think positively during this long, cold night. Iranian friends were keeping watch over Kate. By some miracle, I had been

---

29 Schistosomiasis is an infection caused by parasitic flukes of the genus Schistosoma, occurring commonly in eastern Asia and in tropical regions and transmitted to humans through feces-contaminated fresh water or snails: symptoms commonly include pain, anemia, and malfunction of the infected organ

30 The Peacock Throne, famous golden throne captured from India by the Persians in 1739. Thereafter lost, it (and its reproductions) remained the symbol of the Persian, or Iranian, monarchy.

able to telephone her from the city of Tabriz in northwestern Iran. She told me that the oil company was preparing to evacuate all expatriates from Ahwaz and Abadan. I knew our British and American friends would assist her in getting to the airport. My plan, I told her, was to hitchhike to Tehran, where I would try to get a car, train or plane to Ahwaz and join her before the evacuation.

My situation was actually a lot more precarious. We were in a seemingly docile setting—an abandoned summer camping and picnic grounds—but I had felt safer in Vietnam. At least in Vietnam there was a sense of security. I carried my own weapon. I had my own friends to rely on. We had air cover and evacuation helicopters. In those days, if I failed to make it back to base there was always someone to come looking for me.

Now, no one knew where I was. I had no weapon, no air cover, and no backup and, certainly, I could not expect a dramatic, last-minute rescue by helicopter. If I got out of this desolate place it would be by my own willpower and wiles.

The campground was isolated, several hundred yards off the main roadway. In one sense, our location was good. No one could see us. But if we were stumbled upon by bandits or Islamic revolutionaries, they could easily eliminate us and hide our remains in the hills. The cold caused me to imagine worse-case scenarios.

"Nothing is as bad as the mind imagines it," I kept telling myself, as if this were an Indian mantra. It was one of the many personal mantras I had used to survive in Vietnam.

Since starting out on this journey, the Iranians I'd met had been nothing but kind. They had helped us after an accident in the Zagros Mountains the night before. I recalled our Volkswagen van spinning on its side down a mountain path but quickly put that out of my mind. It had been an Iranian who had warned us not to drive into the city ahead.

The Shah's troops were machine-gunning anyone who moved, he told us. Other Iranians had shown us the way to this campground. It was the old caretaker who opened the gate and allowed us to stay in the hut that now sheltered us. He had even given the woman in our party his only blanket. I lay there thinking about that old man, and how he looked so sorry when he said he had no food to give us.

Other things were also in our favor: the car in which I had hitched a ride was new, and we probably had enough gas to get to

Tehran. We also had a pretty good fix on where we were. The best I could figure, we were less than 10 kilometers west of Qazvin City. This put us near a good all-weather road on a direct west to east drive to Tehran. If all went well, we could drive through Qazvin early in the morning and make the Tehran city limits by late afternoon.

The Near East Foundation's main Iranian office was in the capital. With the help of office staff and a bit of luck, I could be heading to Ahwaz the next day.

It gets dark early in the mountains, auguring a long cold night. The temperature was already in the low 20s. A light dusting of snow carpeted the ground. I wore an unlined blue jean jacket, a light long-sleeved shirt, worn blue jeans and Redwing work boots—hardly the preferred attire for these temperatures.

With no gloves, I had wrapped some dirty old rags I had found on the floor around my hands to keep my fingers warm. My upstate New York experience taught me to breathe down the front of my jacket to help keep my body heat inside, warming my chest.

I tried to relax. I could do nothing about my situation, but I had been through worse. I curled up on a metal lounge chair and considered our shelter. The first thing I looked for was an avenue of escape from the building. Vietnam had taught me well.

We were in a small cinder-block structure with a flat roof. It was divided into two sections separated by a wooden plywood partition and door. Built into the partition was a serving window so that a summertime cook could pass food and dishes from the kitchen on the other side of the wall. The kitchen itself was sparsely outfitted with an old butane-powered stove. Not surprisingly, the butane canister was missing. There was an empty 50s-style refrigerator against the wall, along with several sheet-metal kitchen cabinets painted pale green. Dirty plates and utensils littered a wobbly kitchen table. It was hard to estimate when the last meal had been consumed.

There were four of us in the second room. Eric and his wife Anna were Swedish. Their traveling companion, whose name I could not remember, was from Sri Lanka. The three were partners in a travel business and had been scouting a possible overland bus route to Asia for European tourists. As unrealistic as this bus route seemed to me, I was grateful when they offered me a ride to Tehran.

The room in which we slept contained metal lawn furniture in various stages of disrepair, painted the same hospital green as the kitchen cabinets, but missing the one thing that might have provided at least some comfort—foam cushions. I reclined awkwardly in a love seat I had selected for a bed. My Sri Lankan traveling companion had put the two straight-back chairs face-to-face to form a sleeping surface. The last piece in the set, a lounge chair, was in such bad shape that the Swedish couple had opted to sleep together on the ping-pong table.

Both rooms were lit by a single bare light bulb that was suspended from the center of the ceiling by a frayed electrical wire. The fact that we had electricity at all was amazing to me. After I shared my last Snickers bar with the group, it was decided we should try to sleep. It was dark and only 8:13 P.M; it promised to be a long, cold night.

I lay there unable to drift off, my inner voice asserting itself.

"You idiot," it said, "You have a master's degree in public health from the University of Michigan, a wife who loves you, and here you lie in no man's land, waiting to freeze or get shot. What the hell are you doing here?" My inner voice could be blunt, overly dramatic and self-righteous, but it posed a good question. I certainly had time to think about an answer.

My dreams and ambitions had remained constant since Vietnam. I wanted to work in international public health, to help people, to make a difference. Some things had changed, though. My desire to return to Vietnam was crushed that sad day in April 1975 when the first communist tank had rumbled through the gates of the Presidential Palace in Saigon. America had lost its first war.

What was I doing here? My thoughts receded to my last days in Vietnam, recalling the success I'd helped achieve at An Duong— and the horrors I'd witnessed at Hoi An Prison. In the years since, I had been driven, seeking something, but not sure what that something was.

I received my discharge from the U.S. Army on May 7, 1971 at Fort Lewis. Washington. I had served my country for 31 months and seven days, 25 months of that in Vietnam. I felt relief, even joy, at being safely outside the war zone and was exhilarated about starting my next career adventure.

Although I was physically unscathed, I was bleeding out of the rectum from what I called a "Vietnam stomach." I had hearing loss and a constant ringing in both ears, the result of being too close to the "rockets' red glare and the bombs bursting in air." I had hip and back problems from hours of driving 'off-road' in remote areas of Thua Thien and Quang Nam Provinces. And I couldn't sleep without sedatives or alcohol. And of course, there were my ghosts. Those horrible nightmares.

I wanted to get beyond the war and use my military public health experience and what I had learned in my universities. While I could be proud of what I had done, I could not be proud of what my government was doing in Southeast Asia. It was so important, I believed, for America to learn from returning veterans so our country would never make the same mistake again. How could I articulate what I had witnessed? And even if I could, who would listen?

Still, I felt reborn. From Specialist 5th Class Giannone, I had morphed into Mr. Paul J. Giannone, aspiring college student. My life was before me, and witnessing pain and suffering were left behind. Rarely does an individual have the opportunity to stand on such a wonderfully clean threshold.

My hometown of Auburn is a picturesque community of 30,000 located in rolling farm country in central New York, nestled at the northern tip of Owasco Lake. It is a 20-minute ride from Syracuse to the east and an hour's drive to Rochester in the west.

Auburn is the birthplace of William H. Seward, Lincoln's Secretary of State, who purchased Alaska for $7 million. Harriet Tubman, the former slave turned suffragist who worked on the Underground Railroad, owned a home in Auburn; there is a museum dedicated to her on South Street. The Auburn Correctional Facility on State Street, in the center of the town, is a maximum-security prison. It has the dubious distinction of having been the site of the first execution in an electric chair of a convicted murderer. You can actually purchase a postcard of the prison that points out this little-known historical tidbit.

My first post-Vietnam summer at home gave me time to collect my thoughts and get used to living without the war. There were no air strikes, refugee camps, late night medical evacuations or political prisons. I enjoyed the freedom to go into a restaurant, grocery store or ice cream parlor and buy anything I wanted to eat; the choice to drive or walk around at night and not worry about getting ambushed; the relief of not having to carry a weapon every place I went.

To say that I did not have readjustment problems, however, would be a lie. At first I simply could not get used to not carrying a weapon. I owned a pistol and for a long time I needed to keep it under my pillow to feel secure enough to even attempt sleep.

Talking to women or being around them was most difficult for me. I made a few blunders that I regretted long afterward. I had a tendency to drink too much. Like a rich kid opening presents at Christmas, the gift of survival was too much and I sometimes found myself opening all that was given to me too quickly to really enjoy each one.

I knew I had changed, yet the people of Auburn had pretty much remained the same. Sitting with friends, listening to the conversations at Curley's Tavern and other favorite watering holes, it soon became clear to me. I had come through a very intense time, but the gossip and jokes had not changed in Auburn. Now I found myself hearing about who was sleeping with whom and the latest joke from the prison, whereas the conversations at the Enlisted Men's Club at Dozema Compound in Hue City dealt with hard core politics and very real life-and-death situations.

I didn't blame my friends. It was simply that I had changed radically. I felt different, out of tune, isolated. An invisible wall surrounded me, and I realized that I was seeing the world from an entirely different perspective, one that was impossible to explain to friends or family.

Once I recognized this, Auburn became, for me, a place to be *from;* a place to return to, perhaps for solace, my rabbit warren of protection. But my life was somewhere else. I wondered, even then, if I would ever again call a physical place on earth "home."

I was off to college the last week of August 1971. College felt like a rare and precious gift that I had earned by having survived 25 months of daily insanity. I was going back to school not only for myself but for all the others who did not make it out of the rice paddies and the triple-canopy jungle. I had failed at my first attempt at higher education in 1968, but motivation was no longer a problem. I would do well because I had to. I reached out for the tools that would help me pursue my life's work in public health. Nothing would stop me.

Because of my service in Vietnam, I had two years of solid public health experience, but I did not have a public health degree.

Professors at the State University of New York at Brockport took the time and had the patience to show me the way. Also, I had a support group on campus of more than 800 Vietnam veterans.

College seemed easy and college life was exhilarating. And, I met the woman with whom I would fall in love and eventually marry.

Kate Huntley was an art major. We met on a warm summer night in a Brockport bar at the start of my junior year. She was wearing a halter top, and the romantic person that I was broke the ice by placing a cold beer can against her bare back. Instead of turning and attacking me, she smiled. I asked her to dance.

As we got to know each other, I found Kate to be very independent, with strong opinions on the world, women's rights and political views similar to mine. I was upfront with her from the beginning. I told Kate that she should not get interested in me unless she planned to work overseas, as my plans were to get my degrees and go overseas as soon as I could. I am not sure if she actually believed me at the time.

At SUNY Brockport, like all other campuses across the country, there were demonstrations against the war. I did not participate; I thought it was their right as long as their beliefs were genuine. Unfortunately, so many were so wrapped up into being anti-war and anti-establishment that they wouldn't take the time to listen to those Vietnam veterans who could give them just cause for rallying against what I considered crimes against human rights. Instead, the anti-war protest message seemed to me to be something along the lines of "war's a bummer."

Sitting one night alone in Barber's bar, waiting to meet some veteran friends, I was joined by another vet, a "brother[31]" I had never seen before. We began talking, and I lamented about not being understood by many in my generation. He just looked at me and laughed. He put his arm around me and said, "Now you know what us black folk feel like on a daily basis."

I was shocked and confused by this statement. His tone became more serious as he continued, "Think about it. Use your head. You think these are your people? Man, the only people that are going to be *your* people for the rest of your life on terra firma are going to be other men who wore bush hats and jungle boots. Shit, I can't even talk to other brothers who weren't in Nam."

---

31   Brother was the term used to describe African-American soldiers in Vietnam.

He swung around in his bar stool and with a flamboyant sweep of his arm pointed to the students in the bar. As he turned, I got a good look at him. Like me, he was wearing blue jeans, a faded army fatigue shirt, bush hat and jungle boots. It was our uniform. The Screaming Eagle patch on the shoulder of his sun-bleached fatigue jacket and the Combat Infantry Badge sewed to it indicated that he had been with the 101st Airborne Division and that he had seen combat. An ugly Y-shaped scar on his cheek told me he had been wounded.

"Look at these people," he went on. "They got awfully moralistic the minute the government started drafting more rich Republican white meat for the grinder in Southeast Asia out of the colleges. No one was protesting when poor folk were dying. It was all fine and patriotic for them as long as blacks and Chicanos from the ghettos were being blown into small pieces in the rice fields. Who really cared if a poor white dirt farmer from Iowa or a kid from a steel mill town got his testicles and his legs blown off?

"The minute we started taking their own kind, the war became a moral issue. Our people have so much freedom. They have so many mechanisms for getting at the truth. Yet they ignore what is before them. God bless the draft. The draft was the great equalizer. It was forced equality. It doesn't matter if you're black, white, rich, poor, tall, short or just plain ugly. All of them ended up in the same bunkers. I'm not complaining, though, and you shouldn't either. For one shining moment in history we were all forced to see the truth at ground level. And we dug in our heels and spit the truth back in their faces. For whatever the motive, we have not seen Americans stand up like that since Washington's time. Goddamn this war, but God bless the draft[32]."

His warm dark eyes caught me again as he leaned back against his bar stool. An aura of compassion seemed to surround him: wisdom born of cold steel, fire and blood.

"The government will never make that mistake again," he said. "Mark my words. The next war will be a series of quick ground actions so poor folk like you and me will have the privilege of dying for unethical causes and no one will raise a finger to protest our deaths. The President may even show up at the airport to cry crocodile tears over the body bags.

---

32   Author's note: It should be noted that when the Vietnam War ended so did the antiwar and anti-draft movements. Today few protest the unwinnable wars in Afghanistan and Iraq.

"My friend, I haven't known you one hour but I can love you like a brother."

Raising his glass, this man said, more to the entire bar than me: "Welcome to the coming age of economic and ethnic racism."

He downed his beer in one quick gulp, bought another for me, and walked out of the bar and my life. I would never see him again. I would never learn if he was a student, a construction worker or simply one of my ghosts visiting me.

The cold interrupted my musings and brought me back to the Iranian campground. It was actually a noise that focused my attention and perked my senses. My hips were becoming stiff from lying on that metal love seat. My spinal cord shivered involuntarily. It was only 9:26 P.M. My little sojourn into the past had taken little more than an hour.

I heard the noise again, not a comforting sound. Like a computer, my brain went down the list of noises stored in its memory bank, trying to match this particular sound to a thing or being.

Rats! I was hearing rats. The building sounded as if it were full of them. I should have realized that the scraps of food in the kitchen might attract furry guests. I could hear them scratching at the remaining food. God, how I hated rats, ever since the refugee camps in Vietnam.

My first military compound, in Hoi An, was rife with rats. They would run around the rafters of our barracks all night long. I was unfortunate enough to have a top bunk. Those rodents, some the size of small cats, would scamper along the beams a few feet above my head. If they wanted to take a shortcut they would jump on my bare back and gallop down the length of my body. From there they would fling themselves to a table near my bunk, then onto the floor and out the doorway. I could still feel their rope-like tails swishing along my bare legs. Just the thought made my skin crawl.

Slowly, I got up. There was no light in the room. I groped for a small flashlight in my pocket and beamed my way to the kitchen wire opening. I could hear the others were tossing and turning, unable to sleep. I didn't know if they had picked up on the sound or recognized its source. I decided to say nothing. I found the rectangular service portal with my beam of light. It was slightly ajar and I opened it just enough to look through. As I focused my light at the kitchen table, all I could see were scurrying claws and tails.

There was not much to be done about the rats beyond satisfying my curiosity. I trudged back to my metallic bed hoping that the rats would stay on their side of the building. I knew now that any sleep would be impossible. I had nothing more to do than resume my nocturnal chronology of the events that had brought me here with the rats and freezing cold in northern Iran. Where was I in my reflections? Oh yes, college life, the girl of my dreams, and the challenge of the future.

After graduating with honors from SUNY Brockport, I went on to the University of Michigan for my master's degree in public health. Luckily, Kate was accepted at Eastern Michigan to pursue her master's in education. She was in Ypsilanti, only eight miles down the road from Ann Arbor. At the University of Michigan, I was attending what many in academia considered the number one public health school in the country. I was taught by some of the finest professors in the country, if not the world. Just as exciting to me were the students with whom I associated. At least two-thirds of the 30-odd students in my cohort hailed from foreign countries; several were medical doctors affiliated with ministries of health in Asia, Africa, the Middle East and the Americas.

I learned not only from my professors but from study sessions and informal gatherings with my peers. Our potluck dinners were not only feasts of international cuisine but a laboratory for informal discussions on international development. I was in my element. After 18 months, I had my masters' degree with a concentration in population and family planning. Along with my undergraduate degree in community health services, I felt ready to go out and do some good in the world.

I began applying for public heath positions overseas, but not in Vietnam, now a unified state under communist rule. I sent out hundreds of resumes. I knew that if I could find work overseas I would show people in Third World countries that development and democracy did not come out of the barrel of an M-16. I might be only one voice, but at least I would be a voice.

I received two job offers. CARE had a health administration position opening in Nicaragua. The Near East Foundation had a health administration position available for a schistosomiasis research team in southwestern Iran. Nicaragua was war-torn and unstable. On the other hand, the Shah of Iran, according to government and media reports, was as stable as the Rock of Gibraltar. I accepted the position in Iran.

I would be stationed in the city of Ahwaz, essentially a camel stop, north of the port of Abadan. I joined the University of Tehran Schistosomiasis Research Team I as the sole American. The team was working with Marsh Arabs across the Dash Mishan plain near the Iraq border.

Since Ahwaz was an isolated desert city, there would be little to do for a person who did not have a job. Kate and I decided I would go to Iran alone, establish myself in my work, and look for work for her. If I found her a position, she would fly to Iran and we would be married.

I arrived in Ahwaz in January 1978 and found an apartment in an Iranian neighborhood. I had told myself from the start that I did not want to live in an American "golden ghetto." I wanted to live among the Iranian people, to learn about their culture and as much of their language as possible. I began taking classes in Farsi, though I am the first to admit that language is not my forte.

Luckily, I was able to find Kate a job relatively easily. In fact, I ended up with three job offers for her. A new friend, Ajit, offered the one she eventually took. It was with an American-based company, a language training school with a contract to teach English to oil company employees. Kate was a teacher. The pay was good. The staff she would work with was friendly. And they threw some of the best parties in town.

Next, I had to get Kate to Ahwaz, where we would be married. Myrtle Huntley, Kate's mom, was as strong and independent as her daughter. At her insistence, I would fly to London and meet Kate, her sister Karen and Myrtle. We would vacation for a few days and visit Kate's relatives in England, and then she gave me permission to escort Kate to Iran for our nuptials.

The wedding of Kate Emily Huntley and Paul Joseph Giannone was like everything else in our time together has been: unique. Luckily for us, there was a Christian church in Ahwaz; luckier for me it was a Catholic Church. The pastor was Archbishop John, who looked as if he had walked out of The Adventures of Robin Hood. Short and rotund, with a salt-and-pepper beard, he was a modern-day Friar Tuck, always accompanied by his pet German shepherd.

Of course, Archbishop John, upon finding that my British best man, Michael Wherly, and I were Catholics, insisted that we go to confession. As Protestants, Kate and her maid of honor, Elizabeth Cooper, were off the hook. Kate could not understand why this would throw two non-practicing Catholics into turmoil.

I had not been to confession in years. Michael was an ex-Catholic brother who was gay. There was a lot of tossing and turning for Michael and me the night before confession but we both did our duty in the confessional.

Paul and Kate
entering St Simon Church on September 15, 1978
to take their wedding vows .

We had to leap another hurdle and get special government permission to have the wedding, as Ahwaz and many other cities were under martial law. No mass gatherings were permitted. Our guests had to arrive in small groups and not linger outside the church, an old Gothic-style structure painted pink. Inside, statues of Jesus, the Mother Mary and other saints, strategically placed, stared down at us. Before an assembly of Iranian, British, French, Russian, American and Pakistani friends, an entire two-hour ceremony was conducted in Aramaic. The only words uttered in English were from a biblical verse spoken by a very baritone Englishman called up from the congregation by Archbishop John. He boomed out for all to hear, "Woman, ye shall submit to your man."

So much for woman's liberation and Catholicism. I had planned to get handmade wedding rings in the bazaar but demonstrators had set it on fire, so our wedding bands became the two gold bracelets I had bought for Kate a few months earlier. And so, with tanks and armored personnel carriers rumbling up and down the street in front of the church, we were married.

The cold night and metal furniture again collided with my train of thought. Someone stirred. Rats were still scratching away. I looked at my illuminated watch: it was 10:18 P.M. My hands stung from the cold and were getting stiffer. I had a headache, my hips were sore and my eyes were beginning to run. I shifted my position for what seemed like the thousandth time and my body creaked as pain shot into my hips. That sense of complete isolation seemed to make me colder. And I was on the fringe of a revolution in which anything could happen and no one knew where I was.

I reflected on the wonders of hindsight. The warning signs had been there from the moment I flew into Iran, almost a year before. My survival instincts, honed in Vietnam, had picked up on the mood almost immediately as I felt cold and angry stares like the ones I felt in the Vietnamese refugee camps.

Iran was like a giant pressure cooker. Pressure began to build as items like gasoline, cooking fuel and other cooking staples escalated in price and then disappeared from the market entirely. The Shah's secret police, the Savak, intensified their activities. Students and workers were arrested in their homes, from their places of business, from classrooms and in the streets. Many would never be heard from again.

The Iranian people responded with peaceful demonstrations, work slowdowns, and strikes within government ministries and universities. That the American mission to Iran did not pick up on this and take action—or, if they did sense the unrest but refused to take action — only spotlights how inept our foreign service had become.

I lived in an Iranian neighborhood, had Iranian friends and worked on an otherwise all-Iranian research team. These friends and associates would tell me what they had learned through their informal networks. The demonstrations that were initially isolated were spreading over the entire nation. Strikes were crippling government projects and studies at the universities. There were transportation slowdowns. Marketplaces were burned. An occasional western-style restaurant would be fire-bombed. As the tactics employed by the Shah's military got increasingly more vicious, anti-foreign and anti-Shah sentiments continued to escalate. As the middle-class Iranians ad the students joined the battle against the Shah, the "Rock of Gibralter" was starting to crumble from within.

Rumors were rife in Ahwaz of weapons being smuggled across the Iraqi border into the small city of Dezful. The population of Dezful, about two hours north of Ahwaz, had long been strongly anti-Shah. The probability that Iran's old enemy, Iraq, was supplying weapons to provocateurs in Dezful seemed strong. This worried my Iranian friends since the odds were increasing for the potential of violent confrontation.

At the time, more than 40,000 expatriates were living throughout Iran. If the country erupted into a full-scale revolution, it was not inconceivable that a great many Americans might be in jeopardy. There was no U.S. Embassy in Ahwaz, but once a week an American consular officer would make the two-hour drive to Ahwaz from the port city of Abadan. At the offices at the Iran/American Society, he would see people on a first-come, first-served basis.

I decided to go see him, even though I had lost a great deal of trust in my own government. As I was ushered into his office it seemed as if MGM had been hired to typecast the young consular officer for the role of a Foreign Service Officer. He looked like everything that a U.S. Foreign Service Officer should be: blond hair, blue eyes, perfect white teeth, skin that had never seen a pimple. He appeared to be in his late twenties or early thirties. He was impeccably dressed in a starched white shirt, tie, grey trousers and polished tasseled loafers. He looked as out of place in a desert town in Iran as a Klansman in Harlem.

To play the Foreign Service game you have to be well connected and smooth. But smooth does not necessarily equate to smart and intuitive, although the man who stood before me knew exactly what to say and how to say it. To me the most dangerous person in the world is a newly graduated U.S. Foreign Service officer who believes everything he had been told during training. Still, with anti-

Shah demonstrations intensifying, I felt obligated to tell him what I had heard and seen.

I was concerned about the attitude of the Iranian people toward the American community. If the worst did happen, and civil war broke out, would the Iranians lash out at the foreign communities, especially the Americans? After all, it was the CIA that had restored the Shah and his family to power[33]. That our government had been his benefactor was not lost on the Iranian people.

One incident I related to the consular officer stuck out. One morning my best Iranian friend, Iranshahi, burst into my office. His face was distorted in pain. Tears were running down his cheeks. As soon as I could calm him down he told me that he had just heard that the Shah's troops had used American-made "Huey" helicopters to strafe unarmed women and children demonstrators in Mashhad.

"My God, Paul," he said, trying to fight back more tears, "We don't want violence. We don't hate Americans. How can your government arm these rabid beasts? Americans, of all people, who stand for democracy and freedom, should understand us. I know we won't take it much longer."

After I shared this story and other information, the consular officer, who had been entirely cordial and attentive, escorted me out of his office and reassuringly patted me on the back. He repeated the same pablum that the U.S. government was feeding the American media: "Don't worry, Mr. Giannone. The Shah is in complete control and the nation is secure. There is nothing for the Americans to do in Iran but be patient, wait out the demonstrations and continue to work as best as possible."

In the next days and weeks, the situation grew even more dire. Coming out of my home one morning, I found myself face-to-face with an armored personnel carrier. I soon learned that the Shah had ordered tanks and machine gun posts to be set up in every large city. In Ahwaz, all major intersections were covered, as were all government buildings and schools. Was this a sign of a government in complete control?

---

33   *American Coup.* Directed by Joe Ayella. Performed by Ervand Abrahamian and Ehsan Yarshater. United States: IMDbPro, 2010. Streaming Video. This worthwhile movie tells the story of the 1953 coup carried out by the CIA to topple the popular Iranian Prime Minister Mohammad Mossadegh who had nationalized the oil industry to protect Iran's chief asset. This enraged Winston Churchill who believed England should continue to control the oil reserves it had originally discovered in Iran..

Kate and I began living with our suitcases packed, anticipating the day when we would need to make a hasty departure from Iran. Each night there were massive demonstrations in Ahwaz and throughout the country, with thousands of people chanting, "Death to the Shah! Death to the Shah!" or "Allah-hu Akbar!" (God is great). Each day, just as dusk fell, the faithful gathered at the mosques. Loudspeakers atop the mosques would call them to evening prayer and then command the people to go into the streets to join the jihad, the holy war, against the Shah. For those who perished under the Shah's guns, death meant an ascent to heaven as a martyr for the cause.

I heard chilling reports of parents encouraging their own children to join this holy crusade against the "Peacock Throne" and the Pahlavi dynasty. The mosques became a central meeting place for the demonstrators. By inciting the Iranians to take to the streets in the name of Allah, the mullahs were slowly gaining back the power that had been taken from them years before by the Shah's father with the help of our CIA. The people themselves needed little encouragement, as the corruption and brutality of the Shah's rule reached a critical mass and into almost every home. By invoking the name of God, the mullahs gave the cause religious credibility.

A religious and political tug-of-war was rocking the country. The Shah's army was trying to suppress the demonstrations and sustain a government that had been crippled by strikes. The mullahs were calling the people to the streets, asking Iranian soldiers to desert and telling government employees not to go to work. At that point, both the American and British governments had failed to assess the dangers.

More importantly, the U.S. government seemed willing to bargain with the lives of Americans who were working in Iran. How could our government explain a mass exodus of Americans when it was publicly telling the world that the Shah was in complete control? It was déjà vu all over again. In Vietnam, our government did not want the world to see large numbers of refugees in camps: in Iran our government did not want the press running stories of Americans fleeing that country in large numbers. Politics, control and public perception were more important than human lives and the truth.

As I lay restless in the cold dark room, recriminations assaulted me. Why had I put Kate and me in such danger? Was it in order to honor a contract with my first international employer? I knew, from the history of Iran, that there had been times when the government had been unsteady but had survived. Was this such a time? How many times does a volcano rumble and smoke over the centuries before a catastrophic explosion?

An attack on a British oil company executive was the main topic of conversation when I next met with the American consular officer from Abadan. The incident was common knowledge. It had been covered by the world press. Had not this attack verified what I had been saying all these months? He smiled at me. I knew deep down that he just wanted me to leave him alone. I knew I would get the latest, most politically correct response. Still, I had to try.

He stared at me for what seemed like forever. Finally, his silence was broken, but the smile never faltered. "You see, Mr. Giannone, they were not really trying to kill this man. They just wanted to frighten him."

I nearly laughed in the young consular officer's face. Was he truly such a fool or did he take me to be one? I told him that one lesson I'd learned in Vietnam was that when someone throws a bomb at you, you have to assume that person is trying to kill you. There was no point in talking any further and I left his office for good.

I couldn't be too mad at this boy in Foreign Service clothes. He was lethal. He was dangerous. But he was a product of his environment, blinded from reality by the very precepts of our own narrowly-focused foreign policy and a need to protect his career. Like all the others I had met before, and those that I would meet after, he had been weaned, disciplined and indoctrinated on mediocrity, insensitivity and always "staying the course," whatever the party line was. He was incapable of reacting to or seeing what was before him and thinking beyond his political talking points and his career. From that point on, whenever we heard gunfire in Ahwaz, the joke was, "Don't worry, they're not trying to kill anyone; they're just trying to frighten them."

After the bombing incident, events seemed to escalate. I telephoned a colleague in Tehran who was authorized to attend security briefings at the U.S. Embassy. I asked my colleague what had been said about events in Ahwaz and Khuzestan Province over the past few months. Surprised, he told me that relatively little had been mentioned about activity there for a long time. I shared some of the stories that I had recently told the consular officer. Both of us concluded that either the consular officer did not report them at all or higher authorities in the Embassy had censored them. Not unlike the now famous "Pentagon Papers" the U.S. government was again withholding information that might prove vital to the safety of its own citizens.

Now it was 11:45 P.M. I lay there in the cold and dark. My eyes were open but in the blackness of the room I could see nothing. Still, my senses sharpened as a thought began to take shape. I drifted back to Saigon and my talk with Dennis after the party at the fat man's apartment. I had said that the "road show," the lies, the distortions of truth would go on. What had happened in Vietnam was now repeating itself in Iran. I wanted to believe that Vietnam was an anomaly, a bad judgment call, a fluke in American history. But that would be a lie. We lost in Vietnam, and would continue to lose, because we had betrayed our own principles: that life, liberty and the pursuit of happiness are above all our foundation as a nation. And a nation that betrays its own principles will always fail.

The morning of December 23, 1978[34], right before Christmas, was just another work day for both the Muslim and Christian population of Ahwaz. Out in the expatriate suburbs an American oil company official, the "acting" General Manager for the Texaco Oil Service Company, Paul E. Grimm, walked from his house to his car. His driver was already behind the wheel. The engine was running, the heater on in order to ward off the winter chill. As they started down the road at about 7AM they were ambushed by three men with automatic rifles. I doubt if the American even saw the car that slowly rolled up on his blind side. It was all over in a second. Mr. Grimm was instantaneously killed. The New York Times report indicated that Mr. Grimm was the seventh American to be murdered in Iran in the last five years. To me, the irony was chilling—the reason Grimm was in an acting general manager capacity was that his predecessor, George Link, had been wounded in the bomb attack I had described to the U.S. Counselor official.

That morning in another rich residential Iranian neighborhood, the same scenario was being repeated against an Iranian oil company executive, Mr. Malek Bouroozardi. The opposition had made its point well. In the early morning hours, on the day before Christmas, they

---

34   "Gunmen in Iran Ambush and Kill Two Oil Officials, One from US." *New York Times* December 24, 1978.

had violently told the Shah and the world that they were armed, well organized and determined. The consular officer from Abadan and all the other Americans could take their confidence in the man who sat atop the Peacock Throne and shove it.

The news of the killings hit us hard. Despite the sincerity and kindness of our Iranian friends, despite their efforts to protect us, I knew the time had arrived for Kate and me to prepare to leave. I had already drafted a letter of resignation on December 20th to my employers indicating my rationale for departing the country and sent it. Before leaving I needed to close up my office and pack up files.

My Iranian friends felt it would be a short time until order was restored and we could return. They helped us pack the few household goods that were of value. We put them in three foot lockers and took them to a Tehran University guest house where they could be safely stored until our return.

We began meeting with Kate's boss Ajit and other friends to plan the logistics of an evacuation. The most pressing problem facing us was mobility. We had not been planning an immediate departure. Everyone, including our Iranian friends, had concluded that the opposition had made its point in the December attacks and things would calm down until the "Nowruz"—the Iranians lunar New Year in March. We knew airline and rail service was sporadic because of strikes but they were our first and second choice. Each of us had a car and we could purchase enough fuel on the black market to get the lot of us to a border in a convoy.

Unfortunately for us, the nearest border was Iraq and there was no love lost between Iran and Iraq. One option would be to drive to the Iraqi border and hope they might grant us passage through their country. Another option would be to drive to the port of Abadan, leave our cars there and rent an Arab dhow[35] that could sail us to a safe port of call, possibly Kuwait or Bahrain. However, no one cared to speculate on how dangerous a clandestine boat trip might be. Another alternative would be to convoy our vehicles north to the Turkish and Russian border and then west across Turkey to Greece. This would be a long hard drive over the Zagros Mountains and through the always-volatile Kurdish homeland.

---

35   Dhow (Arabic المراكب الشراعية dāw) is the generic name of a number of traditional sailing vessels with one or more masts with settee or sometimes lateen sails, used in the Red Sea and Indian Ocean region. Historians are divided as to whether the dhow was invented by Arabs or Indians. Wikipedia

We decided that I would accompany Ajit in his Volkswagen van because he had to renew the entry permit for the van from the Iranian immigration authority at the Turkish border before it expired in a couple of days. This would give us the opportunity to scout out this potential exit route and we could be back in four days. We decided to depart immediately.

Ajit was able to acquire the black-market provisions we would need for the trek. He bought two large, heavy-duty plastic storage drums that he filled with black market gasoline. Because it would have been unwise to advertise our gasoline supply, the drums had to be strapped down inside the van. A very dangerous move, which almost proved deadly.

We started our journey early on the morning of December 28th. I gave Kate a hug and told her not to worry; I would see her in a few days. Ajit said his goodbyes to his British girlfriend. I was travelling light. I carried a gym bag with a fresh shirt, change of underwear and toiletries. For security, I took a large kitchen knife and placed it behind the passenger seat. It was really only for my mental security; I doubted it would be much good against bandits or soldiers armed with automatic weapons.

It seemed we were off in our olive-green Volkswagen camper before we even had much time to think of the journey before us. We had maps, fuel, food and the *Best of Gordon Lightfoot* and *James Taylor* blasting out of the car stereo, heading north toward Dezful and the Zagros Mountains. Ajit drove, I rode shotgun, wishing for the first time since Vietnam that I had "Butch," my old M-3 grease submachine gun, in my lap.

Ajit looked like he had just walked out of India. He had very dark skin, curly black hair, a strong, eagle-like pointed nose and piercing brown eyes. When he concentrated on a subject he glared like an eagle. He had played soccer at one of the Ivy League schools. He was a very good conversationalist. His South Asian appearance stood in stark contrast to his American mannerisms, and he talked pure East Coast American.

The road to Dezful was single lane in either direction and fairly straight as it cut a black path over the flat desert terrain. Occasionally we passed the twisted wreckage of a tractor trailer or passenger car. These rusting hulks served as metal altars to the numerous head-on collisions that occurred daily along this highway, as the often-fatal results of overloaded trucks driven at excessive speed by drivers strung out on opium.

I began to pick up other signs of danger as we approached Dezful. I was falling back on my Vietnam survival instincts. There was a feeling in the air of caution and urgency. I had felt the same way before in Vietnam driving down Highway 1 over the Hai Van Pass between Hue and Da Nang. It was as if death was out there somewhere, seeking an easy victim.

We soon began to notice more elements of the Shah's troops and armored units. They were deployed in small units of one or two British or American-made tanks and Russian armored personnel carriers. As we approached Dezful, military concentrations in greater numbers became more visible, and I noticed no small children in the villages or at play in the fields. In Vietnam, we quickly learned to be cautious in areas where no children were to be seen. When trouble is around, parents will always pull children inside their homes.

As we approached Dezful we were halted at an Iranian military checkpoint manned by three soldiers in a U.S.-made M-151 jeep. There was a belt-fed M-60 machinegun mounted on a pole in the rear of the jeep. The corporal manning the gun kept it pointed at me, his finger on the trigger. I could be splattered into the hereafter by a scared Iranian triggering American-donated equipment. It was probably Vietnam-era war surplus. Now there was an irony. I began to develop a real uneasiness about our situation.

The checkpoint team leader, a tall sergeant with a handlebar moustache, was relieved to find we were Americans. Once we identified ourselves he smiled but, with a look of sadness, told us that there was major rioting in the center of Dezful. A gun battle had raged that morning. He indicated that it was now over, but snipers were still firing at moving vehicles. He pointed out on our maps the location of a side road that would skirt the city. We thanked him in broken Farsi and English. He told us to pray for Iran.

As the van began to shift gears and pull us away from the jeep, the sergeant's parting information began to sink in. Maybe the country was in more immediate danger than anyone had thought. As we skirted Dezful I spotted a government building, on the fringe of the city, engulfed in flames. I recognized it as an agricultural extension building I had once visited. Conversation had dried up as we thought the same thing: Will there be a way back to Ahwaz?

Night fell quickly as we approached Hamadan. We had slowly been gaining altitude and it was getting colder the farther north we traveled. Hamadan was a welcome sight. There was a government guesthouse just south of the city, so we did not have to drive into town. We were greeted at the front gate by a security guard. He pointed to the city and indicated in Pidgeon English that rioters had burned down the bazaar earlier in the day. The bazaar was still smoldering.

Ajit and I shared a room that was drab but clean and warm. To our great surprise and relief the telephone line to Ahwaz was working and we called home. What Kate was able to tell us was not very reassuring. On the day of our departure, massive demonstrations and gunfire erupted. Several people had been killed. From all accounts, it looked like the government of the Shah was sinking faster than the iron ore ship memorialized in Gordon Lightfoot's ballad, "The Wreck of the Edmund Fitzgerald." The American and British oil companies in Khuzestan Province were beginning to activate their plans for an evacuation of all expatriates.

We hastily decided on a contingency plan. Ajit and I would leave Hamadan before sunrise to avoid any trouble once the city woke up. We decided to take a less developed road to Kermanshah and then head north to Tabriz and Khoy. If the situation calmed down, we would get the van's permit stamped and head back south immediately. If the situation remained critical, Ajit would take the van across either the Turkish or Russian border, I would take a bus or hitchhike to Tehran and find whatever means possible to get me back to Ahwaz and Kate.

After a sleepless night, we climbed back into the van and somehow found our way to the Kermanshah road. It was still pitch black. Even the high beams seemed to have difficulty piercing the darkness. Icy patches glinted on the pavement, but we decided not to put on the tire chains until dawn broke and we were out of the city.

Beyond Hamadan, the road seemed to rise straight up into the blackness of the sky. The only illumination came from our headlights bouncing off the snow on the roadside. Neither of us was in the mood to talk. At one point, we reached a high pass at the crest of one of the mountains. The snow had been increasing in volume along the side of the road, but the road itself seemed clear.

Once we reached the crest Ajit slowed the van a bit as he tried to make out the road in front of us. I remember seeing a faint glint of light to the east, and felt glad that the sun would soon be up. We peered into the darkness as the roadway pitched almost straight down into another valley. Looking in the valley we could make out distant lights. Apparently Ajit and I made the same incorrect assumption about what was before us. We assumed we were seeing vehicles trying to climb the steep grade using the soft snow on both sides of the roadway. We had both seen this tactic used before.

Ajit decided to cautiously drive the van down the center of the road between the traffic below us on our left and right. The grade was so steep that our van felt like a fighter jet going into a dive. Almost immediately he lost control of the van. The road surface that looked clear instead was covered with black ice. We began to spin, and the van flipped onto the driver's side as the spinning continued.

I found myself on top of Ajit. A great many things jumbled through my mind. As in most accidents, things appeared to be happening in slow motion. Whenever the vehicle spun so that the windscreen was facing downhill I could see the lights of the vehicles below us coming closer. I assumed that we would hit one at any moment. But that was not my greatest worry. The cigarette Ajit had been smoking was now in the cabin. I could see its glow. I could also smell gas fumes from the plastic drums stored behind us. I counted the seconds until we would explode.

Suddenly the van stopped spinning. To my surprise there was no impact and no explosion. Somehow, the van managed to spin straight down the center of the road. I was not about to wait for Ajit's cigarette to ignite the gas fumes. Standing on Ajit, I jumped for the passenger door that was now above me and managed to push it open. Ajit swore at me, then found his lit cigarette and extinguished it between his fingers. Lying on the outside of the van, I reached into the cab and pulled him out. Together we slid down to the ground. Then each of us performed a cautious self-inspection. Miraculously we had a few bruises but no cuts or broken bones.

It took us a moment to get our bearings. We lay against the side of the van feeling the solid ground, adrenaline flowing, knowing how lucky we had been. It was Ajit who first noticed the crowd of 15 to 20 Iranian men surrounding us. Sunlight was just beginning to illuminate the scene at the bottom of the hill and I could see the faces of the men. They looked serious, but I interpreted it as concern for us. After the wild ride down the hill it would be hard for me to believe that we would be killed by an anti-American mob in the Zagros Mountains. We smiled and greeted the group in Farsi.

A university-aged man returned our greeting in perfect English. I breathed a sigh of relief. The young man's first name was Ali. With the aid of one or two other men, he gently helped us to our feet. He kept repeating in Farsi how merciful God was to us. I could hear in the crowd some of the men whispering the praises of Allah.

As we surveyed the scene, it began to sink in just how fortunate we were. It was actually beyond luck, leaning more towards a miracle. Our initial perceptions of what we thought we saw at the top of the hill had been wrong. The lights we thought we saw at the base of the hill were not vehicles coming toward us. They were the front and back lights of a huge fuel truck. The body of the truck stretched across the width of the roadway. Had we not flipped and slid down the road, we would have driven straight into the middle of a gasoline tanker, and the explosion would have incinerated us.

As it was, our vehicle stopped within 20 yards of the side of the truck. I sat back down in the snow and mentally thanked God (or Allah) for sparing my life again.

Ali explained that he and his traveling companions were in a bus that was parked on the other side of the jack-knifed truck. The bus was too big to get around the truck. He was a college student in Tehran. He was returning to his hometown in Khuzestan Province because the strikes had canceled classes.

Ali and his friends volunteered to help us. With great care, eight Iranian men got on one side of the van and pushed it back over on its wheels in one motion. The vehicle bounced a little on its shocks as if it, too, were trying to adjust to being through such an ordeal. The van looked better than we could have hoped. There was a fairly large dent on the side that hit the ground, but other than that, it looked fine. The big test came when Ajit got behind the steering wheel and turned the key. The engine turned over on the second attempt and our Iranian friends cheered. They then helped guide us around the disabled truck, and before we knew it we were waving good-bye to our Iranian saviors continue our trip to the north.

After we departed the scene of the accident, silence enveloped us. Mentally, we both pondered our own mortality, the thin line between life and death.

And something else edged between Ajit and me as the sun began to rise over the mountains. Nothing was said because nothing had to be said. The events of the past 30 hours had spoken loudly enough. It was obvious that it would be foolhardy to attempt to retrace our steps and take the road back to Ahwaz. The road to Ahwaz had realistically closed as an option.

Ajit would take the van across the Turkish border and on to Greece. I would make my way as best I could to Tehran, hoping to find some other way back to Ahwaz and Kate. If I could get to Tehran and back to Ahwaz by train or plane, maybe I could help Kate and Ajit's girlfriend out of the country. Keeping my fears to myself, I consoled Ajit that both were in safe hands in Ahwaz, and that with a pending oil company evacuation everything would be fine.

Ajit tried to talk me into going to Greece with him to await the evacuation from Ahwaz. The offer was tempting, but my responsibility was to Kate. If there was any possibility that I could get south to her, I was going to take it. When we reached Tabriz, we were able to find a room in a government guest house. It was the evening of December 29. After several frustrating attempts, we were able to get a line through to our women. Kate told us that Ahwaz was in chaos and the oil company was in the final phase of planning the evacuation. The oil company was well organized. They had computer lists of all expatriates living in Ahwaz, even those not working for them. All foreigners would be welcome in the coming evacuation.

The company had divided the city into wards and each ward had a designated block warden who was responsible for organizing and evacuating everyone in his or her area. Communications were being maintained by telephone, cars and hand-held radios.

I explained our game plan to Kate. I told her that if the evacuation did start she was to get on the first flight she could. In the morning I would try to find a bus to Tehran, if a bus was not available, I would try hitchhiking. Once in Tehran I would try to get on a train or plane back to Ahwaz. If I heard that the evacuations had started, I would assume that Kate was part of it and I would try and get a flight to Europe. We would then rendezvous in London at the house of a friend. In the interim, I would try to contact her by telephone every night.

It was difficult for us to hang up. Once we lost contact with each other there would be no telling when we might talk again.

Almost mercifully, the decision to terminate the connection was made for us as the line went dead. After another sleepless night, Ajit and I found a small coffeehouse attached to the hotel for breakfast.

As we discussed our plans, a Swedish couple and their Asian traveling companion overheard our conversations. The male in the group, Eric, came over to our table and introduced himself. He explained that he, his wife Anna, and their Sri Lankan business associate had crossed into Iran from the Turkish border the night before. They were driving overland from Europe to Iran, Afghanistan and Pakistan. In Pakistan, at the port city of Karachi, they would travel by sea to Sri Lanka. They operated a tourist business and were investigating the possibility of developing a land and sea route for European tourists to Sri Lanka. I was surprised to hear that they knew little about the turmoil occurring throughout Iran. I wondered if the Western press could still be in the dark about the intensity and size of the revolution.

The "Big Swede," as I began to think of him, offered me a seat in his car to Tehran. I breathed a sigh of relief as a loose alliance developed between this odd traveling group and myself. I was able to hitch a ride to Tehran without hitchhiking and they had my experience of the road, my knowledge of what was going on in the country and my rudimentary grasp of Farsi to get us through any rough spots.

Before I knew it, Ajit and I were hugging each other and wishing each other a safe journey. As it turned out, the journey as far as Qazvin was safe and uneventful. We noted troop movements and signs of insurrection, but we never witnessed any violence. We stopped in the town of Zanjan looking for fuel. The section of the town we were in was obviously not under government control, as citizens in the street were carrying weapons. To my surprise, Eric actually found a gas station that was selling fuel. With two large Nordic persons in the front seat and an Asian and me in the back, our car was drawing a great deal of attention in the long fuel line.

One man carrying a Belgium-made assault rifle approached us. I was leery because he looked like a mullah and the rifle he carried was basic issue for the Shah's troops. He first spoke to me through the back window in Farsi. With my dark skin, hair and beard people often mistook me for an Iranian. I smiled and in broken Farsi told him that I was French. I thought at that point that I should slide my American passport down the back seat but I was too afraid to move. I cursed the fact that I never took French class seriously in high school and prayed that this man did not speak French. Apparently he didn't, and my bluff worked.

The man with the gun smiled. The French government had been granting asylum to Ayatollah Khomeini, so French people were looked upon with favor. The man then focused his attention on the front seat. In passable English he asked Eric where we were going. When Eric told him we were driving to Tehran, he became concerned about us waiting in line too long. He talked to the Iranians at the gas pump and those at the front of the line and soon they were waving us ahead to get fuel so we could be on our way. Again I found myself amazed at the kindness of the Iranians.

It was late afternoon as we approached Qazvin. The road to the city was congested and snarled with assorted vehicles trying to get out of the city. The scene reminded me of black and white photographs of refugees fleeing European cities during the Second World War.

Eric slowed our vehicle and pulled over to a couple of Iranians wearing civilian clothes. These men were unarmed but the thought crossed my mind that we would be defenseless against an angry mob. But they too were concerned about our safety. They indicated in broken English that there was a great deal of trouble in Qazvin. One of the men made a symbolic pistol shape with his fingers while making the sound of automatic weapons. These two indicated that they knew of an abandoned campground ahead and told us it might be best if we spent the night there. It would be safer for us to drive through Qazvin in the early morning as the city slept. And this is how we came to our resting place for the night in this cold, uncomfortable, albeit safe shelter.

I looked at my watch. It was 4:30 A.M. I must have drifted off to sleep for a while. I lay on my back for another hour. By then the others were tossing and turning. The body can only take so much and I knew that my traveling companions were getting anxious to get into their Subaru and get on with their journey. I had less anxiety, perhaps because I had been traveling longer and as a veteran had experience in volatile situations.

Again, I reflected: I had been on this road since Vietnam.

ESCAPE FROM TEHRAN

In 1978 and 1979 countless thousands of Iranian civilians suffered brutalities from American-supplied weapons. U.S. guns killed them, U.S. cattle prods burned them, and U.S. experts taught their oppressors how to torture them.

—Jonathan Kwitny,
Endless Enemies

It was still dark, and I was cramped, having spent the night on the steel frame of the love seat. My new companions and I were partway to Tehran. The Shah's regime was falling. My wife was preparing to be evacuated in a city far from me, and I wanted us both out of Iran as soon as possible.

The big Swede was the first to get up, swinging his legs and massive frame over the side of the ping pong table. As he passed me on his way to the door I rose in unison with the Sri Lankan. Anna remained on the ping pong table for a few more minutes, fighting the coming dawn on her back with her right arm draped over her eyes.

That dawn proved anti-climactic, considering the amount of time we spent awaiting its arrival. We moved cautiously as we walked out to face the day. The sound of gunfire had ceased sometime during the night, and I could hear traffic on the main highway. Even the rats that had harassed us through the long night had ceased their scratching and gone wherever rats go during the day.

The guard from the campground had departed before we awoke, so there was no one to thank as we assembled around an already running and warmed up Subaru. As I continued my journey with this group, it was hard to believe that this cold night had really happened. The mind can be funny like that.

We joined the main highway again, heading east toward Tehran. The big Swede was driving and he slowly maneuvered the

Subaru through the streets of Qazvin. His wife was in the front passenger seat with me directly behind her, and the Sri Lankan was to my left. Calm had set in on these streets sometime in the early morning hours, yet as we drove through the silent city, we felt a sense that events of a violent nature had occurred not long before. It was like being in the eye of a wild political hurricane.

Eventually, we passed piles of debris and smoldering buildings. Eric maneuvered around hastily erected barricades and burning automobile tires, and our hearts did not lift until we were looking at the city in the rear-view mirror.

It was mid-afternoon by the time we entered central Tehran, December 31, 1978. The normally bustling city was still and silent, almost a ghost town. The reign of the so-called "Rock of Gibralter" was about to collapse. There was little traffic. Burned and abandoned vehicles still smoldered. Refuse was strewn in front of ransacked shops. Poster-size pictures of the Shah, ripped and partially burned, were scattered in the street.

It had been mandatory for every shop, business, school and home to prominently display at least one picture of the Shah. Now they littered the streets of Tehran. I would occasionally spot a soldier with his weapon at port arms, ready for who knows what. The soldiers, it appeared, were trying to stay off the main roads. They were hidden in alcoves and alleyways along with a few tanks and armored personnel carriers, as if to avoid some sleeping monster that had roamed the streets at will the night before.

The most memorable image was that of a huge burning hook-and-ladder fire truck in the middle of a major boulevard. In several areas we had seen "Yankee Go Home" scrawled in crude English on shop walls. The burning fire truck and the slogans warned of a disintegrating infrastructure — and of my own vulnerability.

Somehow, despite the confusion of Tehran, my Swedish friend managed to find the hotel where I had stayed on several business trips over the past year. It was within walking distance of the Near East Foundation's main office. My traveling companions, however, decided that Tehran was too unstable for them to spend even one night. Surveying the streets around the hotel, I had to agree with them. The countryside would probably be safer.

"Yankee Go Home" sign on building.

I said my goodbyes and thanks and wished them a safe journey. I would never see them again. Meeting them had been a lucky encounter, and I knew I might have died without their help.

I was now alone, but only for a moment. As I stared up at the hotel, a hand grabbed me from the rear. I twisted low trying to escape the grasp. I heard a laugh and a voice I recognized. My mind was trying to interpret the words, not realizing in my fear that the person behind me was speaking English.

"You truly are a lunatic colonialist!"

The words seemed to assault me.

"And look at you, or dare I say, smell you! Where have you been sleeping, a bloody barn?"

I turned and focused on the man behind me. It was Michael Wherly, the best man at our wedding.

Michael was as glad to find me as I was to see him. He had been in Tehran on a business trip when the trouble escalated. He had also been in contact with Ahwaz, and hearing that I might be heading for this hotel, he had come down from northern Tehran to warn me off it. The hotels in Tehran had become focal points for anti-foreign—and especially anti-American—mobs.

My friend offered me a safe place to stay with him in a villa in northern Tehran. With a wicked glint, he dug into his pocket and dramatically produced a single train ticket.

"Look," he said, "I picked this up today for myself, but we British have never been ones to keep men from their loved ones. The ticket is yours. It's for the train tomorrow."

I wanted to kiss him.

Still, Michael warned me to not get too excited, as the workers had been on strike and the trains had just started running again. Another strike could be called at any time.

Before heading to the villa, I needed to check in at my office— only a short walk from where we stood. A few minutes later we entered the opulent offices of Mr. Farooque. This lawyer represented the Near East Foundation, and he had been a friend and an associate of the foundation for years.

Mr. Farooque was, as usual, immaculately dressed in a three-piece, Western-style tailored business suit. He was the vision of the Iranian elite with his manicured fingers, graying temples and a perpetually lit carved-ivory pipe. Nevertheless, there was something different about Mr. Farooque that afternoon. The hospitality and graciousness were still there but his smile was not quite so bright. He no longer carried himself as assuredly as he had in the past. He looked tired, fatigued, and wary.

Mr. Farooque was of the Iranian "Old Guard." The end was in sight and he knew it. The blood of too many tortured souls had gotten into the waters and now the sharks were circling for the final kill.

Of course, Mr. Farooque was too proud to acknowledge this. At times he acted as if a last heroic gesture by the Shah's Imperial Guard or some "Hail, Mary" diplomatic effort by the Americans would calm the waters and keep the sharks at bay.

When I told him that I had a train ticket to Ahwaz the next day, Mr. Farooque only sighed.

According to his well-placed sources, all train, airplane and bus services within Iran would cease today. There were rumors that some foreigners had been attacked on the Ahwaz train and thrown off as it went through the remote mountains. Whether or not this was true, my newly acquired train ticket was worthless.

At that moment, I knew I had no more choices. I had to get

out of Iran as quickly as possible. My Iranian looks wouldn't protect me forever. I felt like a refugee, being evicted from a country where I had chosen to live. I had no job and no clothes. I didn't know where my wife was. Unlike a refugee, however, I did have a homeland, and I would be heading for the safety of the U.S. as soon as I linked up with Kate in England.

Before I could fully process what Mr. Farooque had told me, he was behind his desk and on the telephone. After a few calls he had secured two tickets on Lufthansa Airlines for Michael and me to Heathrow Airport via Frankfurt, Germany, departing in four days. The tickets would be delivered to Mr. Farooque's office within the hour. He explained that European airlines were safer in the Tehran airport and that the Lufthansa flight was the first one he could bribe us onto. A good many people were fleeing the country these days.

Mr. Farooque gave me some Iranian and American money, from foundation accounts, to cover my expenses in Tehran. When our tickets arrived, Mr. Farooque personally drove us to Michael's friend's villa, my refuge for the next four days. As we thanked Mr. Farooque, I promised to stay in touch with him by telephone.

The villa was lavish. It was a modern hacienda-style building constructed of poured concrete slabs and a green tiled roof. It had four bedrooms and a large open dining and living room area overlooking a swimming pool. The pool was filled with dirty stagnant water.

Michael had been staying with two British Consul friends, Ian and Derek. A third roommate was out of the country on vacation. Besides these two, there was a Pakistani houseboy/cook, "Ahmed," and a groundskeeper.

After a brief hello, Michael mercifully ushered me to my room. It was spacious, with an attached bath. Michael got me some clothes and a sarong to sleep in that night. I stripped, gave my dirty clothes to Michael to take to the houseboy for cleaning, and then quickly showered, wrapped the sarong around me and climbed into bed. I drifted into a wonderful, uncaring, deep sleep. Time and space did not exist. I slept for hours before a hand tugged at my body.

The hand must have been tugging fairly hard because it was the rocking motion of my head that woke me. The room was dark. I could barely make out the features of Ahmed leaning over me. In very crisp English he announced that dinner was being served. I raised myself and followed him along a corridor and down stairs into the dining room.

A fire had been lit in the fireplace illuminating the room. The only other lights were provided by several candles placed about the room on tables. Michael and our two hosts were already sitting at the table, drinking a deep red wine. The color of the wine was accentuated by the light of the candles. I eagerly accepted a glass.

Michael welcomed me back to the world of the living, thanked me for showering and apologized for the dim lights, all in one sentence. He went on to explain that the "rabble had cut off the power supply to the city again but we must, of course, keep a stiff upper lip for the Empire."

We ate an extremely spicy lamb curry over rice that had been prepared by Ahmed on the gas stove. The discussion around the table was light and noncommittal. We talked of home, vacations, travel, former jobs, avoiding the situation in the present tense. None of us needed to be reminded about how chaotic things had gotten. As Michael and his friends joked, I ate. The nap and the shower had perked up my appetite, and I ate beyond full.

I soon became aware of a droning noise coming from somewhere outside. It seemed to build in volume over the course of the meal. After dessert, Ian suggested we go out on the roof to watch "the show."

Derek ran off to his room and came out with a pair of pants, sweater, shirt, socks and open-toed sandals for me. I dressed and followed the group to a door which led to a balcony. We ascended another set of stairs that led to a rooftop terrace. From that point we had a 360-degree view of Tehran. It was obvious to me that the well-to-do lived in the hills north of Tehran. Descending in a southerly direction, I could discern, based on elevation, an established social strata. The poorest of the poor lived in the southern tip of the city. There, all the refuse from open sewers arrived from the wealthy northern section of the city.

I was sure that the architect of this building created this terrace to get the most rent from foreign occupants. The panoramic view was spectacular, and I could make out the contrast between modern Iran and ancient Persia. Mosques, minarets and mud-packed homes competed with soaring glass skyscrapers and modern apartment buildings.

Tonight, the view was accentuated by events taking place in the city. "The show," as Ian called it, had been going on for weeks.

Before us were the sights and sounds of revolution, a slice of history to witness. The Imperial Dynasty was crumbling. To hear and see the drama unfolding below us was almost too much to comprehend. It was as if we were on the fringe of a large movie set.

How strange it is that we live in a world where movies look real and actual events seem somehow surreal.

Far to the south, in the poorest sections of the city, the wave of voices continued its ascent through Tehran. The wave gained momentum among beleaguered merchants and shopkeepers in the bazaar. It picked up fury and vitality with the students at the universities and high schools. The mullahs and the faithful at the mosques added to its thrust. The businessmen and middle-class professionals gave the tidal wave of voices power and credibility.

By the time it surged at our feet the noise was deafening. The volume was so intense that individual words were hard to identify. The monster was released again on the city and the chants, "Allah Akbar, God Is Great, Death to the Shah, Death to the Shah," chilled the already cool night air. The monster was calling for blood in God's name. There would be no stopping it.

Small fires began to break out in the city, following the same course as the shrieking wave of voices. Soon the sky was aglow, with an occasional tongue of flames lashing up to the heavens. The sporadic report of machine-gun and small-arms fire could be heard above the chanting. A line of red tracer rounds would occasionally arc out towards the sky. It was as if this line of red dots was searching the skies for a weak spot.

With my heart pounding and my feet freezing, I headed back downstairs, leaving the others to stare at history. It was nearly 11 P.M. and I thought I would try again to reach Kate. I gave the operator my Ahwaz home number and waited for what seemed like forever, but in reality was only a few seconds. Without warning, there was a sharp clear ringing sound in my ear. After the fourth ring, I heard Kate's "hello."

There was no point in mincing words, not knowing when I might get cut off, so I told Kate to listen to me carefully. There was no hope that I could get to Ahwaz. She needed to get on the first available flight in the oil company evacuation. I told her I did not know how long the Shah could hold out in Tehran and we certainly didn't know if the Iranian mobs might turn on the foreign community. I told her I was safe and filled her in on the course of events that had brought me to the villa. I gave her my flight number and told her that Michael and I should arrive in England on January 4th. If that failed, we planned to somehow make our way to the Russian or Turkish border. In any event, we would still plan to rendezvous in England.

She, in turn, told me that the oil company evacuations were to start at sunrise the following day. Their employees were to be evacuated first, followed by subcontractors and lastly by any other expatriates wanting out. Kate speculated that she would be out of Ahwaz in two days.

After giving her the telephone number of the villa, there was nothing more to say. I heard an "I love you, honey," over the telephone and then a click. The line went dead and so did my heart. As I sat there with my head in my hands, I realized that it was New Year's Eve, our first as a married couple. I thought of the bottle of champagne I had scrounged in Ahwaz and the two expensive sirloin steaks sitting in our apartment refrigerator. I hoped Kate would share them with our British neighbors before she left.

I slept poorly that night. After I finally fell into a deep sleep, in the early morning hours, I was awakened by Michael. Kate was on the telephone. The evacuations were running ahead of schedule, and she was being evacuated that afternoon. She was allowed two suitcases and needed to be ready at a moment's notice. Ajit's girlfriend, who lived nearby, had recruited an Iranian neighbor to take them to the airport. They would pick Kate up on the way. They were then to board a small shuttle plane for the half-hour flight to the port of Abadan. The Abadan airport was being used as a staging area for larger planes to evacuate people to Greece via Bahrain.

I had to see the small humor of the moment. Kate was allowed two suitcases. She said that she would use one for her belongings and one for mine. To her, this must have been a dream come true. I could see her discarding the clothes of mine that she had never liked: my summer suit, my faded wool shirt, my threadbare blue jeans. All would be triaged at the expense of the evacuation.

Our mood was better. Kate would be safe. We said goodbye and rang off. Less than a half hour later, Kate called to say the timetable had been moved up again. She was to leave within the hour. We made small talk until she could delay no longer. A quick "I love you," and she was gone.

Even though I was staying in luxurious surroundings, the next few days dragged every bit as much as that freezing evening in the Zagros Mountains.

Mentally, it was worse. I assumed Kate was out of Iran by now, and I felt like a prisoner. I'm sure that I drove Michael and my hosts' crazy with my pacing. Finally, it was over. It was the morning of January 4th and according to all reports the airport was still open. Michael and I bribed a taxi driver to drive us there. I called Mr. Farooque to thank him for his kindness and to wish him the best. We said goodbye to Ian and Derek. The British Consul and British staff were not being evacuated quite yet.

The ride to the airport was eerie, the city silent and still. The roar of the monster was gone. I immediately saw the wisdom of Mr. Farooque once I got inside the airport terminal. Pandemonium reigned at the Pan Am desk. Angry people surrounded the check-in counter trying to secure a seat on the next flight out—to wherever. They dragged with them an odd assortment of luggage, trunks, golf clubs, stereo equipment and children's toys. It was a study of man's greed in the face of disaster.

Iranian security police, armed with AK-47s, were carefully checking all people boarding the flight, against a printed list and photographs. A transvestite Iranian, carrying a small toy poodle, pushed his way towards the front of the line, and Michael couldn't resist. He looked at me with a deadpan expression and said, "My God, this must be serious. They're evacuating the queen!"

With a burst of laughter we made our way to the Lufthansa check-in. There were only two people at the counter. We produced our tickets and passports and simply walked onto our freedom flight from Iran. A short time later, the Lufthansa jet taxied to the number one position for take-off. I heard the high-pitched sound of the engines being engaged to full throttle. The powerful forward momentum of the jets pushed my body against the back of the seat. Three-quarters of the way down the runway the jet's wheels lifted off Iranian soil. My spirit soared. I hadn't felt a rush like this since I flew out of Vietnam. I knew I would soon be with Kate in England, and nothing meant more to me.

Michael and I ordered double Scotches, saying little to each other. I assumed his adrenalin had worn off and he was reflecting on all we had just gone through and what he had given up. Both of us had committed ourselves to extended stays in Iran and deep down we knew that return would not be possible.

I reflected on events of the last few days and wondered about the Foreign Service officer. He was the kind of person who always gets out clean, warm and safe. He could have done more for the Americans on his watch had he only listened, but he was too self-assured, career focused and indoctrinated to do that. For me, his unwillingness to listen, to assess and to act constituted betrayal.

All animals have a fight-or-flight space, an invisible proximity in which they either challenge or flee from a perceived threat. Societies can be like that as well. They have an acceptable limit or range that they will allow when it comes to persecution. People can only be pushed so far before their flight response reverses into a fight response. I had now observed my government's support of corruption and abuse in two countries. State-supported murder, torture and greed, it seemed to me, were an ingrained part of our new international foreign policy doctrine. I knew this wouldn't end in Iran.

I left Iran on January 4, 1979, 12 days before the Shah's departure. He was destined to die in exile. The Ayatollah Khomeini returned to Tehran from Paris on the first of February to establish a theocratic government. On November 4, 1979 Iranian university students stormed the U.S. Embassy in Tehran, taking 54 hostages and holding them for 444 days.

I learned in Iran that once the revolutionary pendulum starts swinging, it can't be stopped where you want it to stop. My dream that the country would return to a constitution, a democracy and normalcy had been thwarted by a small, well-organized group of religious zealots in the turmoil of the revolution.

The reality is that the people in Iran suffered first under President Mahmoud Ahmadinejad and then Hassan Rouhani, much as they did under the Shah. There are human rights abuses. Elections have been rigged. Poverty and inequality are rampant. And the Iranian government is scorned by its people and is seen as a pariah by the international community for its support of terrorists, its denial of the Holocaust, its threats toward Israel and its persistent attempts to build a nuclear arsenal. A treaty with President Obama on limiting Iranian nuclear weapons capability is the only tangible success since the fall of the U.S. Embassy in 1979.

Our Founding Fathers established a government with a clear

separation of church and state for good reason. There are some in America today who would like to blur that separation. Like Khomeini, Ahmadinejad and Rouhani, some would like to dictate how Americans should or should not worship, what science is, re-write the constitution, and what a woman's place in society ought to be. I have seen how easy it is to rally a revolution based on hate, anger, prejudice and fear. The citizens in Iran had good reason to move against the Shah, but the freedom they thought they were striving for did not materialize. Those who recently voted abrupt change today in America will understand the bitter taste of supporting zealots who preach, prejudice, religious and cultural hate, human rights abuse and militancy. Americans have not learned from history.

Kate and I were reunited on January 4 in England and returned home to America. Three months later, while in Auburn, waiting to go out on an overseas public health assignment in Asia, I received a telephone call from Pan American Airlines. They had three metal footlockers for me. When we retrieved them, the only thing missing from these chests were my size 12 black dress shoes.

I knew my friend Iranshahi had big feet and I prayed that the shoes fit him well. To this day I will never know how my Iranian friends did it; they were somehow able to get my personal possessions out intact from the turmoil that had become Iran. I have neither seen nor heard from these friends since, and their gift to me is a fitting testimony to their kindness. Two Persian rugs lie on my living room floor, mute evidence of the goodness and honesty of the Iranian people.

LAND OF THE BIG PX

The suffering of the boat people is an outrage to our common humanity and an offense to all Christians. But we do not live in a simple world, and subtle political implications follow every benevolent act by religious people. This should not stop them from acting, but it should make them more sensitive to the political realities of the world which they serve.

—Michael Lee,
The Christian Century

Father and child refugee on board Cap Anamour German rescue ship.

I was under verbal attack.

"Can you tell me just what is so wrong with resettling Indochinese refugees into America?" Chad Bennett almost shouted.

"You, of all people. You're a Vietnam veteran and Director of Refugee Screening Operations here. The Vietnamese make good citizens.
They're hard-working. The majority have been very honest and successful in America."

Chad[36] stopped and gulped a breath of air as he stood on the
other side of my desk. A look of puzzled frustration creased his features. I had gotten under his skin again.

I actually liked getting under his skin. We had just left a daily
meeting for senior staff from both the Indonesian and Singaporean
U.S. refugee programs. I had made a joke about the "Unaccompanied Minors Program[37]," suggesting that "minors" should be spelled
"miners," inasmuch as the ones trying to tunnel into America via this
program were too old to be spelled the other way.

Chad was a few years younger than I, and had been active in
the anti-war movement in college in the early seventies. With Chad, I
suspected, resettling refugees was more fad than conviction, though
that did not bother me. What got to me was what Chad represented.

As with the young consular officer in Ahwaz, Iran, Chad
embodied the new youthful self-centered American. The "ME" generation. Toward the end of the 1970s, he had become a Republican
because, as he told me, "it was better for my career."

He had been staunchly opposed to the draft. Let the poor and
the minorities don the uniforms, carry the guns, and take the risks.
He had better things to do in life. Chad's involvement in the refugee program was partly because of career considerations and partly
because it was the "in" thing to do that year. I knew that inside he felt
that "we," the Vietnam veterans, had messed up Southeast Asia and
now his new generation, with their progressive thinking, was on hand
to fix things. Chad bent over my desk, placing his palms flat on the
cool air-conditioned glass, waiting for a response. Moisture outlined
the images of his warm hands.

In a way, I wanted to agree with him. I loved the Vietnamese

---

36   Chad Bennett is a composite of a number of staff I worked with in the US Indochinese
      Refugee Program in Singapore. The majority of people, myself included, become involved
      because a deep compassion for helping people and providing them with certain standards
      for living. But some are involved for ego, power and to improve a resume.

37   The "Unaccompanied Minor's Program" allowed children traveling without parents or a
      guardian special privileges on acceptance into the U.S. and other countries. Refugees do not
      carry documentation such as birth certificates and the youthful looking Vietnamese used it
      to their advantage.

people. Granting entrance to America and the possibility of American citizenship to any Vietnamese requesting would be the easiest way to proceed. To me it was a painful internal struggle between what the heart wanted to do and the cold hard reality of what was right.

Our government wanted us to believe that while we failed to defeat the communists in Vietnam, the Vietnamese people would prefer moving to countries that had democratic forms of government rather than remaining in their communist-controlled homeland. "Voting with their feet" was a popular term at the time. The majority of Americans — and, it seemed, most of the news media— apparently embraced the same view. I suppose we were all eager that some good could be made of that wrong war. Simply said, America wanted the war to fade into history. This made us all vulnerable to manipulation by a U.S. foreign policy that remained unchanged.

I desperately wanted to believe that my country was capable of a benevolent act with no strings attached, and the U.S. Indochinese Refugee Resettlement Program[38] was designed to respond to helping those we left behind. But no one wanted to take a clear and unbiased look at why people were fleeing Vietnam and why there was a three-year delay in the exodus. It was not until 1978 that the massive surge of refugees began. If Saigon fell in 1975, why now?

Chad was right about one thing: in America, the vast majority of Vietnamese made solid citizens, individuals I would be happy to resettle in my home town. But it was wrong to pretend that the refugee program existed solely because our government was so benevolent, and Hanoi was so evil. Like the war itself, the U.S. Indochinese Refugee Resettlement Program had started out with good intentions, but by 1980 the program had evolved into a more political animal.

The flight from communism, the "re-education camps[39]" and

---

38   The Indochina Migration and Refugee Assistance Act, passed on May 23, 1975, under President Gerald Ford, was a response to the fall of Saigon and the end of the Vietnam War. Under this act, approximately 130,000 refugees from South Vietnam, Laos and Cambodia were allowed to enter the United States under a special status, and the act allotted for special relocation aid and financial assistance. This funding melded into a program called "The US Indochinese Refugee Program."

39   Reeducation camp (Vietnamese: trại giáo dục) is the official title given to the prison camps operated by the Communist government of Vietnam following the end of the Vietnam War. In such "reeducation camps", the government imprisoned up to 300,000 former military officers, government workers and supporters of the former government of South Vietnam..

the New Economic Zones[40] were part of the reasons why so many chose to leave. But too many were exiting Vietnam for other reasons. Some had been dislocated from their farms. Two bad years of harvest because of uncooperative weather, along with the U.S.-led economic boycott, had inflicted hardship on the people of Vietnam more than on the communist regime. People were fleeing starvation that had arisen from a war drawn out by America and exacerbated by Mother Nature. Sino-Vietnamese left because of America's new relationship with China and Hanoi's crackdown on ethnic Chinese in Vietnam.

Chad continued to stare down at me and I, in turn, focused on his reflection in my desk. I got the impression he realized that his questions had hit a raw nerve. And they had.

Chad worked for the other Joint Voluntary Agency (JVA)[41] office in the building. We had similar missions. Both of our offices were under contract with the U.S. State Department. Our job was to screen Indochinese refugees to determine if they were eligible to resettle under a U.S. government category system[42] (CAT) into the United States. Chad worked for the American Council for Nationality Services (ACNS) and his office was responsible for Indonesia; I was the JVAR for the United States Catholic Conference (USCC) and directed the office in Singapore.

My eyes went from the reflection to the person, and I sat for a moment appraising Chad. He was well-groomed, with short-cropped

40   The New Economic Zones program (Xây dựng các vùng kinh tế mới) was implemented by the Vietnamese communist government after the fall of Saigon. This program displaced around 750,000 to over 1 million Southerners from their homes and forcibly relocated them to uninhabited mountainous forested areas. Conditions in the "New Economic Zones" were poor. Authors note: by the early 1980s Hanoi was admitting that the NEZs were a failure. In 1986 Vietnam launched a political and economic renewal campaign (Doi Moi) that introduced reforms intended to facilitate the transition from a centrally planned economy to a form of market socialism. Doi Moi combined economic planning with free-market incentives and encouraged the establishment of private businesses in the production of consumer goods and foreign investment, including foreign-owned enterprises.

41   Joint Voluntary Agency (JVA)—in order to avoid dealing with administrative confusion with hundreds of non-governmental organizations (NGO) descending on Asian refugee camps the US Government established the JVA system that elected that only one NGO would represent all NGO's in the refugee processing system. The Joint Voluntary Agency Representative (JVAR) was the director of the office and was responsible to coordinate with the United Nations and the US Embassy/State Department. The JVA would review and process refugee applications for resettlement to the US in preparation for an official review by visiting teams of US Immigration officers.

42   The Category System used by JVA offices in 1980 was a prioritized system for the U.S. Refugee applicants for asylum were prioritized as Category (CAT) 1 – 4. CAT 1 & 2 were the highest for US resettlement and CAT 3 & 4 were lowest priority for resettlement in the USA. Criteria to Establish Priority of Acceptance into the US Long Range Program for Indochinese Refugees, September 10, 1980.

brown hair, sharp brown eyes, a good complexion and straight teeth. Unlike me, he wore a crisp sport shirt, tie, brown khaki pants and loafers with tassels. I preferred the more traditional batik shirt, blue jeans and boat shoes. My hair and beard were long.

I could have told Chad that just because the Vietnamese were hard-working, honest and made good citizens did not qualify them as refugees. How I responded, though, was born out of frustration and anxiety.

"Chad, as you keep pointing out, I am a Vietnam veteran," I said, staring directly into his eyes. "It has taken me a long time to say this, but I am proud of the things I was able to accomplish in Vietnam. I am not proud of what my government did, but a lot of brave men and women answered the call to duty and paid for it dearly.

"Would you be willing to tell my brothers-in-arms that the U.S. Indochinese Resettlement Refugee Program is resettling North Vietnamese infantry and Viet Cong into America? What exactly would you say to the widows and orphans? Or better yet, could you shout it out over the graves at Arlington that this crazy refugee program we work for was resettling the enemy?"

Many of the Vietnamese, I told him, were fleeing failed farms, not a failed government. The farmers hailed from both North and South Vietnam, and some had been the enemy we had fought. They were not political refugees—like any immigrants, they were seeking a better life in America. Our program, however, existed to resettle political refugees, not to serve as an immigration service.

Chad wanted to say something, but in my anger I was not about to give him the chance.

"At this very moment," I went on, "we have a highly decorated, one-legged Viet Cong sitting with his friends less than 20 minutes by taxi from here. If he hadn't been recognized by someone at the Hawkins Road refugee camp, we would have resettled him in America. He would have been telling Americans in California that he lost his leg fighting with GI's instead of shooting at them.

"Whenever I see him, he tells me that he knows of more VC who have escaped or are planning to do so in the very near future. How many VC have we resettled? It's the same problem that perplexed our troops during the Vietnam War: you can't tell the good guys from the bad guys. But can you tell me, why we are using American tax dollars to resettle men who fought against our soldiers?"

In many ways, I felt sorry for the VC. They were even bigger suckers than their American counterparts, and I could understand why they were leaving South Vietnam. Many, like the VC amputee now interned at the Singapore YMCA camp, actually believed they were fighting a war of liberation. What they got instead was occupation from the North and a chance to fight and die in a second war in Kampuchea, now Cambodia.

I shook my head, not really knowing whether I was talking to Chad or just venting.

"I am sure you heard of the highly decorated North Vietnamese pilot who stole a C-130 cargo plane and with his family in tow popped up over the Singapore airport. He was clever enough to fly his plane just above the waves so Singapore radar would not pick him up until it was too late. He was a Sino-Vietnamese and no longer trusted. So when Hanoi told him his flying days and air force career were over; he hijacked the plane in Da Nang and came here to roost. The State Department swooped him up right away. We never interviewed him. The cause of this was directly relating to our government recognizing China in 1978. And surprisingly enough, that year Hanoi turned on anyone who was Sino-Vietnamese causing a massive surge of boat people."

"Last week I interviewed a North Vietnamese official and his wife. Both had economics degrees from universities in the Soviet Union. Neither had set foot in South Vietnam until after the fall of Saigon in 1975. Both were sent to South Vietnam in 1978 by Hanoi to work in reconstruction of the southern economy. And now, two years later, here they sit in Singapore claiming refugee status. Their goal is to go to America. And they would have succeeded had they not told my interpreter their story. Can you believe they were actually bragging about it?

"When I questioned this guy, I was polite enough to him. 'Excuse me, sir,' I said, 'This may be a foolish question, but what exactly are you doing here? Didn't your side win the war?'

"You know what he told me, Chad? You know what he had the gall to say? He told me he had become disillusioned with the system. My interpreter must have laughed for 15 minutes. Disillusioned, my ass! Don't you think that this economist figured out quite quickly that he could make more dollars in Detroit than dong in Da Nang? These people are motivated by the same economic turbulence that transported our grandparents onto American shores, but like my grandparents they are *not* refugees.

"The State Department is offering a deal that my grandparents never got: American citizenship for the price of a boat ride. And to make the package even more appealing, we're throwing in education, welfare and employment benefits that go beyond the norm. Vietnam veterans weren't treated this well. Can't you see the irony here?"

I should have ended there. Chad probably hadn't known any of this, as he had worked most of the time in Indonesia. Yet for me, poor Chad represented what would have been called in the military a "target of opportunity."

"Our refugees know all about the benefits in America, don't they? They hear it from their friends and relatives who write them from the U.S.A." I continued. "The Voice of America and the BBC broadcast success stories of refugees who have resettled in America. They tell of the presence of the U.S. Seventh Fleet and other rescue ships plying the South China Sea, there to 'rescue' the boat people. Our program is actually advertising for refugees![43]

"News reports I've read indicate that Vietnamese who have resettled in America as refugees are now returning to Vietnam on tourist visas. Can someone explain to me how people who claim they must clandestinely escape Vietnam to avoid imprisonment, death or persecution feel comfortable about returning to the same country as tourists? The fact that Hanoi is allowing them to come and go should be raising some questions in Washington about the validity of their claims." [44]

I paused to fumble through the stacks of papers piled on my desk. I grabbed a particular "unclassified" State Department cable and shoved it over to Chad.

"You've seen this," I continued. "It warns all U.S. refugee processing centers in Asia to be on the lookout for Russian-trained North Vietnamese computer technicians. I suppose they're heading for Silicon Valley! Cable traffic from the U.S. Mission in Hong Kong points to a dramatic rise of Indochinese boat people arriving there from North Vietnam. A recent newspaper article and cable traffic say

---

43   Draft Unclassified Cable: To: George Cosgrove, From Joseph Chudzik, Subject: BBC and VOA Broadcasts Regarding Mercy Ship Activity—Personal Files

44   Kamm, Henry. "Vietnam at Geneva Parley, Urges U.S. to Accept More of Its Refugees." *The New York Times*. July 21, 1979.

as many as 60 percent of these boat people are North Vietnamese. And remember, it was the North Vietnamese who fought against us, who tortured our pilots. We condemned Jane Fonda for visiting them. Hell, now we're importing them!"[45]

I sat back, feeling a bit guilty for my tirade. I regretted my sarcasm, but knew I was telling the truth.

"Don't you put any significance in the fact that these people are taking part in a very dangerous boat ride regardless of whether they are coming from North or South Vietnam?" Chad asked. "Aren't they making a political statement in their departure? Can't there be political persecution in North Vietnam?"

The same questions had occurred to me more than once. I tried to calm myself before answering him.

"I would accept the argument about political persecution more readily if we were getting large numbers of Chinese from North or South Vietnam. The Vietnamese are persecuting their Chinese citizens, trying to eliminate them. Yet I study the data and the Chinese refugee numbers have been declining since late 1978. [46]

"Secondly, I would accept the argument of people fleeing the evils of communism or any other dictatorship who deserve our assistance, if only the State Department would democratically apply the concept of persecution. At this moment, more than 25 percent of the world's refugees are lingering in camps in Africa. Yet in 1980, our government, using the same definition for refugees, has targeted 169,200 Indochinese for resettlement in the U.S. and only 1,500 refugees from the entire continent of Africa. In 1981 the resettlement targets are 168,000 Vietnamese and only 3,000 Africans." I repeated again for emphasis, "That's the entire continent of Africa.[47] Are people fleeing Ethiopia or Angola any less persecuted than the Vietnamese?"

What was also getting to me was my own war history with Vietnamese refugees. I had seen too much of the U.S. government's apathy and manipulation toward Vietnamese refugees during the war, like the starving babies in Vietnamese refugee camps in Quang Nam Province or my unwilling participants as we had moved those poor refugees up the "Street Without Joy" to "save them" just ten

---

45   "Unclassified Cable sent to all U.S. Refugee JVA posts in Asia, Subject: Ethnic Composition of Hong Kong Refugee Arrivals, "drafted by Cary Kassebaum, 2/24/81, Personal Files

46   Singapore Office Arrival Data tabulated indicated of the 9010 refugees processed only 601 were ethnic Chinese or .06%, Personal Files

47   Refugee Reports, American Public Welfare Association, January 30, 1981, page 2

years before. And now America was saying to the world that we need to save the "boat people." If they showed this much concern for the people of Vietnam during the war, especially refugees, maybe we would have won more "hearts and minds," and maybe the outcome would have been different.

Chad drifted over to the fake-leather easy chair in my office and sat down. I couldn't tell whether he wanted to hear more or was waiting for his chance to disagree.

"What about this?" he proposed as he crossed his legs and settled in. "This program has accomplished a number of very positive things. It has saved lives. It proved to the world that, right or wrong, America would come to the aid of a fallen ally. And moving Vietnamese out of first asylum countries like Indonesia, Malaysia, Singapore, Hong Kong, the Philippines and Thailand has relieved the political strains in these nations. Massive numbers of refugees landing on their shores and crossing their borders have been an enormous political, economic and cultural problem for them. Do you discount that the Hanoi regime has had some part to play in the drama that is unfolding before us on the South China Sea? Just look what the Kampucheans refugees are going through on the Thai border!"

The "plight of the boat people" was the media's favorite refrain. Few in the world realized that all the drowning-at-sea stories so graphically depicted in the Western press most likely did not occur in the sequence related by sympathetic reporters. Many in the first waves of boat people did make it to what they thought of as "safe" foreign shores. Once they had landed, they often scuttled their craft to avoid being evicted by their reluctant hosts.

There were fears on the part of governments in Southeast Asia that the Vietnamese might try to infiltrate communist agents among the refugees, as well as concern that the Hanoi regime might use the fact that Indonesia and Malaysia were harboring Vietnamese political prisoners as an excuse for invasion. The fact that the first 1978 wave of boat people had a high percentage of Chinese did not help. Both Indonesia and Malaysia had bumiputera[48] laws that discriminated against Chinese.

For these Asian countries, it was now obvious that America

---

48   Article 153 of the Constitution of Malaysia grants the Yang di-Pertuan Agong (King of Malaysia) responsibility for "safeguard[ing] the special position of the 'Malays' and natives of any of the States of Sabah and Sarawak and the legitimate interests of other communities" and goes on to specify ways to do this, such as establishing quotas for entry into the civil service, public scholarships and public education.

could not be counted on to help Indonesia or Malaysia if the fears of invasion became reality. We had shown ourselves to be only a fair-weather friend. We had merely watched as Pol Pot and his Khmer Rouge executed hundreds of thousands in Kampuchea, and then supported and funded Pol Pot's efforts because Pol Pot was pro-Chinese and anti-Vietnamese[49]. Vietnam fielded the fifth most powerful army in the world, and no other Southeast Asian government could afford to anger them.

So, Indonesia and Malaysia began putting the landed boat people into whatever refugee craft were still floatable, if not always seaworthy. These flimsy vessels were often overloaded with boat people and either pushed offshore or towed out to sea. Many would capsize. And so the world would be told that 50 percent of the boat people were drowning at sea. They were not hearing that they were being towed by the very countries where they had landed seeking safe haven.[50]

Chad had also known a bit of the history of the refugee program, and that it was through the early efforts of some American expatriates that the initial program was successful and humanitarian in focus. These government and NGO aid workers had come in at a time when a high percentage of boat people actually were refugees. They aggressively negotiated with Southeast Asian governments to accept these lost souls and halted these governments from pushing them back into the sea. They had set up the camps in each first asylum country; provided food and health care; and established the resettlement and processing system that we were now using. We had "won," and lives were saved.

And yes, many of these people would have died had it not been for the intervention of the U.S. government, the United Nations, other governments in Europe and non-government agencies (NGOs). But, by 1980, the reality had changed, and the documentation and data we now had clearly revealed this change. Yet the lie continued, and I wanted to know why.

"Chad, I can't say the program hasn't saved lives. We can be

---

49   Formerly classified 1978 U.S. diplomatic cables released by WikiLeaks show that the U.S. government essentially supported the Khmer Rouge, in order to maintain "stability" in Cambodia and weaken the Vietnamese communists. The U.S sent a cable to six U.S. embassies in Asia on 11 October 1978 claiming, "We believe a national Cambodia must exist even though we believe the Pol Pot regime is the world's worst violator of human rights." May 29, 2015

50   "Malaysia Reports 13,000 Refugees Driven out to Sea," from the Associated Press, reported in *The New York Times*, June 26, 1978 1:3.

proud of that. Our program did help to stabilize Southeast Asia, and we did show that America could be counted on to help a fallen ally. Those objectives have now been met. So why is the program continuing?"

The data, I told him, didn't lie.

"During my master's degree program, I studied the population dynamics of the mass movement of people. I have tracked the demographics of refugees arriving in Singapore for almost two years. I have kept data on almost 10,000 Vietnamese arrivals[51]. Right now, Vietnam has three million or more people unemployed, but when arriving Vietnamese are asked about their occupation, less than .03 percent indicate they were unemployed. That statistically makes no sense to me. Yet 4082 refugees, or 44%, claim their status as "students." I guess Saigon University is on spring break. They claim this status because they have been told that if they were students in Vietnam then they can go to school in America for free once they are resettled."

—John Soucy

Rescue at sea.

"If you combine the occupational categories of student, farmer/fisherman, housewives/babies, and small business owner you have 82% of those who we have interviewed in Singapore. The days of massive numbers of Sino-Vietnamese escaping persecution from Hanoi are over. At present, less than .06% claim ethnicity as Chinese.

"As for the joke I made earlier about "unaccompanied minors," when we looked at the age of this refugee population we found that

---

51   These are part of my available, personal files.

84% were born between 1956 and 1980. It is now 1981, meaning the oldest in this cohort was 19 years of age when the America withdrew from Vietnam in 1973. So, what kind of significant role could these kids make in our war? Now we believe the claimed ages are actually higher as we suspect the Vietnamese are lowering their actual age to qualify for U.S. welfare benefits and hopefully be accepted as a Cat IB 'unaccompanied minor.'

"Even the United Nations High Commissioner for Refugees (UNHCR) is contending that the Indochinese are economic migrants and not refugees. They have developed a safer mechanism to extract true refugees out of Vietnam. Their Orderly Departure Program[52] is a mutual agreement between the U.N. and Hanoi to allow U.N. personnel to come to Vietnam to screen Vietnamese and fly out those who qualify as refugees. No more drowning at sea, rape and pillage by pirates. No more family separation.

"If the Hanoi regime is allowing this, why aren't we involved more in that program? The first asylum countries are now telling us they want no part of a long-term Vietnamese immigration program.[53] Here in Singapore the government tried to evict the Vietnamese from the Hawkins Road refugee camp.[54]

"You've seen the interoffice memos," I said, as I searched my desk again for a State Department unclassified memo originating in Singapore. It was entitled, "REASONS FOR LEAVING VIETNAM: NEWLY EMERGING PATTERNS[55]." I read part of it out loud.

> Most refugees who desire to qualify for the U.S. program are well aware of our criteria for acceptance and rejection. These refugees are deliberately calculating their responses to enhance their qualifications for acceptance and to reduce their vulnerability for rejection under the U.S. Program.

I skipped down a few paragraphs and continued.

---

52   The Orderly Departure Program (ODP) was a program to permit immigration of Vietnamese to the United States and to other countries. It was created in 1979 under the auspices of the United Nations High Commissioner for Refugees (UNHCR). The objective of the ODP was to provide a mechanism for Vietnamese to leave their homeland safely and in an orderly manner to be resettled abroad. Wikipedia

53   Kamm, Henry. "Five Asian Nations Bar Any More Refugees," *The New York Times*, July 1, 1979. Kamm, Henry, "Asian Nations Divided on U.S. Doubling of Refugee (acceptance) Quota, *The New York Times*, June 30, 1979.

54   Singapore Housing Urban Development Board from Estates Officer, Lim Huat Eng to Miss Luise Druke, Head of UNHCR Sub-Office Dated: September 12, 1980—Eviction Notice for the Hawkins Road Refugee Camp, Personal Files

55   Memorandum/Unclassified; From Joseph Chudzik to George Cosgrove, "Subject: Reasons for Leaving Vietnam—Newly Emerging Patterns, "March 26, 1981, personal files

When asked why they leave Vietnam many refugees initially provide a stock phrase such as, 'I was persecuted by the communists' or 'My family was discriminated against by the communists.' The rhetoric used is nearly identical. This indicates that some type of coaching or rehearsing has been employed.

I glanced away from the memo and back at Chad.

"Do you have any idea," I asked him, "how many Vietnamese in the last year have told me, when they found out they were being resettled to Europe, that they would not have left Vietnam had they known they would *not* be going to America? Is that your definition of refugee?

"My master's degree in population planning made me curious about one important criteria for resettlement in the United States— family reunification. As you know, immigration law is very clear here. If a refugee has an immediate family member or what we call an 'anchor,' meaning a father, mother, spouse or sibling, living in the U.S., that refugee is considered a high priority for resettlement. I asked my interview teams to do another step in the interview process. I told them if they were interviewing a refugee who claimed to have an 'anchor' in the States, they were to ask what year their 'anchor' had departed Vietnam. If the 'anchor' left after 1975, as a refugee, what refugee camp did he or she process through to get to the U.S.?

—John Soucy

Vietnamese family being safely brought on board
the Cap Anamur rescue ship on the South China Sea.

"With that information, I would cable the first asylum country where the claimed 'anchor' went to and ask the JVAR (The Joint Volunteer Agency Representative), to fax his or her family statement to me. This project has been going on for months and you know what, Chad, in almost 90 percent of the cases, the anchor's family tree and the new refugees' family tree do not jibe. This is called immigration fraud.

Sea rescue of boat people.   Japanese sailor feeding refugee boy.

"When we query the refugee family here about their fraudulent claim, they usually fess up that the father in the U.S. is actually a third cousin or a neighbor or they were told by friends in the U.S. to claim this person. In fact, our investigation has found that some refugees have anchors in other countries that they are not telling us about because the only place they want to go is America."

I stopped there, put the memo back on the pile of papers and looked up at Chad.

"This last line in the State Department memo is the most puzzling of all to me, the part about being coached. We have known for a long time that, besides the UNHCR-negotiated Orderly Departure Program (ODP) that takes Vietnamese directly out of Saigon, the communists have organized their own boat departure program. They have out-processing centers under the jurisdiction of their

Public Security Bureau in the Interior Ministry. One reason we keep seeing the city of Rach Gia listed on our resettlement forms as the place of departure from South Vietnam is because that is where the communists have set up a major out-processing center. Have any of our Asian 'experts' in Washington or here in Asia asked why this is happening[56]?

"And our refugee resettlement program seems to be helping the communists. The way I see it, the communists only saw this boat people affair as a blip on their international reputation radar. Domestically, the program couldn't have been better for them[57]."

I paused, then continued, "Just like during the war, our adversaries capitalized on a bad situation. In public statements the Hanoi regime complains about the 'brain drain' caused by the departure of the boat people. Yet our program serves them as an economic pressure-release valve. Hanoi uses our program like a big vacuum cleaner to sweep up their economic dead weight and political troublemakers. First, they evicted the Chinese; next it was low-level ex-military, dissidents and businessmen; and then the old, the sick and women and children. They made these people pay in gold for the privilege of departing the country in leaky boats. This has allowed Hanoi to profit in the face of our embargo.

"If there had ever been a hope for a resistance movement in South Vietnam it was flushed out of the country on refugee boats. You may find this strange coming from me, but I think the biggest losers are the Vietnamese themselves. Think about the women who are raped by pirates and sold into prostitution; think about the men, women and children who drown at sea, or those blown apart by landmines crossing hostile borders. What about them? Who cares about them, when even those who made it to the Land of the Big PX didn't seem to care?

"What was the price for this failure of American foreign policy? The price for admission to the U.S. is that you give up your

---

56   (Government Supported) transit camps catering to those preparing for departure sprang up all along the southern coast. The Rach Gia camp, was one of the largest. It consisted of about fifty buildings that could hold several thousand persons. Wain, Barry. *The Refused: the Agony of the Indochinese Refugees*. Simon & Schuster, 1981, p. 86.

57   "Vietnam Profits from Refugees Plight," Jay Mathews. A top official in the Hong Kong government has estimated that Vietnam will earn $3 billion in foreign exchange through continued massive expulsion of refugees to Southeast Asia and the United States, *Washington Post* June 9, 1979. "Indochina: Five Years After Communist Rule" by Gregory T, "The Vietnamese government was fully involved in a well-organized system to force "undesirables" to emigrate It has been estimated that Hanoi $15 million in 1978 alone, which was 2.5 percent of their GNP April 30, 1980

homeland, your culture and the ancestors you worship. In one or two generations your children will be westernized, no longer true Vietnamese. Someday it might dawn on them just exactly what we had stolen and how we betrayed them a second time.

"There are other losers: the American taxpayers and our veterans. During the war they were asked to economically prop up numerous corrupt Saigon regimes. They paid further in the blood of their sons and daughters. And finally, they paid for a refugee program with American tax dollars that wasn't resettling refugees."

I looked down at my desk again. "Two times in my life I have volunteered to help my government and the Vietnamese people, and both times I've been lied to."

Chad shifted in his chair, looking uncomfortable. There was a long silence between us. We had talked the better part of the afternoon. The light began to turn a crisp gold. The sun was setting on another day in Singapore.

"I don't need to tell you the obvious," Chad interjected, breaking the silence. "You're overworked and overtired, maybe you need a break.

"I'm not saying a rest will cause you to change your mind," he added cautiously. "You have a number of good points, some of which I agree with, but there are limits to what anyone can take mentally or physically. Get out of the office for a while. Take a long weekend, get drunk, and be with your wife."

I smiled. "You know, Chad, I might take you up on that."

Even as I said this, though, I knew full well that free time was impossible and alcohol only made it all worse. I blessed Kate for putting up with my prolonged absences from our apartment and my sleepless nights.

As Chad got up to leave, I said to his back, "I hope you realize that beyond all these doubts and questions I am still committed to the Vietnamese people. Once they've made it to our shores they deserve to be treated as any other refugees. America has created a mess and it doesn't matter whether they were 'pushed' or 'pulled'[58] out to sea, they deserve all the help this office can give them."

---

58 A push factor is an event or government policy that "pushes" citizens to leave their own country such as a drought or Vietnamese government re-education camps. Pull factors are foreign government policies that encourage citizens to leave their home land. In the case of the boat people placing and advertising the US Navy 7th fleet off the coast of Vietnam ready to pick up "refugees" was a pull factor. According to Reuters News "Refugee Rescued by 7th Fleet Say Carter's Directive Spurred Exodus," July 29, 1979; "U.S. Navy Tells 7th Fleet to Watch For Refugees" NTY, July 24, 1979."

Chad turned slowly as he reached the door and smiled, then opened the door and left. I swiveled around to face the Singapore skyline. As the sun set, from my 30th floor office I could see the beautiful pastel skyline and the port begin to light up. Electric and neon lights blinked here and there like stars in the sky. Lights glittered from ships in port.

When I first joined the refugee program, I was apprehensive about working in a comfortable air-conditioned golden tower 30 stories above the streets of Singapore. There was the risk it might distance me from the people I came to help. I laughed to myself, wishing that I could have cried instead. Somewhere out there in the real world, my platoon mate, mentor and refugee manager extraordinaire, Mike O'Neal, was having the last laugh.

The lights of the merchant ships at anchor in the harbor once again caught my eye. Somewhere out there beyond those bobbing lights, desperate Vietnamese people—men, women, children, the old and the sick—clung to small wooden boats on hostile seas. They were the human flotsam of a lost war and a failed and bankrupt U.S. foreign policy. They were paying the price for American folly, and yet they still were drifting, placing their hopes and dreams into the arms of America—heading for the Golden Door. The land of the Big PX.

Some months later, I sat in Singapore's Paya Lebar Airport waiting for the Thai Airlines flight that would take me to Bangkok. In six days I would be in Khartoum, Sudan, on a new refugee assignment. My luggage had been checked and I sat pondering my fate with my feet resting atop a large battered file case. My hat was pulled low over my eyes. Kate and I had said our goodbyes three hours earlier and I was already beginning to miss her. The plan was that Kate would finish out the school year at the Singapore-American School. She would join me in Khartoum in a couple of months.

As I sat in the waiting area, several Vietnamese refugees filed into the room. I could tell they were Vietnamese not only because of their physical characteristics but because they were carrying refugee travel documents in the familiar plastic bags that had ICEM (Intergovernmental Commission for European Migration) stamped across the front. As I looked at them with their expressions of joy and relief as they prepared for their journey to America, I was both happy and apprehensive for them.

I'd been perfect for the position that I held these past two years. I was one of the few staffers in the refugee program who had actually worked in Vietnam during the war and I was one of the few who had actually worked with Vietnamese refugees. Having studied the dynamics of population movement at the master's level, I knew about the "push" and "pull" factors that influenced the movement of refugees. I understood the differences between refugees and economic migrants. I had studied the phenomena of why there were movements across the globe from rural to urban settings and from developing to industrial nations. I knew the statistics of population movements.

Or maybe I knew too much, because the data did not lie. The hundreds of interviews I sat in on with refugees could not be ignored. I knew from my time in refugee camps in Vietnam and my experience on the Street Without Joy how refugees could be used by our government for political purposes.

Others also saw what was happening in the program I was leaving and chose to ignore what they knew for their own reasons, but the new senior U.S. government official in charge of the Singapore and Indonesia refugee operations decided to do something about it. George Cosgrove was a brash Foreign Service officer, a former Green Beret and a professional football player. He was aggressive, fair and a topnotch manager. He had Robert Redford's looks and smile and a sense of humor that reflected his time in the military and the world of sports. He did not mince words. He represented a refreshing change from the politically correct acolytes and their politically correct ways of doing business. He was also a staunch Republican and supporter of Ronald Reagan.

George became one of my mentors and a close friend. Our relationship proved to me that people with divergent views—me, a liberal Democrat and he, a conservative Republican—could work together, be friends and achieve significant results. George and I played squash every day we could despite the noonday heat in Singapore. He always beat me. Did I mention he had been a professional athlete?

With George in the lead, the stage had been set for an incredible drama. Ronald Reagan was newly elected. He was recognized as staunchly anti-communist and anti-welfare. George ordered a few staff in each of the Indonesia and Singapore refugee programs to help him draft a cable for the president that explained the refugee situation in Asia. The cable basically told President Reagan that the U.S. Indochinese Refugee Resettlement Program had accomplished its mission but now it had become rampant with immigration and welfare fraud. The cable bluntly indicated that the program was actually resettling an unknown number of Viet Cong, North Vietnamese military and communist political figures as well as civilians from North Vietnam.

I never saw the final cable, only the draft. I was told that the cable was sent classified to the White House. How George pulled this off without going through proper channels, I will never know.

George, in his admiration for what Reagan stood for, felt the President would take action on this situation. And action was taken immediately—George was relieved of his command. In my two years in the program, I had never seen such a flurry of cable traffic between Washington and Singapore after the classified cable was sent to the White House. Secretary of State Alexander Haig would send a carefully worded, politically correct cable[59] to all U.S. Indochinese Refugee Resettlement Program offices in Asia instructing them to basically suppress or cover up any embarrassing revelations.

The truth drowned with the children in the South China Sea that year. America still needed to justify the loss of all those Vietnamese and American lives at the cost of billions of taxpayers' dollars and did not want the spotlight turned on our foreign policy failures that had been staring us in the face now for more than 10 years.

During my research, I found a *New York Times* article from 1975. On page one, President Gerald Ford is quoted about how much we owed the people we left behind in Vietnam. Further back in the same issue a much smaller article reported that the United States was cutting off all food, medical and other essential aid bound for South Vietnam.

America was going to punish the Hanoi regime through the people to whom President Ford said we owed so much. The Vietnam War was not ending. It was simply taking on a new form. This time there would be no witnesses, no press, and no soldiers to give testimony.

To think that no one could have figured out what would soon happen was delusional. Vietnam was a potential train wreck. During

---

59   Press guidance cable CSM article alleging change in character and motivation of Indochinese refugees. EA Press Summary, March 27, 1981

the war, American planes intentionally defoliated much of the south of vegetation to deny the enemy food as well as concealment. Chemical sprays had destroyed about one-third of the south's rice paddies. Two-thirds of the rubber trees were unproductive. Four million acres of forest had been destroyed. Three-quarters of the land used for coconut production also had been decimated.

The chemical sprays had destroyed about one-third of the South's rice paddies, two-thirds of the rubber trees were unusable. Four million acres of forest had been destroyed and three quarters of the land used for coconut production. We left in the landscape 26 million bomb craters that serve as stagnant reservoirs for malaria and 150,000 tons on unexploded munitions. Estimates put the number of homeless at 15 million, three million unemployed, one million handicapped by war, a million drug addicts, 800,000 orphans, 600,000 prostitutes and an untold number suffering from the effects of Agent Orange. The entire nation was greatly dependent on America for their food supply. A United Nations team in 1976 found that in Vietnam $432 million in foreign assistance was urgently needed.[60]

As I sat in that cool airport waiting area, I thought about all that I had learned. The devil was in the details, and the details were in the data we had collected and the research I had done. But our government did its collective best to bury this information and "pull"[61] Vietnamese onto dangerous waters and across borders. And the media missed one of the great stories of the war, the last lie of the war; the last body count.

I was awakened from my musing by a figure standing over me. I looked up and recognized the silhouette of Chad Bennett. I assumed he was here to see off the Vietnamese. Chad couldn't resist a jab.

"So, have you mellowed out at all over these past few months?" he said with a calculated smile. "Look at all these happy faces," he continued, using a sweep of his hand to indicate the room full of waiting Indochinese. "Certainly this has got to warm your hard Vietnam veteran heart."

"Sure, I can be happy," I replied, and said nothing more. I took

---

60　"Vietnam – Still at War", Sydney Lens, *The Progressive*, December 1981, p 45

61　There were numerous other "Pull" factors that the US government used to encourage Vietnamese departures such as the resumption of US postal, air and surface deliveries to Vietnam (1975); 1/15/78 US Treasury Department allows Vietnamese in the US to send money to relatives in Vietnam for "the purpose of immigration." The question is how? There would noy be a US Embassy in Vietnam until 1995.

a paper out of my file case, with two quotes on it and handed it to him. It read:

> My God, when is America going to overcome its adolescent pique at losing the Vietnam War and begin to display some common sense and genuine compassion for the beleaguered Indochinese people rather than transparent posturing over the plight of the boat people? Although there is plenty of blame to go around—for the Vietnamese, for the Cambodians, perhaps even for the Laotians—the culprit responsible for the ongoing horror show in Southeast Asia is the United States.
>
> —A former officer of the US AID mission
> in Cambodia and Vietnam.

> Our government is refusing to recognize the government of Vietnam and making it difficult (for a time impossible) to ship even medical supplies and agricultural equipment to Vietnam. Such vindictiveness against this rural country only augments the already tarnished image of the U.S. as a land of justice and freedom. Vietnam will not go away, nor will the U.S. gain moral leadership in the world until we confess our responsibility in a very great tragedy, open our hearts and hands with generous efforts to provide the equipment and resources to rebuild the war-torn land and discover that efforts of reconciliation on our part will lead to mutual understanding and friendship.
>
> —George Weber,
> Chairman of the National Steering Committee

I shook Chad's hand, but as I walked away, I was thinking of an old friend and mentor, Dr. Do Van Minh, the Public Health Province Medicine Chief for Thua Thien Province during the war. He once told me he believed that the Americans would never leave him. I heard a few months ago that Dr. Minh had been taken into custody after the fall of Saigon in 1975 and went insane while in captivity.

FALWELL'S FOLLY

"The Beja boy is dying," that's what they said to me,
and they took me by the hand and led me there to see,
to where he sat on seats of grass, still and very cold,
with his face the mask of an aged man,
but he was less than one year old.
Flies crusted round his nose and hands,
He did not move, he could not move, just gazed across the sand.
With milk, with food, with tender care him surely we could save,
It seemed after all only fair, in a tiny boy so brave,
So I resolved at least to try, to save this little one,
But when I came back in a very short time, the Beja boy had gone.

—Dave Ellaway,
British Red Cross volunteer

The wheels bit into the surface of what an optimist might have called a road. The contact of tire on earth spewed a maelstrom of red dust and sand around the Toyota Land Cruiser, making it impossible even to make out the bright Red Cross and Red Crescent decals pasted on the side doors and hood.

I could not imagine how Jean could see from behind the wheel. Actually, it didn't matter much. He was experienced in this type of terrain, and had learned long ago that a slow speed did not cushion the bumps. It was just as well, if not better, to accelerate through them.

Besides, he was fighting against time. Difficult enough during daylight, these roads became treacherous to navigate after dark. Even worse, there was always the possibility that armed bandits might choose this night to ambush us.

The noise inside the vehicle was deafening, a combination of high engine torque, the crashing as the vehicle bounced along the road and the rock n' roll that Jean liked to blast from the stereo cassette deck.

Red Cross feeding operation for Baja nomads.

"We Are the World" may have been the number one pop song on two continents, but for Jean the music of the day was the Talking Heads. The cab of the vehicle was stiflingly hot and filled with the same dust that enveloped us. We couldn't afford to shut the windows and use the air-conditioner because we needed to conserve our precious supply of diesel fuel.

I sat next to Jean, braced for the roller-coaster ride. My right hand tightly gripped the strap over the passenger door, my left hand hooked under the seat. My feet were jammed forward but I was cautious that I didn't smash a knee or shin against the dashboard each time the vehicle bounded back to earth. Why they had sent us these brand new Land Cruisers without safety belts I would never know. I felt more like a cowboy riding a rodeo bull than a refugee worker.

We looked laughable. My bush hat was pulled low over my brow, and I wore the darkest prescription sunglasses I could find to deflect the glare of the desert. An Arab headdress, a *kaffiyeh,* was wrapped around my mouth in a vain attempt to keep the dust out. The sweat on my shirt, mixed with dust, made an unsightly reddish paste.

Jean wore tan cotton pants, a short-sleeved shirt and yellow aviator-style sunglasses that seemed to cover his face. An ever-present cigarette dangled from his lips. He might have looked like he was heading for a picnic in his native Belgium, except they didn't have this dust in Belgium.

We were both in poor physical shape, the result of no time for meals, 14 to 16-hour work days without a break and a good case of giardia, an intestinal disease caused by drinking contaminated water. I was gaunt, having lost 25 lbs. Compared to Jean, though, I was in good health. He was recovering from a bout of malaria and had pains in his chest. Jean had also lost a great deal of weight. The loss of flesh on his skull made his eyes appear to bulge out of his head. None of our clothing fit properly. It was hard for me to imagine what Jean looked like three months earlier.

If we had been in a war, we would have been tagged as "walking wounded" by the medics. In fact, this was war, and the enemy was a ruthless adversary. Mother Nature had declared war on everything that lived in this region, and she had both time and the terrain on her side. Over and over, she put obstacles in our way as we raced to locate a nomadic group that had reportedly been bogged down by lack of water about two hours northwest of the city of Kassala.

Jean was the head of the League of Red Cross Society (LRCS) sub-delegation in Kassala. He was a male nurse with vast Red Cross refugee field experience, and was now responsible for coordinating League of Red Cross efforts at three Ethiopian refugee camps and Sudanese feeding operations in the immediate area around Kassala.

When we first received the report about this group of nomads, Jean and I were the only two people at the LRCS offices. There was no choice but to find these people, evaluate their situation and, if necessary, arrange for food and water to be trucked to them the next day.

With no portable radios available, Jean wrote a note to his second in command, a German Red Cross delegate named Franz, about where we were heading and why. Before I knew it, we were off. We started our search about 2:30 P.M., so most likely our return would be after dark.

I looked over at Jean and smiled: with the noise and dust in the cab it was difficult to talk. I yelled to him that with the condition his lungs were in, smoking cigarettes was not the best thing he could do for himself. Jean had one of the nicest, broadest smiles a man could possess and he used it on me now.

"Aw, come on, Paul," he drawled, accentuating my name, "Let me die my own way."

We both laughed. Then Jean resumed total concentration,

scanning the road and the land before him. The point in this type of driving was not so much to stay on the road as to select a path of least resistance.

By consulting a Sudanese government outpost in a small village we had passed a while back, Jean had a pretty good fix on where we were going. Now it was a matter of following a crude map—and a bit of luck. We had given ourselves until 5:00 P.M. to find the group. If we had no luck we would return to Kassala and try again the next day, this time using two vehicles.

The lyrics from the cassette blasted at my ears: "*This ain't no party. This ain't no disco. This ain't no fooling around*[62]." So true to our situation. I could not believe I was back in refugee work. And, of all places, I had chosen Sudan. Again. But this time was different.

I reflected on the situation that had brought me here and how I had been dealing with it over the past few weeks. I had decided by the fall of 1984 that I had to join the "professional" world. I had completed my research and background studies on refugees for a book I wanted to write about my experiences in Singapore. I had been working part-time with the Lutheran Immigration Services on resettling refugees (from Vietnam, Cambodia, Laos and Eastern Europe) in Rochester, New York. I also toiled as a house painter to earn enough money so that Kate and I could survive. Her teaching salary was not enough.

Still, I wanted to use my education and my international experience, so I began to send out resumes in November of 1984. I got the call from the American Red Cross in early December, asking if I'd consider a posting in Sudan.

Refugee work in Sudan had beaten me badly in 1981. I had gotten a severe sinus infection that took months to heal, and now I was being asked to climb back into the ring. I learned that the League of Red Cross Societies was desperately in need of people with field experience in refugee relief—and especially those who had field experience in Sudan. It was to be a six-month assignment. My wife could not accompany me. They wanted me to leave as soon as possible. I told the person on the other end of the line that I wouldn't make such a decision without consulting Kate. This would be as much her decision as mine.

---

62   Lyrics from the song "Life During Wartime" from the Talking Heads album "Stop Making Sense"

I hung up the telephone and sat for a long time. Why Sudan? Why refugees? It was almost as if God was calling my bluff. I had been researching my book and trying to get my thoughts down on paper. I am not a particularly religious man, but I believe that privileged individuals and governments have a moral duty to come to the assistance of those less fortunate. The international laws on refugees actually defines it and mandates action to be taken by governments.

I had read the newspapers; I'd seen the reports on TV about the suffering in Africa. Every awful thing that I and others had predicted back in 1981 when I had last worked in Sudan—about the potential for catastrophe if not cataclysmic events there—started coming true in 1984.

I knew the terrain. I knew the government of Sudan. I knew all the refugee agencies and I knew I could help. I also knew what Kate's answer would be, "A person must do whatever is right." So one snowy day in mid-January of 1985, I kissed Kate goodbye for six months. A friend drove me to the airport to begin a journey that would take me to the American Red Cross offices in Washington, D.C., then to the League of Red Cross Societies (LRCS) headquartered in Geneva, Switzerland, and finally to Khartoum, Sudan to join the LRCS field delegation.

Remembering it all as I sat in a bouncing Land Cruiser, covered in dust, I thought of the Phil Collins song "One More Night." It had been playing in the background as I said goodbye to Kate. How I wished I was home at that moment for "one more night." I was sore, dirty, lonely for Kate and hungry. I so missed my wife. But I had to focus on trying to save lives.

This time, the experience in Sudan turned out to be positive. Although my time in Singapore had gotten me off track, I was now able to reconnect with why I had become involved in public health work in the first place. At its essence was the simple desire to help people, but what truly made a difference was the opportunity to be effective. What separated the professional from the "humanitarian" was an ability to make crucial decisions in a professional manner. I had proven I could do that.

The big difference about being in Sudan this time was the Red Cross and Red Crescent badge of the LRCS pinned onto my shirt. That badge said that I was neutral. I was with an organization with no governmental or political strings. The Red Cross had the funds and personnel to act quickly.

By this point I had become convinced that organizations like the Red Cross, the United Nations, the European Economic Community and some of the apolitical voluntary organizations (such as British and American Save the Children Foundation, CARE, International Rescue Committee, Oxfam or Doctors Without Borders) were the answer to this type of work. LRCS had the speed, the human resources and the funds to react quickly to the drama unfolding in Sudan. So did the U.N. and some of the larger voluntary agencies.

I was recruited as the LRCS coordinator for all operations in Sudan. This involved not only the care and feeding of Ethiopian refugees but of drought-affected Sudanese as well. Originally, during my briefing in Geneva, I was told that I would be coordinating the activities of 17 Red Cross delegates and that we would be feeding 60,000 people. Before the operation was over, I was coordinating the activities of more than 70 Red Cross delegates from 17 countries.

We had at least 55 vehicles and were utilizing the services of four and sometimes five C-130 military aircraft that had been donated by European air forces. LRCS was feeding an estimated 240,000 Ethiopian and Sudanese. At the time, it was the largest such operation in the world. LRCS had field teams all along the eastern border of Sudan and a major team in the west. Khartoum and Port Sudan served as distribution points for food, fuel, medicine and other relief supplies.

The Red Cross had maintained a consistent feeding and support operation in Sudan during the early 1980s. Nevertheless, not even they were prepared for the devastation that would befall the area. Drought, famine and conflict had engulfed the land. From the air, the land looked as if an atomic blast had been detonated there. The earth was barren as far as the eye could see. Sometimes you could spot what used to be a farm by the fence outline, now covered by sand or dust.

One day, flying over the southeastern region of the country near Shuwak, we spotted a moving mass of people. As the plane banked to give us a better view, what I saw were hundreds of people digging in the sand attempting to find the smallest drop of water in a dry river bed.

While the media focused on the plight of Ethiopia, by 1985 the drought had caused widespread famine throughout Sudan, as well. The battle with Mother Nature recognized neither political nor geographic boundaries, and people like me were thrown into the breach.

At times, I felt like a combat commander trying to hold the battle lines. We needed to keep the Sudanese people in their homes and villages, as opposed to migrating towards larger cities and forming "internally displaced" camps. Such camps would only contribute to the spread of disease and, if the drought ever did break, we wanted them in a position to resume their livelihoods.

The trick was, keeping the Sudanese in their villages meant that the Red Cross had to travel to the people to deliver relief. We had to try to locate whoever needed help, estimate their numbers and needs, and set up food and water distribution points. At the same time, the number of Ethiopians crossing the border was increasing by the thousands every day.

New campsites were being selected by the Sudanese government, usually in remote locations. I had learned over time, though, that there is no perfect site for a refugee camp. All the "perfect sites" are already inhabited.

The Red Cross and other NGOs rapidly deployed medical, administration and logistical teams to these border refugee camps. Our supply lines were overstretched and our volunteers went stoically into the field without many of the bare essentials for survival. The Red Cross teams literally lived off whatever they could purchase from local markets. I would send young, strong, able individuals out to do battle with disease and starvation—and while many would return weak and sick, they did this work time and time again, rarely with any complaint. No one quit. I would often lie awake at night wondering what motivated such extraordinary people and where they came from.

Our battle to save lives was much like the tank battles conducted in the same region during the Second World War—supplies were essential to achieve victory. The western border was in desperate need of food, and there were no paved roads in that direction. There was, however, an old airfield that had been used by Allied bombers against the Axis at Al Fashir. It was now used occasionally by Sudan Airways, the Red Cross and other agencies. Still, we knew that an air bridge of food could not possibly supply the thousands of tons of supplies needed in the area on a weekly basis. Planes can't carry enough cargo.

Besides the roads, the only other option was a single rail line. This actually connected the city of Kosti, due south of Khartoum, with Nyala in the Darfur region to the west. The newest part of the rail line was more than 40 years old. Since it had been built by different companies from different countries over a long period of time, it was actually made up of several different gauges of track. Rolling stock had to be transferred from one gauge track to the other. Equipment was old and in disrepair and service was, at best, sporadic.

Despite all this, the U.S. government aid program, USAID, determined that this rail line could serve as the sole lifeline for food and medicine to the Darfur region. Just about everyone else I knew disagreed with that opinion, including myself. The U.S. government began to give the Sudanese large sums of money to purchase railroad equipment. Because it would take months to purchase and install the new equipment, however, this was not an answer to the immediate problems of food and medicine distribution. The other issue was volume: the sheer weight of that much new rail stock on a daily basis would cause a great deal of wear and tear on those ancient tracks. The tracks could not be repaired quickly enough to maintain service.

Eventually, a consensus was reached between the American government and the chief delegate from the LRCS. We would use the rail system, but we also secured alternative sources of transportation, which enabled us to diversify our transportation planning. We used rail, trucks, planes and even camels. Our operations were not dependent on one system to re-supply the western or eastern borders. It was comforting to know that the Red Cross had the power to make its own decisions and not be influenced by a single government entity.

Although the roads to the west were poor, there were a considerable number of lorry drivers in Khartoum who could help move significant volumes of food and medicine in that direction. These drivers were skilled in desert driving and often knew alternate routes if there were problems with the main roads. It was a case of using locally available resources to solve problems. LRCS, along with other groups like British-based Save the Children, successfully moved supplies this way.

As everyone predicted, there were difficulties with the rail system from the beginning. Because a number of agencies besides the U.S. government were involved in using the trains, there were problems in scheduling and prioritizing shipments. The flow of commodities, even when the trains were operational, was disjointed.

Mountains of food began to stockpile at the railhead in Kosti. This eventually led to food riots in that city. The poor residents of Kosti, it seemed, did not understand why they could only gaze at such large mounds of food that were being sent to Darfur for free distribution. The people in Kosti were starving, too.

The U.S. government eventually agreed that distribution by rail was not effective, but the delay had made the alternatives more costly. The local lorry drivers knew how badly they were needed to move the stockpiles, and their fees rose. Companies were hired from abroad. A huge contract was signed with the Transamerica Corporation to move supplies to the west by land and air. My thoughts about all these events leading up to my ride in this dusty Land Cruiser were interrupted by Jean's yell to "Hold on!" I looked up to see a large drift of sand that stretched across the road. It was about one meter high and bracketed the road for twenty meters in either direction. There was no missing it.

The wheels hit the outer edge of this wave and ricocheted off. Everything seemed to move in slow motion as we left the ground. I thought to myself that if this metal box had wings we would be flying. As we arched upward I noticed that Jean was trying to keep the wheels straight so that when we hit the ground there would be no chance of snapping an axle or breaking off a wheel. The front wheels hit first. Then the back and then the front wheels again. The engine stalled and died. Even Jean's music abruptly stopped. We sat still, quietly inspecting ourselves, taking a physical inventory and waiting for the cloud of dust behind us to catch up. Other than a bump on the right side of my head, I seemed to be all right. I knew Jean was okay because he started to laugh.

I took off my bush hat and hit Jean over the head, succeeding only in raising more dust. I knew it wasn't his fault but I couldn't resist the chance to give him grief.

"Jesus H. Christ! I got through two tours of duty in Vietnam and the evacuations from Iran only to be killed by a Belgian cowboy in North Africa. Do me a favor. Die from either old age or smoking, but don't take me with you."

This made Jean laugh all the more.

"Aw, come on, Paul," he dragged out in his Belgian-French accent, "that was only a little bump."

We sat in silence for a moment more. Jean grabbed the water bottle and got out of the vehicle to stretch. I joined him as he leaned against the front hood of the Toyota. The vehicle had come to rest near the dried-up carcass of a cow. We had seen a number of dead animals over the past hour. Most were cattle or sheep, although occasionally we saw the remains of camels. If the camels were dying out here, I mused, what must be happening to the human inhabitants of the region?

My eyes went from the animal carcass to Jean, but I said nothing. He read my thoughts.

"Don't worry, my friend, we'll find them," he said.

We climbed back into our vehicle. I was beginning to realize just how sore I was. My right hip ached with a new intensity. If I was sore, I wondered how bad Jean must feel, since he was a great deal weaker.

Jean keyed the ignition. The engine started and died. He tried again, and again it started and again it died. On the third try it finally caught with a loud noise as diesel smoke billowed out of the exhaust pipe. Jean howled with delight, readjusted the volume on the cassette in the tape deck and yelled, "The Belgian cavalry to the rescue!"

As tired as I was, I had to laugh.

As Jean got us back on course, I tried to regain my train of thought. I began thinking about my run-ins with representatives from the U.S. government, one of my favorite topics. And there was my one and only encounter with the Reverend Jerry Falwell.

One day, I had traveled across Khartoum in 120-degree heat to meet with a Red Cross colleague. It was always odd, walking into the air-conditioned lobby of the Khartoum Hilton. The hotel was a mecca of efficiency in an extremely inefficient land, and just being in that building made me feel guilty. In a country where people were dying of starvation less than two miles away, the Hilton's $155 a night rooms seemed incredibly decadent.

I didn't hold the hotel responsible, though. It was expensive running an operation such as this in North Africa. The Hilton staff and management had done me and other refugee workers many kindnesses. The hotel had even let refugee field workers stay free of charge for two nights to give them a rest.

I had heard that Reverend Falwell was in Khartoum, and it was no surprise to learn that he and his entourage were staying at the Hilton. Most relief workers were staying in far less luxurious accommodations.

My search for my Red Cross colleague in the lobby failed, but then I noticed a gathering in front of the conference rooms just off the main lobby. That's where I saw the leader of America's "Moral Majority." The Reverend had just finished a press conference and was answering some questions from the press corps.

Reverend Falwell was expounding on his plans for bringing Christian relief to the starving people of the region. When he mentioned the Red Sea Hills, my ears perked up. The Red Sea Hills is a barren region that runs north to south from Port Sudan to Kassala along the Red Sea in eastern Sudan. It is populated by subsistence farmers, herders and nomads.

As part of a coordinated effort between the Sudanese government and the assisting international relief agencies, this area had come under the responsibility of the LRCS, Save the Children Foundation, the World Food Program (WFP) and a small group from the Saudi Arabian Red Crescent Society. WFP was primarily responsible for supplying food. Save the Children and the Saudi Arabians were conducting some feeding operations in refugee camps along the Port Sudan-Kassala highway.

LRCS had overall responsibility for this area. We managed most of the refugee camps and had a very effective food distribution system targeting Baja nomads in the mountains. At the time of Falwell's press conference, the Red Cross had feeding and blanket distribution operations based out of the villages of Sinkat, Haiya and Derudeb in the Red Sea Hills. Our mission was to utilize local government officials to travel by four-wheel drive trucks, locate starving people and establish feeding points.

At this point, our main concern was that only the healthy individuals could come down from the hills to pick up food, water and medicine. The less able were marooned up in the hill areas waiting to die, despite the often superhuman efforts of Red Cross volunteers who risked life and limb to locate those in need.

In his media event, Falwell had suggested the use of ultralight gliders to send food into the Red Sea Hills. His idea was that a fleet of these metal and canvas mechanical angels would quickly and efficiently bring supplies into this isolated terrain. I could only imagine the thought of celestial, Christian, mechanized angels going forth to feed the backward Muslim peasants.

What a sales pitch the Reverend could make to the faithful of the electronic church back home!

However, it seemed that Reverend Falwell was long on sales-manship but woefully short on aerodynamics. I had crossed this area several times in twin-engine Cessna's flown by veteran pilots. A Cessna is huge in comparison to an ultra-light glider, yet I remembered that all my experiences in flight in this area were at best "uplift-ing." The problem was the principal of heat rising. The sun in these hills is merciless, baking the region in 120 plus degree heat. The heat rises vertically off the desert sands and shoots skyward in tremendous gusts of wind.

Flying in a Cessna, I would often find myself being uncontrollably forced against the ceiling of the plane as we entered a thermal updraft and back down again as we passed out of it. I often feared that the wings would snap off or that wind shear would force the plane against the cliffs below us. Even flying at 20,000 feet in Sudan Air 727 passenger jets, the pilots occasionally fought for control and passengers were bounced around brutally. I had no doubt that Falwell's fleet of angels, not unlike Icarus, would have their wings shorn off for flying too close to the heat of the Red Sea Hills. Oh yes, and the bonus question that no one thought to ask the Reverend at the press conference, "How much food could a single ultra-light carry?"

Amused by the Reverend's uninformed plans, I turned and walked out of the conference room, feeling relieved that these ludi-crous dreams would never be put into action. Although this brief encounter with televised religion was strange, I knew that the checks and balances that allowed refugee assistance agencies to operate in Sudan were sufficiently in place by the Sudanese government to pre-vent Falwell's people from working in any area without government approval.

What I did not know was that behind-the-scenes politics were in play. The Vice President, George H. W. Bush, arrived in Khar-toum on a fact-finding mission at the very same time. In politics, very little happens by coincidence. By 1985 it seemed to many that the Moral Majority was positioning itself to become the religious rep-resentative of the American government—and, indeed, the Rever-end Falwell's arrival in Khartoum on the heels of the Vice President's trip seemed to juxtapose his organization with presidential politics. I later heard unproven rumors that Falwell had actually joined the Bush fact-finding mission.

Everyone was much too busy in our frantic food distribution efforts to pay much attention when Falwell and his people showed up at the remote village of Derudeb. Their intentions were obvious. Falwell arrived with a film crew and began to shoot a promotional video in front of our staff working in the area. The video appeared to be a fund-raising tool to share with the folks back home in America. It seemed to me that the Reverend had smelled the money and prestige famine relief could bring and had jumped on the bandwagon to save the starving in Africa and fill his pockets with gold.

Most professional refugee workers tend to be a bit skeptical about trying to feed starving people with food in one hand and a Bible in the other. I had seen the wealth that organized religions had often accumulated but somehow neglected to distribute to the faithful in developing countries. During my war, I had heard of incidents in Vietnam of wounded Buddhists being refused treatment in "Christian" hospitals.

Still, had Falwell and the Moral Majority come with a plan for relief assistance, brought in experienced workers or offered their assistance to join forces with one of the established relief organizations, they would have been welcomed with open arms. The drought had taken a toll far worse than anyone had envisioned. Our organizations were spread thinly, and there were many regions in desperate need of volunteers and extra hands.

But Falwell did not seem to be placing the needs of the local people or the refugee organizations above his own. From what I had heard from my field officers, the Reverend and his people were targeting a specific site in the Red Sea Hills where they wanted to set up a Christian relief community. The site was a stone's throw from Red Cross and Save the Children offices but neither he nor his acolytes made any effort to coordinate with them.

No one knew why Falwell had selected this area. The staff he brought with him had no relief or international experience. They were kids, really, and probably had not a clue on how to conduct even a basic needs assessment. Perhaps he saw Derudeb as a unique opportunity for fund-raising. After all, the Red Sea Hills region was newsworthy. Senator Edward Kennedy and other VIPs had visited the area. The site itself offered conditions ideal for recruiting volunteers.

At Derudeb, there is an abandoned Italian road construction

camp. Although it was pretty rundown, many of the construction bunkhouses and warehouses were still inhabitable, and the Red Cross and Save the Children were using some of them. I was told by those who witnessed Falwell shooting his promotional film that the camp was to figure predominately in the video.

Derudeb gave the Reverend an amazing public relations opportunity. Not only could he show the world starving refugees but the abandoned Italian construction camp was an excellent recruitment tool. It had houses, a sand filled swimming pool, an outdoor theatre and a recreation center. All in disrepair but very photogenic.

We heard that Falwell had plans to renovate the site. It could be a North African theme park just slightly warmer and dustier than Jim and Tammy Bakker's Heritage U.S.A[63]. Of course, this would take money.

Some relief workers started referring to Falwell's people as "Jerry's Kids." The group of Falwell workers consisted of about 20 college-age volunteers. From what I gathered from my team's reports in Derudeb, almost none of Falwell's volunteers had experience in refugee relief operations or feeding programs. The humor of Falwell's Folly had suddenly ceased to amuse me. He was willing to put lives on the line, both his own volunteers and the refugees they ostensibly intended to serve, in order to fill his bank coffers.

During those desperate months when we were over-extended, even the Red Cross had put volunteers in the field with minimal refugee relief experience. However, inexperienced volunteers were always paired and mentored by highly experienced pros. We would never field an entire team with so little field experience. The resumes of many in the Red Cross delegation read like a history book of disaster relief operations spanning the past 20 years. Delegates in our group had relief experience in Vietnam, Thailand, Malaysia, Indonesia, Ethiopia, Uganda, Angola and Lebanon. Others were trained in desert operations; still others were skilled in dietary feeding. The Red Cross and other agencies had been working in the region for years and knew their stuff.

Still, this was dangerous work. Even with our field experience, our personnel had some close calls. Often, I would have to ask the delegates to live and work under the most difficult conditions. The

---

63   Heritage U.S.A. was an American Christian theme park, water park, and residential complex built in Fort Mill, South Carolina by PTL Club (short for "Praise The Lord") founders televangelist Jim and Tammy Faye Bakker

17-person medical/logistics field team at the Ethiopian refugee camp at Girba North was living in conditions far below what American GIs lived on firebases in Vietnam. But the delegates were professionals. To save lives they were willing to take risks. In my professional opinion, it was pure negligence on the part of Falwell's organization to send these kids into the Red Sea Hills without the proper training or backup.

And what of the refugees themselves? It takes more than good Christian intentions and a little bit of food to save starving people. You have to be careful about what food and medicine is given to a person who has been weakened by disease and starvation. The wrong combination or concentration could do more harm than good. Food delivered to the wrong areas could create friction between groups of desperate people.

I had been told by the Red Cross delegate in Derudeb that "Jerry's Kids" had come to him to ask how to set up feeding operations. He had to tell them that there was simply no time for him to begin to teach novices the elements of science-based nutritional feeding and food distribution. Eventually, the Save the Children group did give Falwell's people some training support. I praised Save the Children for their efforts. Their operations were in fixed locations inside refugee camps. Falwell's people could come to these sites for instruction.

I was very disturbed that the system of checks and balances had been by-passed on how refugee relief sites were allocated to incoming relief agencies by the Sudan government. I went to the official in charge of the Sudanese Office of Drought and Rehabilitation and asked him how a group of people could come into Sudan with no credentials and establish themselves in feeding operations. I asked what had happened to the coordination procedures established by his government. The rather solemn official explained that his government had received "unusually strong pressure" from senior officials within the American government.

The request had been made during a recent visit to Khartoum by officials from Washington. He mentioned no one by name but it made me wonder about the rumors of a Falwell-Bush rendezvous in Khartoum.

Luckily, "Jerry's Kids" would be removed from Derudeb by the Sudanese government because of their striking ineptitude. Still, once again, I asked myself about the U.S. government's involvement in this dangerous game. Was Vice President Bush foolish enough to support such a thing? He may have helped to unknowingly unleash a group of kids on Sudan who could have harmed themselves and others. Could a man running for the presidency in America be so influenced by conservative splinter groups? That in itself was frightening.

I am a strong believer in the separation of church and state. I was evacuated from Iran and the mess created by a pure Islamic state. There are too many examples currently and historically of what happens when politics and religion mix. If George Bush and Jerry Falwell were conspiring in far-flung Khartoum, what were they plotting in the U.S.? To think that Americans back home could be so easily drawn into and used in these political maneuvers greatly concerned me.

"I think this is it, Paul," Jean said to me, as he downshifted gears.

I was not sure how Jean had determined this. All I could see were a couple of men near a thicket in the barren landscape. Jean drove the vehicle slowly towards them.

The two men approached. They were tall with very dark skin and tribal scarring on their faces. One had a hand-made wooden comb stuck in his afro-style hair. They were dressed in the traditional loose-fitting white garb worn by nomads. The only other distinguishing thing about them was that they both carried very long double-edged swords sheathed in leather cases.

I jokingly told Jean to keep smiling. We knew that these people were not shy about using the swords. Jean went toward the elder of the two and gave him the Arabic greeting, which was returned by both words and smiles. I relaxed a bit. Jean inquired if there was one among them who spoke English. We usually had an interpreter with us but we had been told that there were one or two men with the nomadic group who did speak passable English. After a discussion between our hosts, the younger of the two turned and ran back into the bushes. In a moment he returned with an even younger man in his late teens. This man knew a bit of English.

We asked to be taken to the group's leader. Jean and I were led on foot through the thicket to a clearing where five or six men had gathered, sitting near a few dehydrated camels. After identifying the leader, we asked about their situation. They related a story that

Jean and I had heard many times. About 60 percent of their herd had died. The old and the very young were getting weak; some had died. With the herd dying off and so many people sick, these nomads had lost their mobility. They were using their few remaining camels to send men out to their next watering point to bring water back. It was a 12-hour round trip.

From the appearance of an old camel, a few feet from me, I speculated that their treks for water might not last much longer. They had notified the Sudanese government of their plight by messenger. The government promised to send help. That had been more than four days ago.

It would be speculation on our part as to why the government had not sent out immediate assistance. Maybe they had no food or medicine in local government warehouses, a fact not hard to believe.

There could have been a breakdown in communications. The request for assistance could still be sitting on a desk in the province headquarters in Kassala. Or it may be that *we* were the ones who were asked to provide aid. We had never identified the messenger who brought us news of this group earlier in the day. It didn't matter now. We knew these people were in trouble. Our Red Cross field office would come to their assistance until Jean could get some government support for them.

We asked to see the village. We wanted to assess what medical and food issues we would be facing. This triaging would determine the number and types of staff we'd need to send.

The village was little more than rudimentary. The nomads had created makeshift shelters by laying grass mats over tree branches. Possibly they had lost or could not carry their own equipment when the herds began to die. Hopefully this vital equipment was safely stored somewhere.

As the village elders had told us, the old and the young were in rough shape. Jean found one baby that nearly fit in the palm of his hand. Some of the children were reduced to skin and bones. Their skin was dry and leathery to the touch, signifying severe dehydration. Their stomachs bulged, which indicated starvation. This was both sad and frightening. We gave the village elders what little supplies we had brought with us and told them that the Red Cross would return the next morning with food, water and other supplies. We gave our respects, jumped into our vehicle and headed back to Kassala.

Jean holding nomad baby.

Jean was silent for a very long time. He didn't even play his music. Finally, as if he wasn't really talking to me but to himself, he muttered, "Where am I going to get extra staff and equipment to come out here?" I had no answer for him. We had no reserve staff at headquarters back in Khartoum.

He went on, "The medical team at Girba North is working seven days a week. They worked 12- to 16-hour days, and those are the good days. Because of water shortages they are permitted to bathe once every three days. Have you ever spent three days covered in sand in 120-degree heat? They are lucky if they get two meals a day. They have to contend with unrelenting heat, sandstorms, scorpions, venomous snakes and camel spiders the size of your hand. The camel spiders are the worst. They crawl onto your skin at night and inject something akin to Novocain. You can't feel them. Then they would commence to eat your flesh.

"The group at the refugee camp at Kilo 26 is in a similar situation," he said. "Most of them are covered with sand flea bites. All have gastrointestinal problems. We are using all of our vehicles to re-supply these two groups along with the Swiss Red Cross team working at the refugee camp at Wad Sherife."

Calm came over Jean's face. I knew he'd been desperately deciding how he could rearrange staff to accommodate this new emergency.

"Don't worry, Paul, it will get done, he said, "but you need to get me more supplies and staff ASAP." I told Jean I would do what I could. This encouraged a smile. "Another case of the Belgian Cavalry to the rescue!" he yelled out.

Heading back to Kassala that night, I relied on the capable driving of Jean and decided to sit back and relax. I was too tired to care if we got into an accident. Yet I felt somehow renewed. Sitting next to Jean and experiencing what I had today I knew why I had become involved in this type of work. I had met so many good people, people who cared, who had compassion for other beings who shared the planet with us. At that very moment I knew that there were men and women throughout the Horn of Africa and in other lands going beyond their limits to save lives.

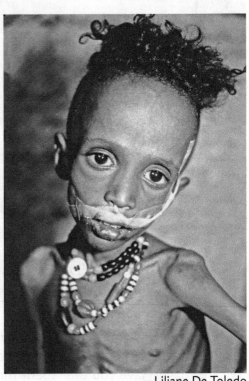

—Liliane De Toledo
The face of cholera.

I found in the heat and shifting sands of Sudan a dignity in humankind that is often overlooked in our "modern" world. I saw it in the face of an elderly Ethiopian refugee being helped across a camp to a medical aid station. One night in the Girba North refugee camp, I saw a three-year-old child triumph after a night long fight with death during a cholera epidemic. Both the elder Ethiopian and the child and others I had witnessed had lost almost everything. Yet they still maintained a measure of pride—and a will to survive.

Man helping father walk.

It is easy to criticize governments and organizations for their policies, their narrow-mindedness, their arrogance, and their bureaucracy. I drew my strength from the survivors and the caregivers. I could return home and renew my own life from what I had seen in those unforgiving months in Sudan.

When I got home to Rochester, I wanted to impress Kate with the tan I had. I took off my shirt and when she saw the skeleton I had become, she cried.

THE DAY
THE MUSIC DIED

Between 1994 and 1996 ---- the U.S.A conveniently ignored the Taliban's own Islamic fundamentalist agenda, its suppression of women and the consternation they created in Central Asia, largely because Washington was not interested in the large picture.

—Ahmed Rashid,
Taliban

After my return from Khartoum in 1985, I sought another position where I could apply my international and public health skills. I came across a listing for the role of Regional Coordinator for North Africa with Family Health International.

FHI had tried to recruit me before I went with the Red Cross. At that time, I had interviewed with a woman named Joanne Lewis, so I contacted her again and was hired. Based at FHI headquarters in Research Triangle Park, North Carolina, my work involved coordinating and evaluating family planning and maternal and child health research projects in Kenya, Sudan, Egypt, Turkey, Yemen and Pakistan.

FHI is a not-for-profit institute that seeks to aid the most vulnerable in a society, utilizing strong scientific research and planning skills. The operation then was small and had the "family" atmosphere embedded in its culture. It was well respected by the U.S. government, the United Nations and ministries of health throughout the world.

At FHI, I worked with some of the sharpest minds in public health research. I tried to absorb everything I could—the basics of research methodology, statistical analysis and data collection—on a

steep learning curve. The FHI projects on which I worked strengthened my management, planning, research and cross-cultural skills. I
spent half of my time traveling, covering three to five countries per
trip.

Since computers were still in their infancy, I always carried
two suitcases. One contained clothes and toiletries: the other held
reams of FHI documents. Because each of "my" countries differed
culturally, economically and politically, I had to have the flexibil-
ity to "change gears" quickly. My counterparts dressed differently,
interacted differently and had different working habits. These counterparts were people who went above and beyond the call of duty,
particularly to protect the health of women and children.

By my third year at FHI, with the AIDS epidemic raging in
the headlines, FHI had already begun to focus on AIDS research and
planning. When a position opened for a coordinator of the AIDS programs in Asia, I applied for the position and was accepted. I segued
to a new learning curve, working with ministries of public health in
Thailand and the Philippines, the World Health Organization, USAID
and private organizations in the effort to slow the spread of what was
then an ultimately fatal disease. The textbook had not been written
on what to do to prevent and control AIDS. We were all learning
together.

My offices in Asia became the bars, massage parlors, brothels
and back alleys where HIV-infected people could be found. My clients
became an odd mix of prostitutes, drug users, bar managers, pimps,
police officers, public health doctors and nurses, medical researchers
and lab technicians.

In many ways, this work was more difficult, psychologically,
than refugee work. Seeing so many infected young people, the
burden of disease exacerbated by the stigmas associated with it, was
beyond difficult.

On my last trip to Thailand for FHI, I was on a four-person
survey team investigating why the northern Thai army had such a
high rate of HIV infection. Recruits came from rural farm fields and
should not have had the same exposure to the disease as their urban
counterparts. But in the city of Chang Mai, we were astounded to
find at least 100 brothels. These were not the fancy houses of plea-
sure on Pot Pong Street or Soi Cowboy that catered to tourists in
Bangkok, but rather dark, dirty back-alley affairs, each with six to ten

very young prostitutes whose clientele were local Thais. As we surveyed these establishments we were also shocked to find that, in most of those that we visited, half of the prostitutes were HIV-infected. At the time the government had only rudimentary health education information and was not even telling these girls that they were infected with the disease. Our team spent a sleepless weekend in a hotel room developing the draft boilerplate strategy for a health education program for the ministry of health.

No matter how much I loved working for FHI, however, Kate and I were talking about having children. Very logically and patiently, Kate pointed out to me that in order for us to produce a child the two of us had to be in the same country, the same city, and the same room at the same time. If we were going to get pregnant, I had to find a position that did not demand constant travel.

Then a friend in Rochester, New York, who knew I was looking for other options, sent me a newspaper clipping indicating that the Rochester-Monroe County Chapter of the American Red Cross was looking for a Director of Emergency Social Services. This was intriguing. I was a former Red Cross delegate, and I was interested in honing my skill set in emergency management. The work would be domestic and we could be close to our families and friends in Auburn, Rochester and Fairville, New York.

I applied, flew to Rochester for an interview and soon was offered the position. That marked the beginning of the second phase of my love affair with the Red Cross/Red Crescent Movement. It also sent me into another steep learning curve, this time in emergency management. I used my own skills in capacity development and team building to expand my new department's local and national emergency response capability. I was soon given the responsibility for leading emergency planning for 15 other American Red Cross chapters in western New York and helping to develop formats for both the state and chapter Red Cross emergency operations plans.

While performing these duties, I took all the Red Cross training available in emergency management, logistics and communications. I was invited to attend the newly developed Red Cross Disaster College for emergency managers. Soon I was noticed by the national headquarters because of my background in large-scale international emergency response, and I was put on their list as a first responder for national operations.

On the home front, the journey to produce a child was not as easy as I had anticipated. In my macho Italian mind I figured the formula to have a baby was to cease family planning and a baby would appear. I soon found that God does not follow formulas. It took us more than four years to conceive our wonderful Kara. I so wanted a girl and was delighted with what God, nature and medical science had given us.

Kara was born on September 16, 1993. Both mother and child did well. I, not Kate, had post-partum depression. Thankfully, Kara inherited the good looks of her mother and not the Sicilian appearance of her father.

At 4:30 A.M. on January 17, 1994, four months after the birth of our daughter, the residents of the Los Angeles metropolitan area were awakened by what would be known as the Northridge earthquake. I had already served as a Red Cross Center manager at Hurricane Andrew in 1992, and I was deployed to the disaster site in LA to put into practice my experience and my training in dealing with disasters of this magnitude. In my five years with the American Red Cross I would also serve in emergency operations for tornados in Oklahoma and Alabama, floods and tornados in Missouri and Illinois, floods throughout the Midwest, and coastal flooding and ice storms in New York.

I loved my work with the Red Cross and the volunteers and staff associated with that organization but with the now-thriving Kara as part of our life, I felt compelled to get back to working in the international public health field. Perusing the New York Times one Sunday morning I spied a job advertisement for the Atlanta-based CARE/U.S.A, the international relief and response organization. CARE was recruiting for a Deputy Director for its Emergency Group. In such a position, I could not only apply my international and public health skills but also utilize the emergency preparedness and response skills I had further developed with the Red Cross. I applied for the position, was interviewed and accepted. In 1995 we moved to Marietta, Georgia.

In the 12 years since leaving the relief effort in Sudan I had the opportunity to work with people from many different cultures, countries and beliefs. They were Muslims, Christians, Jews, Buddhists, and Hindus, conservatives and liberals, military and civilians, Republicans and Democrats, Shiites and Sunnis. What always struck me was that in times of crisis these people were able to not only put aside their differences for a common good but learned from those differences and built sound programs from divergent points of view. All this was bouncing around in my brain as I flew out of Pakistan. There was new turmoil in the world. Opinions were polarizing. Schisms between groups were widening.

In international relief work, as in medicine, we abide by the precept, "Do No Harm." This concept was popularized in a book by Mary Anderson, *Do No Harm: How Aid Can Support Peace—or War.* Its essence is that foreign aid and assistance, whether provided by government agencies or private not-for-profits, should not exacerbate the current economic, social or political situations in a country. This philosophy evolved despite the reality that foreign funds and supplies often end up in the hands of local power brokers who use them as leverage to increase their hold over the populace.

Never has this "Do No Harm" philosophy been put to the test more than in the April 1994 genocide in Rwanda and the establishment of huge refugee camps in Zaire and Tanzania. Exiled extremist Hutu forces from Rwanda co-opted the food and other aid in order to exert control over the camps' refugee population. The Hutus used these refugees as human shields, turning the camps into forward bases for attacks against civilians, as well as soldiers in Rwanda.

In other words, the camps became a destabilizing force. Although they sheltered the very people responsible for the genocide, they received more foreign aid than the struggling Rwandan government, trying to rebuild itself after a devastating war.

But the acid test for "Do No Harm" would come in Taliban-controlled Afghanistan in the late 1990s. The Taliban, when they seized power, openly warned the international donor community that they were going to be a strict fundamentalist Islamic government. Through daring military action, they swiftly won control over most of Afghanistan. They soon issued edicts banning the playing, selling, and broadcasting of music—and for all intents and purposes, music died by edict in Afghanistan that year. Taliban street patrols would stop cars and search for music tapes. If such "contraband" was found, they smashed the cassettes on the spot in front of the horrified drivers. Across the city, bouquets of audio tapes dangled from lampposts, fences and poles.

The Taliban proclaimed bans on flying kites (a national pastime), on having pet birds, on men going beardless, on having American-style haircuts, and on women washing clothes in streams or going to a tailor. They also issued directives on when and how to pray.

More ominous was a ban on women working or even receiving an education, and strict enforcement of dress codes for women by berating or beating them in public. This was paired with a penchant for public execution. With the government in disarray, interpretation of any of these laws varied from street to street in Kabul. Roving Taliban foot patrols determined what the law was and how it was to be interpreted. In some cases, they even seemed to make up new laws on the spot.

The Afghan government broke down. The Taliban were a radically conservative, even reactionary, rural army trying to run a government from Kabul, a city with a population estimated between 800,000 and 1,000,000. Similar to Pol Pot's Khmer Rouge, the Taliban were backward-thinking in their ideas about development, with neither the systems nor interest to run a modern government.

Years of war had taken its toll on the Afghan infrastructure. Water and electrical systems had become inoperative. Roads and farmland had been heavily land-mined. Industry no longer existed. All this created a volatile situation in which experts predicted that between 60 and 80 percent of the population of Kabul was vulnerable.

An initial goal for international agencies was the establishment of clean drinking water in Kabul to reduce the spread of disease. Several water-pumping stations were built with foreign aid. Once completed, the pumping stations were handed over to the Taliban authorities, by then the internationally recognized government in Afghanistan. This gave the Taliban power over the people who drank the water. It also had the unintended consequences of violating "Do No Harm." In one instance a battery was stolen from a pumping station office. To punish the thief, the Taliban cut off water for 10 days to 10,000-20,000 people in the district where the pumping station was located—even though they had no idea if the thief even came from that district.

The most vulnerable women in Kabul were the 30,000 war widows. The Taliban prohibited them from working, which meant they could not earn money to feed themselves or their families. Some could not even afford the traditional dress, the burkha that the Taliban required them to wear to go to the market. Many were forced into abject poverty, prisoners in their homes.

NGOs made these women a priority for feeding programs, especially in the winter months, since food donations had become their only means of survival. But even this relief could be interpreted as violating "Do No Harm." Feeding the women let the Taliban off the hook. Because the women did not have to work to pay for food, the feeding program served to make them more dependent. It also gave the Taliban even more power over them, as the programs could be stopped on a Taliban whim.

On balance, survival took precedence over dependency, and many NGOs had to balance the presumed effects of "Do No Harm" with "Do Nothing at All."

I, as a new Deputy Director for CARE/U.S.A Emergency Group, was given a short term assignment to travel to Kabul and assess the emergency planning capabilities of CARE, the U.N. and other NGOs. There was still serious fighting going on in the country with the Northern Alliance[64]. There was conflict that could be heard on the outskirts of Kabul at night. The Northern Alliance also had jets and occasionally attacked Kabul, targeting the airport and military installations.

At that time, the only gateway to Kabul was by road from Peshawar, Pakistan, through the historic Khyber Pass. For some, traveling to this picturesque capital in the mountains would be an adventure. For me, the eight-hour trip was part of the job. Our 4-wheel drive Land Cruiser took us along precarious roads. We careened around steep curves with no guard rails. The roadway had been ground up by the treads of Russian tanks or crunched by the endless truck caravans that convoyed into Kabul from Pakistan. It was so rough I seemed to spend more time off my seat than on it. My hips and back ached from the pounding.

We passed through rugged snow-capped mountains that jutted up into a crystal-clear blue sky. Deep mountain gorges revealed snow-fed rivers and streams. It was all very picturesque —and potentially very deadly. I rode in a single vehicle in hostile territory, with-

---

64   In 1992, the Northern Alliance was established in opposition of the communist government led by President Najibullah. In 1997, the Taliban had launched a large-scale offensive against the Northern Alliance, capturing several of the positions it held to the north of Kabul. Thus began the back and forth war between the Northern Alliance and the Taliban

out radio communications, where ambushes by bandits and head-on crashes were not uncommon. The sides of the road were heavily mined; warning signs were everywhere. If you had to relieve yourself, you did so on the road.

We passed burned-out hulks of Soviet tanks and armored personnel carriers. Like altars to the god of war, they stood as an ominous sign to me and any other foreigner who thought he or she could come into Afghanistan and tame a people who had never been conquered.

After eight hours, we finally reached Kabul. I was not there long enough to learn much about the culture or the Afghan people. My memories are little more than snapshots in black and white. I see Kabul the beautiful: majestic mountains, ancient buildings, exotic cultural dress. Then I picture Kabul the dangerous: a two-man Taliban foot patrol. The men carry AK-47 rifles and swagger along the street. I think about the thin line between life and death.

The strict, if ignorant, interpretation of some archaic Islamic law can prompt these men to abuse, beat and even pull the trigger of their weapons to eliminate a "perpetrator." Prison or torture can start with a tap on the shoulder. I see an image of a war widow and her child waiting in the cold with hundreds of other war widows for food rations to be distributed by relief workers. Armed Taliban are vigilant. They ensure that no woman talks to a man who is not her spouse or relative at the food distribution sites[65]. I see a man missing both legs, probably a veteran of the war against the Russians. He is sitting in the street begging for alms in the name of Allah. Wherever I look I see bunkers and buildings fortified by layers of sandbags to protect them from in-coming air strikes and artillery fire.

Nights seemed to last an eternity in Kabul. With no electricity in most buildings and a Taliban-imposed 9:00 P.M. curfew, there was little to do. Yes, there was the U.N. Club, where I could get a western-style meal and be served a beer, but I was also told that Taliban agents inside and outside the club took notice of those who visited there. I avoided the U.N. club.

I stayed in a relief worker's safe house. It was rudimentary and only rarely had electricity. The building was large, a cavernous

---

65   CARE and other NGOs, in order to interact with the female population in Afghanistan would hire local females willing to work under dangerous circumstances. These were tough, educated women who did their work daily. They were also a high profile target for the Taliban. In one instance female employees were taken off a bus by the Taliban and publicly beaten.

cement structure with five bedrooms. Each bedroom had a bath. Occasionally I got cold water to shower. At night, the temperatures dipped well below freezing, and there was no central heat.

A dangerous-looking kerosene heater warmed my bedroom. I assume the fumes would either kill me or the heater would simply explode one night. Dinner was generally consumed directly out of tin cans: anchovies and lunch meat shared under freezing candle-light with whomever was staying in the house that night. Each night, I got into bed, cold and dirty, and listened to a sporadic serenade of machine gun and small-arms fire, occasionally accompanied by a mortar blast.

I listened to this, knowing that somewhere, out in the sub-urbs, human beings were trying to kill one another to gain some illu-sionary advantage. But I was also comforted, knowing I must spend only a few nights in Kabul, unlike others spending months and years. That usually allowed me to fall into a restless, dreamless sleep.

The Northern Alliance, the main enemy of the Taliban, was still able to strike at Kabul from northern bases and managed to keep the Kabul airport closed to civilian air traffic through regular strikes from aircraft and artillery. I was in a U.N. meeting discussing disaster preparedness and planning during one such attack. We sat there, as if we were at the United Nations Plaza in New York City, sipping our coffee and tea, while an anti-aircraft battery blasted away a short distance from us. The sound was deafening, stinging the eardrums. It is a strange marriage— war and international planning.

"Well, I think that rapid assessment teams (boom-boom-boom-boom-boom) are essential for early (boom-boom-boom-boom-boom) response planning."

A shouting, almost comical, conversation ensued as one or two aging fighter bombers swooped over the airport and released their lethal loads. All across the city, Taliban anti-aircraft guns and heavy machine guns opened fire on the attacking planes—and con-tinued firing long after the attackers had gone to their tea breaks in a Northern Alliance airport. I keep wondering, "With all this heavy metal from the anti-aircraft guns going up into the blue heavens, where is it coming down?"

The one color image I have of my brief sojourn in and foray into Kabul is that of the women. The Afghan women I was allowed to see are an inspiration to their gender and our race. In the face of incredible adversity, they went on living, caring and helping one another. They faced daily harassment, arrest without warrant, and random beatings by Taliban foot patrols. Yet they seemed strong and resilient.

As I think about these women, I think, too, about my daughter. I want Kara to understand about these women and their courage and humanity. I want her to know that people's rights must be held sacred above all else. I look with disdain towards countries that actively or passively oppose the advancement of women and deny them their rights. I want my daughter to think, as she grows up, about the role she must play to ensure that the rights of women are never compromised or abused as they have been in Afghanistan and in so many other sad societies.

In 1997, in Kabul, the music that the relief agencies played was a silent song of survival, dedicated to the thousands of women and children who were trying to survive a desperate situation. Sometimes relief workers are the only witnesses and the only musicians.

WHAT DO WE DO WHEN THEY COME FOR THE CHILDREN?

While he was looking at me sternly, he took the bayonet from its scabbard and attached it at the muzzle of his gun. I trembled so hard that my lips shook. He smiled without emotion. The rebels, none of whom were over 21, started walking us back to a village we had passed.

—Ishmael Beah,
A Long Way Gone: Memories of a Boy Soldier

The jumping-off point for rebel-controlled southern Sudan is Loki-chokio, also known as Loki in northern Kenya. It was here that the United Nations, the United States, other governments and numerous NGOs had set up operations in a battle against the impact of war, poverty and disease.

The Loki base resembled a military operation — everything, that is, except weapons. It contained a mess hall, motor pool, warehouses, and huts where personnel could bunk. Airplanes carrying vital food, medicine and aid workers were constantly landing on the tarmac runways. Truck convoys braved bad roads, landmines and bandits as they rolled in and out after an arduous trek to/from the north. The air bristled with the background crackle of radio communications.

My assignment was to travel to southern Sudan with two experts to teach local CARE staff, aid workers, and village elders how to mitigate the dangers of land mines and how to initiate effective security planning. Our team consisted of Bob MacPherson, a 20-year veteran of the U.S. Marine Corps with vast military experience from Vietnam to Somalia, and Fred Steele, who was a Maori[66] from New Zealand and had spent nine years in their military as an explosives expert. We carried with us a case of land mine models and instructional booklets on "mine awareness."

We had planned training exercises in the rebel-controlled areas of Tambura and Bor counties in southern Sudan, but the only safe way to get to either site was by light plane. The landing strips in Sudan were rough bare fields. As our twin-engine craft bounced through the clouds on the first leg from Loki I peered down and saw the beginnings of the Sudd.

In *The White Nile*[67] Alan Moorehead describes what I was seeing. He writes, "There is no more formidable swamp in the world than the Sudd. The Nile loses itself in a vast sea of papyrus ferns and rotting vegetation, and in that fetid heat there is a spawning tropical life that can hardly have altered very much since the beginning of the world; it is as primitive and as hostile to man as the Sargasso Sea. Crocodiles and hippopotamus flop about in the muddy water, mosquitoes and other insects choke the air. This region is neither land nor water. Year by year the current brings down more floating vegetation and packs it into solid chunks perhaps twenty feet thick, strong enough for an elephant to walk on."

If our plane went down, there would be no survivors, even if we survived the crash.

My mind drifted back to my first visit to Sudan as a representative of the U.S. Catholic Conference in 1981. I had flown to northern Sudan, landing in the capital, Khartoum. My assignment was to help U.N. and U.S. Embassy officials set up a refugee screening operation similar to the one I help establish in Singapore. The program would relocate Ethiopian refugees to Europe and North America.

Khartoum, at the confluence of the Blue and White Nile rivers, was a shock to my system. It was surrounded by desert, excruciatingly hot, and hit 120 degrees or more during the day. It had few paved roads. Violent sandstorms, called haboobs, would spring up out of nowhere. I quickly discovered in this extreme climate that the

---

66   Māori people: https://en.wikipedia.org/wiki/Māori_people; The Māori are the indigenous Polynesian people of New Zealand. Māori originated with settlers ... Early Māori formed tribal groups based on eastern Polynesian social customs and organization. Horticulture flourished using plants they introduced; later, a prominent warrior culture emerged.

67   Moorehead, Alan. *The White Nile*. New York, NY: Harper Perennial, 1960

Sudanese people were among the warmest, friendliest, and most hospitable people on the planet. It is not uncommon for people you meet on the street to invite you home for dinner.

My next visit to Khartoum was in 1985 as a Red Cross delegate. Again, I was to work with the influx of refugees escaping the bloodshed in Ethiopia and the Sudanese displaced by the horrible drought. In 1983, the Sudanese government had proclaimed Islamic law, forbidding dancing and the consumption of alcohol. The law placed restrictions on women. The friendly people were still there but the music and socializing were now hidden behind closed gates in private homes.

The enforcement of Islamic law triggered and gave momentum to a war that had been dormant in 1981 between the Muslims in the north and Christians in the south. The enforcement of Islamic law in the south was a provocation to the Christians and other non-Muslims, and by 1997, when Bob, Fred and I were flying over the Sudd, an estimated two million lives had been lost and extensive dislocations of the population had occurred because of the war.

To paint this war as a conflict between religion and race, however, is a mistake. It was more about oil[68], although other factors fueled the conflict as well. In 1989, Lieutenant General Omar Hassan Bashir seized power in a military coup. His regime was criticized for human rights violations: slavery, torture, and the use of child soldiers. He put his country on a collision course with the United States and Europe by harboring terrorist groups.

Now here we were in 1997, flying into a war zone to provide security instructions to CARE aid workers who were trying to help millions of displaced persons. As our light plane banked and headed for a landing in rebel-controlled South Sudan, two feelings came over me. First, I wondered if the friends I had made in 1981 in Khartoum would consider this act of collaborating with the enemy. The second was more immediate. The pilot initiated a rapid descent, probably to avoid ground fire, but I saw nothing that looked like a landing strip. I couldn't believe he was putting the plane down there, but he did. We held our stomachs and gave silent thanks as we bounced onto a dirt strip obscured by grass.

---

68   In 1978 - Oil is discovered in Bentiu Province in southern Sudan; in 1983 - President Numeiri declares the introduction of Sharia Islamic law also in 1983 civil war breaks out again in the south involving government forces and the Sudan People's Liberation Movement (SPLM), led by John Garang. Time line at: https://www.bbc.com/news/world-africa-14095300

Our first stop was Tambura. In isolated southern Sudan, each landing is a community event and the local people crowded around the plane. Once on the ground the three of us shook so many hands it felt as if we were running for public office. The heat, humidity and flies were intense and, even worse, it was obvious to me that we were in a hostile environment. Men and boys were carrying assault rifles. There were bunkers to dive into during the occasional air raid. The locals pointed out bomb craters. Spent shell casings littered the ground.

Even without the war, the slightest injury could be life-threatening. We carried "quick-run" kits that contained survival gear in case our encampment was over-run by bandits or enemy troops and we were forced to flee. A gunshot, an infected appendix, or snake bite at dusk or at night could easily result in death as planes could land only during the day. The smallest accumulation of rain could close the landing strip for days. The nearest hospital was in Nairobi, three to four hours away by air.

Rebel-controlled South Sudan was on the fringe of war and in the cusp of time. There, distance was not measured in miles but by how many hours it would take to walk from one point to another. One CARE staffer had walked more than twelve hours through swamps to get to our training session. There was no electricity, no running water. Money was useless, as it had no immediate relevance to survival here. Barter was the way the locals acquired what they needed and even CARE's locally hired staff did not want money but took payment instead in blankets and other tradable items.

The village administration was not a building but rather a cleared place under a tree. The school was a one-room shack abutting a swamp. The most popular methods of communication were drums and runners.

CARE's living conditions in the field ranged from Spartan to primitive. In Tambura, a stone fence enclosed the compound of bungalows. They had a generator for electricity, running water and even a sit-down latrine. This is where we stayed. We knew that living in bungalows was "upper class."

There was an air raid bunker behind the bungalows. Looking into its darkened entrance I wondered if I would dive into that hole if bombs began to fall. Bunkers were dens for snakes and scorpions. I might just take my chances with the ill-placed air strike.

A Russian-made Ilyushin 76 cargo plane could be seen high above us. The planes kept their distance because the rebels had anti-aircraft weapons that could easily shoot down a slower low-flying cargo transport. Was this plane on a supply mission, surveillance or a bomb run? The Ilyushin would lower its rear cargo doors and the crew chief would roll a bomb out of the back door. While this was not a very accurate system it could still be lethal.

We spent a few days in Tambura, meeting with the area rebel leader to get approval for our mission. Garbed in camouflage clothing, with dark sunglasses shielding his eyes and a black beret, he looked like an African version of Che Guevara. He had a pistol in a shoulder holster, a large knife on his belt and three bodyguards, each with an AK-47.

I could tell by the way the guards carried themselves and the way they cradled their weapons that they were professionals who meant business. I also had no doubt that if their leader told them to shoot us, there would be no delay in carrying out the order. But our meeting with the African Che was cool and cordial. He wanted to know why we were there and where we were going. Bob and Fred explained our land mine training mission, and Bob added that any mines removed from the ground should be immediately destroyed; a UN recommendation.

We knew, of course, that these rebels would re-use the mines they had dug up to strike back at the government that had put them there in the first place. We invited "Che" and any government officials to attend our training. We knew they would show up, invited or not.

In Tambura, we had a makeshift classroom to teach CARE staff, school teachers, healthcare personnel, and rebel government staff about the dangers of land mines and unexploded ordnance (called UXOs). The UXOs in the area included artillery shells, mortar rounds and grenades. We taught them what UXOs were, what they looked like, how to get out of a minefield and how to avoid minefields. We emphasized that UXOs were never to be picked up or touched by the untrained. We re-emphasized that because mines and UXOs are lethal and unpredictable they should be removed only by ordnance experts.

We suggested that villagers mark off the perimeters of minefields or areas where UXOs had landed or were stored. These markings could be made by whatever was available—stones, paint or traditional warning symbols. We urged them to instruct villagers, especially curious children, not to go into marked areas.

Late one afternoon, some of the village elders approached us. They told us of a minefield near our encampment that had killed some people—including children—and animals. Bob and Fred gave each other a look that said, "We have to do something," and we asked the villagers to lead us to the minefield.

Using knives and screwdrivers, Bob and Fred probed the ground attempting to locate the edge of the field. They probed as far as two large trees, and calculated that beyond the trees there were mines. The villagers indicated that they were, indeed, at the front of the hazard zone. Each man took out a can of red paint that we had brought with us for the training. They marked both trees with the word "MINE" and painted a skull and crossbones sign on each which is universally recognized as a land mine warning. I stayed a safe distance away, taking photographs, hoping that my camera would not take a picture of a friend blasted by a mine.

Bob and Fred were being neither brave nor stupid. They were trained for this and we were there to train villagers how to do what they were now doing. Besides, there are times when human beings must try to help other human beings, especially if they are the only ones with a skill that can make a difference.

Bob persuaded the elders to call a town meeting to warn people not to walk beyond the tall trees with the red marks on them. For that effort, we received a gift of three bracelets, one of which I still wear today. The bracelets were fashioned from spent artillery shell casings. Three days later, our plane returned to pick us up and take us to Bor. The team had provided the basic training and know-how about mines and UXOs to a number of people. How this was applied, or if it had an impact, we would never know.

I had heard stories about CARE's Bor encampment and knew that the next four days would be rougher than the previous four. Our plane bounced along the Tambura landing strip and gained enough momentum to just barely clear the trees at the end of the runway. I said a silent prayer as we made the next approach, as that landing zone looked more improbable than the last one.

All I could see was a large swamp, surrounded by trees, and I held images of Kate and 4-year-old Kara in my mind. If we crashed, that would be my last memory. Again, the pilot maneuvered brilliantly to a small strip that paralleled the swamp. There was no margin of error in this landing. As we got out of the plane, I noticed the swamp was barely 12 meters away.

We were welcomed by another mob of the curious, necessitating the shaking of dozens of hands. John Berkman, the senior CARE person at Bor, greeted us in English with a thick German accent. Porters who would take our bags followed him. I imagined I was on the set of a 1950s Victor Mature safari movie.

Our entourage hiked directly to the CARE compound where we would sleep and eat. It was next to the swamp and enclosed by an eight-foot-high wall made of grass mats. There was a circular mud-packed hut with a thatched roof, a bungalow called a tuku. This served as a kitchen, sleeping quarters for two, and a place to keep the chickens. Nearby was a screened-in cabana with tables that functioned as the dining room. It served, too, as a respite from the swarms of malaria-carrying mosquitoes that seemed to be everywhere.

In the corner of the compound was an area blocked by a grass mat. The door to this tuku was so low that you had to crouch to get inside. In the center of the enclosure was a hole in the ground, about three feet deep with several rolls of toilet paper next to the hole. This was obviously the latrine. In the opposite corner was another walled-off area. Behind the wall were two buckets filled with water. This served as a makeshift bathing area.

My teammates and I slept on the ground in one-man pup tents. The temperature in the tents must have been over 90 degrees, but at least we were somewhat protected. Since the tents had a floor and were completely sealed, no snakes, scorpions, spiders, or centipedes could get in during the night. The camp staff slept under the stars on cots covered by mosquito netting held up by poles and taped or bolted to the four corners of the cot frame. The sun sets early in late summer, about 6:30 P.M., and from that point on, we had to be in a tent, in the cabana, or under netting. Otherwise we would be eaten alive by insects.

Since the compound was on the edge of the swamp, it was not smart to go barefoot. I carried a flashlight to be on the lookout for snakes and scorpions. I went to bed to the sound of hyenas, the occasional rifle shot in the distance and the bumping of insects against my tent. Sometimes the number of insects hitting the side of the tent was so thick it actually sounded like rain.

My four-night stay was further bedeviled by some type of lung infection I'd picked up. I couldn't stop coughing. It was worse when lying down. During those steamy nights, in that cramped tent, I tried to sleep upright. I got through these miserable nights by playing a mental game I called, "I wonder what Kate and Kara are doing now." It would be seven hours earlier on the east coast of America. I imagined Kara in school and Kate teaching class. Somehow, thinking of Kara playing in a schoolyard calmed me.

The interaction between the CARE field staff and residents was both impressive and fascinating. In a Bor County village called Paliau, John Berkman gave an impromptu planning meeting to village elders on CARE's plans for the area. Using his foot, he mapped out the area, indicating villages, swamps, paths, fields and battlegrounds. He explained which secure sites could be considered for development projects like agricultural farms and irrigation ditches. These sites were eligible for relief aid, including emergency food rations or food for work projects in which workers were paid in food for repairing bomb-damaged bridges and roads.

What impressed me was that this plan was participatory. This was not a situation in which a white CARE worker told the locals what to do. The elders gave their own suggestions and comments. There was open discussion and negotiation, adjustments were made to the plan from the elder's suggestions and finally a course of action was mutually arrived at. It reminded me so much of my construction committee in the village of An Duong, and reinforced my belief that all development projects should be run this way.

In Bor County, our training site was under a tree. The lectures were always full, some people walking eight to ten hours to partake in the training. The heat was stifling, and aggressive flies replaced the night mosquitos. Any slight breeze was a godsend. Yet, everyone took the discussions and demonstrations seriously, because mines and UXOs were a life-and-death issue for them.

At both Bor and Tambura, we asked if there were any mines or UXOs in the area. At Bor, one man raised his hand shyly and asked about the "metal" by the swamp. We walked over to the location he had indicated. Lying in high grass were about a dozen mortar and rocket-propelled grenade rounds. Another man then took us to a neatly stacked pile of land mines. This is part of the problem in war zones. Live ammunition that can kill and maim becomes part of the background. People become accustomed to these "pieces of metal" and do not see them as implements of terror and death. Children played in this area, oblivious to the danger.

Identifying mines.

One evening after training, I spotted an elderly gentlemen reclining in a metal chair near a wall outside our compound. He had been at the training that day. He was tall, with short cropped hair. Draped over the chair with his long legs, relaxed and reclining, he had a regal air. His face, though weathered and lined, had a peaceful aura about it. His hands were long and, when he spoke, gestured elegantly.

I asked one of the locals to interpret for me and we talked. We talked about families, farming and the war. He picked up on the fact I felt we could do so little when there were so many problems in the area. He reassured me that what CARE was trying to do with land mines and development had ensured the livelihood of many of the children who had been playing around us. I hung on the words "of many" because even he knew that neither CARE, God nor any government could save them all.

In Tambura, a school teacher told us how his daughter recently lost her right hand to a land mine while playing in a field. The teacher was of slight build and stood out among the Dinkas who towered over me and my 6-foot frame. His face was weather-beaten.

His white shirt and blue pants were tattered but immaculately clean. His sandals had been broken and repaired many times. I could not help but compare this teacher to my wife who is also a teacher. Both had the same enthusiasm for their students and teaching, but Kate was paid well. She worked in a comfortable environment. Getting to work was not a life-threatening experience. The Sudanese teacher was paid little for his labors. His workplace could hardly be called comfortable, and simply getting to work could have life-ending consequences.

Practicing prodding for mines S. Sudan 1997.

The personal experiences we heard during the training touched the heart and the soul. They were related neither dramatically nor out of anger, which affected me even more. I realized what brave, stoic survivors these Sudanese are. In my journey I had evolved in my thinking about heroism and bravery. When I was a boy my hero was John Wayne charging up the beaches in *Sands of Iwo Jima*. In Vietnam my heroes were my fellow soldiers and the Vietnamese who persevered in the most difficult of circumstances. Now it was the brave women of Afghanistan and these humble people before me who went about their daily lives with a courage that few Americans can appreciate.

Our trainees were wise to nature and humankind, although both had been punishing to them. The questions they asked were no different than the questions I had asked as a soldier in Vietnam 26 years before.

"By running fast, can you out distance yourself from the blast of a land mine?" "Is there a clicking noise before the blast?" "Can you see the mines in the dirt?" "What color is the trip-wire?" "What do I do if my child brings an unexploded bomb into the house?"

One gentleman asked why the United States would not sign the treaty to ban these horrific weapons. Another told us that many villagers knew how to track and that in moist soil they could trace their own footsteps out of a minefield. Some of the most poignant questions were about personal safety. They were questions with no answer. "What if the enemy comes to rape my wife?" "What do we do when they come for the children, to make them slaves or soldiers?"

Certainly, the issue of rape and the abuse of children is not unknown in America. But in the United States there are outlets for help—the police, social services, social media organizations such as the "Me Too" movement and the religious community. In Bor County, these bleak questions yielded stark answers, underscoring the help-lessness that had befallen these people.

When it came time for us to leave, there was both tension and excitement at the landing strip. The team was tired and dirty. What if the plane did not arrive? What if we had to stay here longer? My chest still hurt from the coughing and my throat felt raw. Finally, we heard the distant drone of a twin-engine plane. It came in fast and bounced along the strip. In attempting to turn the plane around the wheels got stuck in soft soil and a number of us were recruited to push it out of the muck. We did so eagerly. Before we knew it, we had said our goodbyes and were airborne.

There was little conversation among us on the plane. We were deep in thought over what we had experienced in a little over seven days. I tried to take my thoughts away from Bor County and think of Kate and Kara. But Bor County had invaded my consciousness. I imagined my wife and daughter in their beds sleeping as groups of heavily armed, faceless men descended on our home. Being so far away I would not be able to help.

Plane stuck in mud.

As we headed back to Loki I kept thinking about the question, "What do we do when they come for the children?" Sometimes, I know, there are no good answers. I knew the work we had just accomplished was relevant. We taught people how to protect themselves and others from land mines, even if we could not eliminate all the threats they faced. Even if frolicking children might set off a mine. Even if the enemy might come to rape, pillage, kidnap, and kill.

I knew that it would always be important to use what I had learned to help those who needed help to fight their foes, and that I would not fight this fight alone. There was some comfort in that.

THE VILLAGE OF MANY WIDOWS

"When I came back in 1991, I was too scared to farm my land. One of my neighbors tried to take the mines out of his land and he was killed when a mine exploded in his face." Phoeuk Soem, Battambang Province, Cambodia.

—Shawn Roberts and Jody Williams,
*After The Guns Fall Silent:
The Enduring Legacy of Land Mines*

In a small village bisected by a dusty road, an old woman sat in a flimsy lean-to that protected her from the unmerciful heat and humidity of Cambodia. As my partner, Bob Archer, and I approached her with our interpreter, we pressed our hands together as if in prayer and bowed[69]. It was the traditional Cambodian greeting and a way of showing respect. Through our interpreter, we politely inquired if we could ask her some questions about the village.

Village widow.

She smiled broadly. I imagined she was curious why these white men with big sun-burned noses would care to talk to anyone about this village. She gestured to us to sit down on a raised bamboo

---

69   In Cambodia it is called "Sampeah" and there are 5 different versions of this prayer like greeting depending on the social ranking of the person you are meeting. In Thailand a similar friendly greeting is called a "Wai"

mat at the back of the lean-to. With our shirts already soaked we were more than happy for a respite from the pounding sun.

Behind us another woman, also elderly, sat. Between her legs was a small child of about five. Soon another old woman joined us. She wore a flimsy top and skirt and carried a child on her hip. After discarding a smelly hand-rolled cigarette, she squatted on the dirt floor of the lean-to and looked up at us, smiling.

I tried to guess the age of the elderly woman who beckoned us in. Her face said many things to me. The lines, the dry leathery look, the sad-happy smile, spoke to me of years of hard work, poor harvests, bad weather and war. If you could count the lines on her face like the rings in a tree, she would have been hundreds of years old. Yet there was also strength, perseverance, dignity and the will to stay alive. Somehow she had managed, by luck or skill, to survive a 20-year-long game of death that had been playing out in this land.

We were in Cambodia as part of a team dedicated to identifying and isolating areas at high risk for land mines and unexploded ordnance (UXO). Our plan was to locate and map the largest minefields in the area and apply for U.S. or European governmental or United Nations funding to hire mine clearance teams to remove and dispose of the buried explosives. There were enough people in Cambodia missing limbs.

We asked this woman if she knew the location of any minefields or if they were a problem for life in the village. She gestured vaguely with her hands towards the west. There were many minefields out there, but the Cambodian government came and destroyed them, she indicated.

Are people still hurt by land mines, we queried?

"Not recently," she said through our interpreter. "But we know there are mines near the river where we get water. And some of the wooded and hilly areas have mines in them. We are careful where we walk."

We pressed on.

"Water is a problem," she told us. "The river is four kilometers away. It is a long distance for an old woman to fetch water for crops, washing and cooking. And we have to be careful of the mines. Sometimes I don't have enough water to clean myself or the children.

"Also the weather. Last year the monsoon did not come. If it does not come this year, I don't know what we will do for food."

She told us that the children had no place to go if they are sick.

"The school was far away," she said. "Many of the children don't attend because they have to carry water and do other chores. Many are sick from malaria and have stomach problems from drinking bad water."

I asked where the men were. The ancient one told me that you could call Boch Non the "Village of Many Widows." In the time it took the interpreter to translate her words, both old women were laughing about their new name for the village. Our hostess went on to add that while we might see some male children or teenagers, most men had been claimed by the wars. Pol Pot had murdered many of them, and others who were still alive were forced into migrant labor in Thailand or other parts of Cambodia.

I asked if I could take her picture, and she proudly posed for me. Her neighbor, the older woman, quickly ran to get a nicer shirt to put over her flimsy blouse. I snapped her photo as well. We thanked them for their time; they asked nothing of us in return. Soon we were bouncing down the dusty road to another village.

We spent a week traveling through Battambang Province. The area was formerly Khmer Rouge territory that quickly ricocheted from war to peace when the local Khmer Rouge leadership "defected" to the government side. Displaced persons, refugees and those living in towns rushed back to claim land for fear that others might homestead it.

Maintaining land ownership was difficult in the province. The Khmer Rouge destroyed all land records and deeds. Land was now controlled by the government, the police, the military, and the people who homesteaded it. Some may have title to a given piece of land. In other cases, the government had given out plots to refugees or displaced people. In some ugly instances, high-ranking officials had taken over large sections that had been cleared by government de-mining teams.

Battambang Province, with its rich soil, precious gems and forests, once produced enough food to feed the entire country. Now, the major harvest was land mines and unexploded munitions. Still, the province, now at peace, provided opportunity. Villages were springing up wherever road improvements were made. People were homesteading, regardless of the risks posed by land mines and buried bombs or the fact that there was little infrastructure, such as schools or health clinics, to support them.

We were told that the failure rate of the farms was high. Many people enthusiastically left the cities and refugee camps to get land for a home but it takes more than enthusiasm to settle a harsh environment. Those who couldn't cope ended up back in refugee camps or destitute in the larger cities.

Traveling the dusty, rutted roads of western Battambang, we learned a great deal in a short amount of time. Bob and I were there to address the problems of land mines, but we discovered that this issue was only one bad thread interwoven through the harsh fabric of life on the fringe. Malaria, cholera and other gastrointestinal diseases were threats; so was drought and malnutrition. I began to feel that the very environment was a threat to the human and animal populations in Battambang Province during these past 20 years.

Huts being built on minefields.

Everywhere we went, the story was the same. Moving back onto the land was risky, but the risk had to be taken. I witnessed huts being constructed and children playing on land that was clearly marked with the familiar red skull-&-crossbones signs. These signs warned, in English and Khmer, "DANGER LAND MINES."

Wherever we went, we asked about what problems people were facing. The answers were repetitive: "We need water..." "We need agricultural support..." "...health care," "...our children need to go to school." Mines were present but often not mentioned in the conversation unless we pressed the issue. They had become a part of the accepted landscape, like a road, river or poisonous snake.

Yet mines and unexploded bombs prohibited the digging of wells, the improvement of irrigation systems, and the expansion of agricultural lands. Schools and health centers could not be built, or if they could, getting to them might be fraught with danger. What infrastructure that was still standing had been mined by Pol Pot forces. This included schools, government buildings, temples and public wells. In one area where there was a school, the children couldn't attend full-time because they needed to haul water, navigating the minefields as they went about their chores.

The specter of mines was everywhere. In one village, a woman told us that a man had been killed by a mine that morning while searching for firewood. As she related the story, a procession of people came by carrying a hastily-made coffin with the latest mine victim in it.

In another village, while talking to another woman, I spotted an anti-tank mine under the stairs going up to her hut. This device could destroy her home and everyone in it. When we queried her as to why she had such a device under her home, she said she didn't know why; her husband had brought it in. She didn't know if it had been defused. Not wanting to touch the mine for fear of setting it off, we urged her to tell local de-mining teams about its location and have it removed.

Anti-tank mines under hut stairs.

I assumed, as in rebel controlled southern Sudan, the locals had become so accustomed to the sights and sounds of war that they became only background noise and images. That day we had passed by several rusting artillery pieces and a tank lying by the side of the road, waiting for the jungle to envelop them.

It was not that the Cambodian government and international NGOs working in Battambang Province didn't understand the situation. The Battambang Provincial Development Plan recognized land mines as a major impediment to development. They also recognized that in order to tackle a problem of this magnitude, everyone had to be involved in eliminating them—individuals, villages, communes, districts and provincial leadership, as well as local and international NGOs and trained de-miners.

The Battambang Provincial Rural Development Committee and the United Nation's Cambodia Area Rehabilitation & Regeneration Project strategy called for a bottom-up approach that empowered people through village and commune development committees. These approaches were designed to bring former enemies together while removing this deadly detritus of war.

It is natural to begin a process of healing after a war but in order for there to be action plans and development strategies, it is important to get things organized politically.

Long after the war is over and life has resumed with some semblance of what it was before the fighting, the effects of war persist. I bear the scars of Vietnam, even though decades have now passed. Many lose their possessions or their land. Others continue to cope without a limb or even worse, without a husband or father who was lost to the war. In the case of land mines, though hostilities have ceased, the war goes on claiming additional casualties.

Suffering injury and death for a dispute that has already been settled is even more senseless, it seems to me, than suffering these injuries during war.

THE MUTILATED OF SIERRA LEONE

All that is necessary for the triumph of evil is that good men do nothing."

—Edmund Burke

The woman sat in the hot office of the United Nations High Commission for Refugees (UNHCR) facility, answering my questions about her journey through terror.

The room was humid, but her eyes chilled me. She looked through me, as if she could see beyond the cement to some monster lurking outside. I recognized the stare. She was only 24 years old, but she had seen enough horror for five life times.

She was the fourth person I had talked to that morning. Each had told tales that were remarkably similar, albeit each with its own wicked twist.

This woman had come from the village of Makeni, across the border from Guinea in Sierra Leone. She and her husband were small-business traders. When Revolutionary United Front (RUF)[70] rebels had surrounded her village, she and her 3-month-old baby were able to conceal themselves. But from her hiding place, she saw her husband tortured and killed. She saw women—some were pregnant—gang-raped until they died. Villagers who tried to escape the onslaught were shot.

Once the rebels withdrew, she and other survivors retreated to the safety of the Guinea border. On her journey, her child died. She found two other children who had been abandoned, so she picked them up and was now caring for them. Her village was destroyed and her only relative, a sister, was somewhere in Sierra Leone—if she was

---

70   Revolutionary United Front (RUF) was a rebel army that fought a failed eleven-year war in Sierra Leone, starting in 1991 and ending in 2002. It later developed into a political party, which still exists today. The three most senior surviving leaders, Issa Sesay, Morris Kallon and Augustine Gbao, were convicted in February 2009 of war crimes and crimes against humanity.[1]

still alive. The woman was obviously under great stress, her future uncertain. Still, she told me that, "Thanks to God and the UNHCR Health Center," she was being encouraged to "live day by day."

The small enclosed compound was a ten-minute ride down a busy street from UNHCR headquarters in Conakry, the seaside capital of Guinea. Run by UNHCR in partnership with the Guinean government and a German NGO, German Agency for Technical Cooperation (GTZ), its hallmarks were compassion and respect for human life.

There, I met Peter Kono, a Sierra Leone refugee, who ran the center and explained its function. Refugees from Sierra Leone who had been mutilated or psychologically scarred by RUF rebels were brought to the compound for medical treatment, counseling and for a measure of hope.

I had heard about the mutilations and the facility created to address them, but I could not understand why, if the stories were true, the world was sitting mutely by. As a soldier, I had seen the effects of torture, but what I had heard and seen this morning numbed me. I had spoken with 12 people who had been either tortured or mentally abused, half of the census at the center that day.

By 1998, Sierra Leone had been at war with RUF rebels for more than seven years. The situation escalated in May of 1997 when Sierra Leone army troops overthrew the democratically elected President, Ahmed Tejan Kabbah. The insurrection leader, Major Johnny Paul Koromah, invited the RUF rebels to join him in the Sierra Leone capital of Freetown.

After fruitless negotiations, Nigerian-led army units, part of a West African peacekeeping force known as ECOMOG[71], launched a counter-attack. ECOMOG succeeded in ousting the rebel junta and forcing RUF forces from the capital. President Kabbah was re-installed and remnants of the ousted junta and RUF forces fled to the diamond-rich northeast of the country, with ECOMOG forces in pursuit.

In the northeast, the ECOMOG troops and the rebels came to a stalemate. For three months, the rebels began a reign of terror on the innocent local population. In a "scorched earth" policy, villages were surrounded and their inhabitants massacred. A few able-bod-

---

71   In an attempt to end the bloody civil war in Liberia, in August 1990, a group of West African nations under the auspices of the Economic Community of West African States (ECOWAS) took the unprecedented step of sending a peacekeeping force into Monrovia. This force, known as the Economic Community Cease-Fire Monitoring Group, (ECOMOG). "Waging War to Keep Peace 1993", https://www.hrw.org/reports/1993/liberia/.

ied civilians were kept alive to serve as porters or were forced into the rebel army. Perhaps worst of all, some people were mutilated to serve as human signposts of the continued power of the rebel forces.

Doctors Without Borders reported in May of 1998 that as many as 128 mutilated victims had reached the capital of Freetown. According to Amnesty International, women and children were being rounded up and locked into houses that were then set on fire. There were widespread reports of gang rapes, as well as the mutilation of men, women and children, usually the amputation of an arm or hand. In some cases, rebels would amputate both arms OR hands.

As I interviewed the victims, I sat numbly as they related their tales of terror in the same passive manner as the 24-year-old woman. This was reminiscent of the bland, quiet way of telling stories of horror related to me by land mine survivors in southern Sudan. I could only hope that the damage to these people's minds was not as severe as the damage to their bodies.

Here is some of what I heard:

A man who worked in the diamond mines was captured when rebels attacked his village. He was unsure of the status of his mother, father and sisters. He was used as a bearer to carry loot away from his village to a rebel stronghold. Of the 13 men captured from his village, four were released and five were taken away, never to be seen again. The four remaining prisoners were tied up. The rebel commander told them that they were to be executed. The 38-year-old miner was to be first.

The rebels brought them to a place where they said they killed people. Here, at these "killing fields," the miner saw numerous corpses. The captives were told to stand and wait to be executed.

For some reason, however, the commander decided to mutilate this man instead. He was taken to a tree, and as one rebel held a gun to the back of his head, another put his right hand against the tree and chopped it off with a machete. Next they cut off his left ear. He was then told to run or he would be shot. He was instructed to go to ECOMOG and tell them that the rebels were ready for them.

The miner made it to an ECOMOG base and was transported first to Freetown and then on to Conakry for care. He knew that if he returned to Sierra Leone and was caught by the rebels, he would be executed. The miner did not know about his future since he was "right-handed and now that hand was gone."

A 36-year-old farmer was captured by rebels while helping his brother with the farming. He was in a group of 12 with his father, mother and three sisters. He was forced to watch as rebels gouged out his father's eyes, burned his face, amputated both his legs and eventually beheaded him with a machete. Eight others in the group were killed, including his mother and sisters.

The three remaining captives were kept alive and forced to serve as bearers and—in case of an attack by opposition forces—human shields. The farmer was bound for three days, the bindings so tight that blood circulation to his hands was cut off and his hands became deformed.

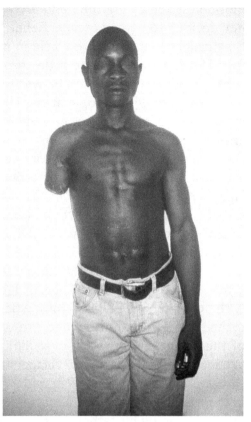

Mutilated refugee.

The rebel commander gave the three prisoners a choice of death or mutilation. They chose mutilation. One man's lips were cut off. The other's ears were cut off. The farmer's finger was cut off and his hands were put in a fire. The men were instructed to run to ECOMOG to serve as a warning that the rebels were still active in the area. They were told that if they were seen in the area again they would be killed. The farmer did not know if he would be able to ever use his hands. Conakry did not have the medical expertise to do much more for any of the patients than keep them alive.

A 28-year-old farmer from Lelehun village was captured with two others in a rebel attack. Because he belonged to the Mandingo tribe, the tribe of the current Sierra Leone president, the rebels beat him with their gun butts until they thought he was dead. He lay motionless for a long time and after hearing no movement around him decided to try and escape. Rebels were still in the area and when they caught him they threw acid in his face. Then they told him to run. The farmer could see little through his acid-scalded eyes. He took off and wandered until he was found by ECOMOG forces.

According to people at the UNHCR facility, the acid did not totally destroy his eyes but did weld his eyelids together. There was a chance that he might see again, if he had access to a medical facility that could provide the kind of care he needed.

I also spoke with an unmarried 27-year-old man from the village of Kabala who worked in the diamond mines. Rebels killed his father during the 1996 elections because of his involvement in the democracy campaign. Now, in 1998, rebels had captured him during a pro-democracy rally and amputated his arm.

As a father, possibly the hardest story for me was that of a 5-year-old boy from the village of Igbeda. The boy was in a house with 19 members of his family when rebels attacked. The rebels rushed the house and opened fire with machine guns. The father of the boy threw his body over him and died in a burst of bullets. When the attack was over, villagers came to the house and found the wounded boy crying, lying under his father's body. All the others in the house were dead. In a matter of seconds he had lost his entire family, including his father, mother, four brothers and eight sisters.

As I left the compound, most of those I had interviewed were gathered together in a small courtyard, talking. My last view of these souls was the man who'd had acid thrown in his face. He was standing there clutching a Bible he could not read. The murder of civilians and the torture and maiming of these people brought no strategic gain or tactical advantage to the RUF rebels. No intelligence was gathered. The opposing forces were not weakened by these acts. They represented man's inhumanity to man at its most raw.

The 20th century saw two world wars and hundreds of other conflicts. The end of the Cold War did not bring peace, but merely fomented hot geo-political conflicts. In Africa colonialism was replaced by violent tribalism. Humanity seemed to be crawling into the new millennium unable or unwilling to learn from past mistakes.

The U.N. and NGOs have often been criticized for not doing enough for those savaged by war, even of creating more harm than good. I have sometimes been one of those critics. To me there is a vast difference between the staff that sit in international headquarters and those who do the dangerous humanitarian work, such as Mr. Kono at the Refugee Counselling Office in Nongoa, Guinea.

I am not an expert on U.N. policy, but efforts I witnessed from the U.N. and several NGOs in this case during my short trip to Guinea were nothing but commendable. The government of Guinea, one of the poorest countries on earth, was a gracious host to one of the highest concentrations of refugees in Africa, caring for as many as 600,000 Sierra Leoneans and Liberians who were forced to flee their homelands.

After my interviews, I stopped by the UNHCR office because I wanted to shake the hand of the U.N. protection officer and commend him for the job he was doing. He sadly announced that he had just received a report that five more mutilated persons had crossed the Sierra Leone border into Guinea. I had come to realize in this trip that the criticism of others, myself included, leveled at the U.N., international governments and NGOs often is directed at the executive level of these groups and some field leaders driven by ego and power instead of humanitarian concerns. At the field level there are often found the unrecognized heroes of humanitarian efforts.

I am a professional refugee worker and former soldier who had seen much of the terror and brutality of war. But that night at dinner, sitting by myself in my hotel, I was unable to shake the horror of what I most recently seen and heard.

After the Holocaust, the Jews said the world must "never forget." Had we forgotten? Or was it too easy not to notice?

A CHICKEN DINNER IN KIGALI 1998

I listened to a young boy who told me that he had been mutilated, that the militia had cut him all over his body. He managed to escape and found a hiding place in the bushes where while he was hiding he saw militia members and soldiers rape his mother until she died. When he saw dogs come to eat his mother's body, he could not chase them away because he was afraid that the militia would then see where he was hiding.

John A. Berry and Carol Pott Berry, witness testimony **of**
Lazare Ndazaro, Ministry of Rehabilitation
Genocide in Rwanda: A Collected Memory

Kigali is lovely.

It sits in the center of Rwanda, among rolling hills. The crest of each hill looks out over a green landscape dotted with the red-tiled European-style chalets of the middle class and the silver-tin roofs of the working classes. A brilliant blue sky overarches it all.

Unlike other cities I have visited in Africa, the main roads here are in excellent shape. Drivers pay attention to driving regulations. There is little litter on the streets. The city has a low crime rate. Although there is poverty, as in any urban center, it is not as apparent in this capital. The citizens take meticulous care of their land. Driving to work, you can see legions of people cutting the grass with long machetes.

The Rwandans I met during my short visit were polite, self-determined, and extremely friendly. The sky, the landscape and the people all project an image of tranquility. Rarely have I felt so at ease in a new place. And yet this is where the unthinkable happened.

Rwanda, and Kigali in particular, is where a nation ran amok and devoured itself. Neighbor turned against neighbor, teacher against student, priests and ministers against their own parishioners. Those who so meticulously cut their lawns with machetes used these same tools as instruments of terror—and before they finished cutting, a million people were mowed down in the landscaped grass[72].

Today, one can only wonder how the people and the government survived this catastrophe. In my talks with officials, I was impressed with their honesty. I was even more impressed with the "can-do" attitude that the government and its citizens seem to share. Rwanda received international donor assistance but did everything it could to become less dependent on outsiders. I had come there to discuss emergency assistance and preparedness, and in most cases I was politely told that they would "handle the problems ourselves."

Such a response is unusual. Most governments do not miss an opportunity to collect the food, equipment and money that might flow into a country from outside operations after a disaster.

When I visited, Rwanda was working on an ambitious social restructuring. The compassion and determination applied to solving the many internal and external challenges they faced was impressive. I was in Kigali too briefly to say how this approach came to be. Was Rwanda assuaging its guilt over the tragedy that had blackened its standing in the international community? Or, as in Israel, were Rwandans trying simply never to let such a tragedy happen again?

A major target of the social restructuring was Rwanda's rural area. Traditionally, there were few villages outside the capital. Families liked to live on their own homesteads, separated by great distances. Their cultural pattern was akin to that in the early American West, where the nearest neighbor was somewhere over the horizon. But the Rwandan government initiated a system of what it called "village-ization," which encouraged people to move into small communities.

The number one rationale for such a drastic move was security. During the 1994 genocide, people living in isolation were easy targets for their killers. Today, with rebel forces crossing borders, this kind of isolation still makes for a poor defense.

The other rationale was more realistic and forward-thinking.

---

72 The Rwandan genocide, also known as the genocide against the Tutsi, was a mass slaughter of Tutsi in Rwanda by members of the Hutu majority government. An estimated 500,000 to 1,000,000 Rwandans were killed. Additionally, 30% of the Pygmy Batwa were killed. https://en.wikipedia.org/wiki/Rwandan_genocide.

The government realized that it was nearly impossible to provide much-needed social services—such as health care, basic education, water and electricity—to an isolated population. With villages come social services, and with the provision of such social services comes development.

Certainly, there are downsides to bunching people together in communities—the spread of disease and crime are two potential drawbacks — but the government clearly believed that the positives outweighed the negatives. It was hard to join a gathering of people at the time I was there and not discuss the events that had occurred four years earlier. Still, present and future problems facing the Rwandan people were equally popular topics for discussion.

Especially difficult for me was trying to be sensitive to the survivors with my desire to find out how this worst of human horrors impacted them and how they survived. The massacre in Rwanda was a subject that could not be mentioned casually, and I learned much of what I could through observation.

One night during my week's stay there I attended a dinner party. I had known our hostess, Julia, for several years. Every time we met we greeted each other with a knowing smile of acceptance of two people who once had walked over death. It was an acceptance that we—two, clear-thinking, college-educated adults—had once walked into a minefield together in Angola.

At that time, Julia was a senior manager for the CARE Angola Country Office. I had been visiting Angola, a nation of 10 million people and 10 million land mines, in order to train our staff in mine detection and avoidance, as well as to develop proposals for the U.S. government on land mine removal projects.

Each time I saw Julia, we laughed about our foolishness. I would automatically flash back to the event that could have drastically altered, if not ended, our lives.

At the time of my visit to Angola, land mines were suspected everywhere—bridges, schools, wells, farmlands and former battlefields—and we were visiting a village encircled by mines on three sides. A retired British military explosive ordnance disposal (EOD) expert traveled with us.

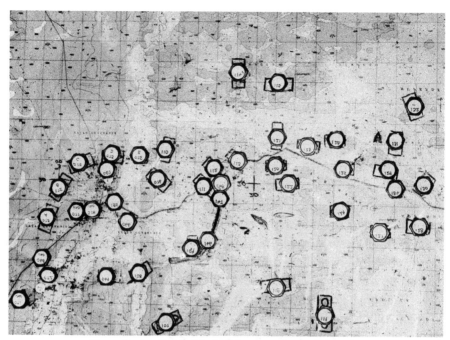

Map of mine fields (circled) in a province of Angola.

We had been sitting in a community building with the village chief and village elders trying to determine the scope of the land mine infestation. We were also curious about the types of mines that had been laid in the fields surrounding the village to determine how lethal and sensitive they were, and how to remove and neutralize them.

During our discussion, the chief verified that they were surrounded on three sides by landmines. He said that the village had a water point nearby but that it could not be used because of the mines, forcing village women and children to travel a long and circuitous route to another location.

We talked about the war. We talked about those in the village who had been maimed and killed by mines and warfare. In my public health mind, land mines should be treated like a socially-spread disease. To fight a disease you locate it, define it, isolate it and remove it. And I felt that this is what we should be doing with land mines and unexploded ordnance (UXO) in Angola and other countries.

The village chief suddenly asked if we might like to "see" some mines. The EOD man was quick to say, "Yes." Our little patrol began at the side of the village. There was the village chief, one of the elders, myself, Julia and the EOD man. The EOD man showed the most sense by going last. Four others walked the path before him. I should have known better. In Vietnam, I learned, because of mines, never to be the lead vehicle in a convoy, especially if I was heading out first thing in the morning.

I knew the area could be lethal when we passed the village trash dump and the EOD man pointed out a loaded surface-to-air rocket launcher sitting in the trash. We walked down a well-worn path and veered onto another less traveled. Then that path disappeared and the column stepped into a field. We were quite a way into the field when I started to get nervous, but I foolishly assumed the village chief knew what he was doing. My Vietnam self-preservation survival experience clicked in and all my senses heightened. My eyes picked up an anomaly in the field.

Then I got scared. What scared me were two things I saw in front of us. Just off the path about 20 yards ahead was a rusting grenade booby trap. This was a grenade attached to a stick with a rusting trip wire crossing a stretch of land. The second was about 50 yards further ahead. I could see remnants of trench lines and pillboxes, signaling this had been a defensive position. Such areas were always mined in Angola.

I immediately stopped the column. As calmly as possible, I asked the village chief where the mines he planned to show us were. He stretched out his arm pointing and turned, completing a 360-degree circle. We were surrounded by land mines. I looked hard and, sure enough, I could see the telltale humps in the soil that land mines leave over time. I had experienced this before in Sudan, Cambodia and Vietnam where the locals have become so accustomed to the death that surrounds them that they no longer regard them as threats.

I caught Julia's eye, seeing shock, fear and the thought of, "Gee, aren't we unusually stupid today." In the back of my mind, I kept assuming that the village chief knew what he was doing, knew where the mines were and had not put us in danger. I knew too that we had to get out of the field. I got the column turned around and started retracing our steps.

Can you see the mine?

That day we had broken every rule in the land mine removal book I was helping to write as we slowly, carefully—make that, *very* slowly and *very* carefully—retraced our steps back to the main trail. To this day, if only for my sanity, I like to tell myself that the village chief did know exactly what he was doing and that we were not in any real danger.

This is how I met our hostess and probably why she invited me to dinner. The other two guests were a German and his Rwandan wife. The conversation was light, mostly about work and office life. But the oddest thing happened at the start of dinner. Our hostess went into the kitchen and returned with the first course of our meal. First came soup and potatoes. The next course was a large platter of barbecued chicken.

As we began to pass around the dishes, I noticed that one plate remained empty. It was that of the Rwandan woman, to whom I passed the chicken. As the platter was set down in front of her, she shuddered, as if she had seen a ghost. She quickly raised her hand to her mouth, as if she were about to vomit. In a casual way, her husband explained that "she did not like to eat or see chicken bones."

Naively, I commented that I did not like to eat chicken bones either. After an uncomfortable pause, the German politely corrected me, explaining that it was really just the sight of the bones that disturbed his wife; and to ease the tension, he told of a similar instance when something like this had happened in a restaurant.

When I finally realized the implications of what had just occurred, my heart sank. How could I have been so unthinking? This woman had seen bones, lots of them, thousands of them, and they were not chicken bones. They were the bones of her countrymen who were being buried or reburied, having been removed from mass graves so that their souls could have dignified burials. Without making an embarrassing issue of it, our hostess graciously moved the platter to the other side of the table, and the dinner continued.

I saw the strength and the suffering of the Rwandan people during that meal. It gave me a glimpse into how deeply the cut had penetrated the soul of the country. I wondered how others, especially children, who had seen the killings and the bones, reacted when they saw food that reminded them of human remains.

It took me back to a scene aboard the refugee rescue ship, Cap Anamur[73], in Singapore harbor in 1980. The refugee children were given chalk to play with, and five years after the fall of Saigon, they still drew tanks and war planes. I then realized how deeply war cuts into the mind of everyone who witnesses it. How long would it take the Rwandans to recover? Could this generation possibly cope at all?

That night I lay on my bed in my hotel room, unable to sleep, and thought about that dinner. The strangest saying kept coming into my mind: "It is not only the food, but how the meal is presented."

There are many real and imagined bones throughout Rwanda. Its government was trying to present a meal that would satisfy everyone. It can be done, and I think the government is on the right track, but needs to be careful about its presentation.

Leaving Kigali for Nairobi, Kenya, my mind drifted to what had happened in Kosovo and Bosnia. The Balkans was another example of genocide that not only the Americans, but the entire world, had promised would never happen again. Instead, "chicken dinners" were served from Kigali to Kosovo. And the bitter taste of genocide taste hangs on the palate forever.

---

73   Cap Anamur is a German humanitarian organization and a ship with the goal of helping refugees and displaced people. The journeys of Cap Anamur (and her sister ships afterwards) were a huge success: 10,375 boat people were rescued on the open sea and an additional 35,000 were medically treated. But were they also a "pull" factor encouraging refugee departures?

NUNS, CLOWNS AND REFUGEES

How far you go in life depends on your being tender with the young, compassionate with the aged, sympathetic with the striving and tolerant with the weak and strong. Because some day in life you will have been all of these.

—George Washington Carver

Left to Right: French Transport Officer, Paul Giannone, Peter (CARE Kenya), Marine Security Officer.

Climbing into the U.S. Marine Chinook helicopter headed for Fier Prefecture, a sense of déjà vu came over me. I was back in Vietnam, as an army medic hunkered down in a pit, waiting for an evacuation helicopter to save a dying, legless South Vietnamese soldier.

Then I was jolted back to the present. The smell and the ten-

sion felt the same, but I wasn't. For one thing, I was older. I had letters after my name and a wife and a child waiting for me back home.

Was I wiser? After all, I voluntarily got on a U.N. plane and the
military helicopter for a free ride to Europe, Albania and Fier Prefecture. But when the U.N. offers a free ride, the destination is usually a
place that most people would not want to go.

In the belly of the helicopter, I was surrounded by heavi-
ly-armed U.S. Marines. I was entering a war zone as a humanitarian
worker. I wore a bush hat, T-shirt, and blue jeans. Instead of a rifle, I
carried a suitcase and a computer. We were flying south away from
Tirana, the capital of Albania, to Fier Prefecture.

At first I thought the name, pronounced "fear," was a joke. It
wasn't.

The world was on the brink of a potential major land war in
Europe. Hundreds of thousands of innocent men, women and children had been violated, uprooted and displaced by a despotic ruler. I
thought of my own family. What would it be like for them if someone
put a gun to their heads and told them to leave their home in the
middle of winter, abandoning all their belongings, and force-marched
them out of their country? If this happened to Kara, or my mother-in-law, or my own aging mother, surely, they would die. And if I
were not there, wouldn't I pray that someone would be there to help
them? I was that someone. That's why I was on the helicopter.

I was joining an international CARE team supporting the U.N.
refugee relief effort. As an American with both refugee and military
experience, my task was to help establish Camp Hope, an American
military/civilian-sponsored refugee camp.

The camp was designed to accommodate approximately
20,000 refugees. The strategy was to use camps built in the south
of Albania to draw refugees away from the northern border. This
would keep them out of range of Serbian artillery and make room for
a NATO-led land invasion if that became necessary.

We landed in a grassy field, about a quarter-mile from the
camp. The rolling hills reminded me of where I grew up in the Finger
Lakes region of Upstate New York. We came down military-style—
very fast. As soon as the big chopper hit the ground, the troops
deployed quickly out the back ramp. Disembarking Marines joined a
security cordon that was already on the ground.

I got that cold feeling in my gut. Why so much security this far south? I grabbed my computer and suitcase and headed toward the dirt road.

There was a hot, uncomfortable wind, and the air was suffused with dust that settled in my nose and throat. Heavy-construction equipment and lines of high capacity dump trucks churned up the ground. The activity was intense. Vehicles and personnel scurried about as helicopters carrying personnel and equipment buzzed overhead. The threat of a land war seemed more real each day. The camp was only fifteen percent complete, yet already filled with about 2,000 refugees. Winter was fast approaching.

Camp Hope was a major construction project: building a refugee camp is the same as building a small city. In an ideal situation, the entire infrastructure for essential services like sewage, water, and electricity should be in place before the refugees start to arrive, but I have never seen an ideal situation.

In Fier, relief workers and camp managers were juggling to meet the immediate needs of the refugees while still working on setting up infrastructure. As I walked towards Camp Hope and the hustle and bustle of equipment, I had to wonder how people were living under all that dust.

I wish I could say the construction of the camp had been done efficiently, but this was not the case. The contractor designed a military camp for refugees, but refugees do not use a camp like the military. They are not as structured. Nor are they as organized or disciplined. I immediately noticed that the tents were spaced too close together. If a fire broke out in one, it would sweep swiftly through an entire row of tents and possibly the entire camp. I had seen this happen in Vietnam.

There were no spaces allocated for recreation, worship or garbage disposal. Nor had anyone yet thought about the inevitable need: a place to bury the dead.

The camp was situated in the middle of an irrigation system. It was only after the site was under construction that someone asked officials what the ditches were for. They were told that when the valves in the hills were open in late May water would stream down from the surrounding catchments and the camp would be flooded.

Drinking water was a major concern. According to U.N. guidelines, a refugee should have 15 liters of water per day. To house 20,000 refugees, Camp Hope would need 400,000 liters every day—yet the closest supply of potable water was nine miles away. Attempts at drilling wells had failed, so the contractor was bringing water in by trucks, an expensive, slow operation. Because the soil was not the right type for leach-field latrines, cement-vault latrines had to be built that could be pumped out. However, no pumping trucks were available anywhere in the country.

Therefore, trucks had to be brought in from Europe, along with more portable latrines. Although specifically requested, the portable latrines shipped in were not culturally acceptable to the refugees, nor were the designs of the showers. The refugees were accustomed to ceramic squat-style latrines, not the western toilets that had been delivered. Modesty in Muslim cultures and separation of males and females for bathing were cultural norms to be respected, yet the shower set-up consisted of a simple tent, in the middle of which someone had hung a thin plastic flimsy sheeting to separate the men's shower from the women's. This type of shower arrangement might be fine for a U.S. Marine but not for a 70-year-old Muslim grandmother.

Lighting in the camp was poor at best. Some areas were not lit at all. Safety and security are major concerns at refugee camps, especially for women and children. The incidence of rape is high in refugee camps, and women are most vulnerable in poorly lighted areas.

For some unknown planning reason the refugee clinic had not been accorded a high priority for construction. It was not ready when refugees arrived, forcing the NGO responsible for medical assistance to operate under makeshift conditions. No schools had been constructed, but schools are important because there is always a high percentage of children in a refugee population. They help create stability for the children, keep them busy, and distract them away from mischief that could be dangerous at this camp under construction.

And there I was, in the midst of this chaos. Refugees were streaming in. Construction on the camp was far from finished, and what had been completed was utterly inadequate. And the person responsible for modifications or changes in the construction plan was under contract to the U.S. government and was sitting in an office in Germany. This meant delay and more delay whenever we suggested a major design change.

The one saving grace was the administrative structure. The

camp was run by a joint civilian/military command. The military side was led by a very competent civil affairs U.S. Army major, supported by a Marine guard detachment. CARE was chosen by the U.N. to be the administrative lead for Camp Hope.

The CARE effort was led by Carsten Völz from CARE Germany. Carsten and I would become longtime friends. He stood about 6"5', sported a blond ponytail and had the build of an American football lineman. Although younger than I, he was one of the best managers, decision-makers and camp diplomat with whom I have ever had the privilege to work.

Camp management morning planning session in
Civilian/Miitary Operations Center.

There were three others with our CARE team: a Kenyan, a Canadian and another American. All had years of international disaster response experience. Although each of us had an assigned function, we acted as an integrated team and addressed whatever came up on any given day.

The rest of the camp functions were sub-contracted to other NGOs. Water and sanitation activities were handled by Action Against Hunger (ACF); Catholic Relief Services was in charge of food distribution; Save the Children/UK was responsible for education and social services; and health care was under the auspices of British-based Merlin. All were staffed by extremely competent professionals. Each morning at 8:00 AM, functional leaders met in the tent designated as the Civilian Military Operations Center for a briefing, led by a Civil Affairs major, to plan out the day and to discuss any problems that each group might have been experiencing. We did not always agree on issues, but these daily meetings were valuable. We would have a wrap-up at 5:00 PM to prepare for the evening and the next day.

What I found out later was there was a great deal of talk about my arrival at the camp as to the purpose of my mission. At the time I was the Deputy Director for CARE/U.S.A's Emergency Group, probably the strongest CARE among the International CARE Federation. The CARE team at Camp Hope wondered, "Was I being sent to the camp to take over camp administration from Carsten? Was I sent to conduct an aggressive assessment?" Many thought they had no real time for this American "outsider" and an unwanted investigation. When I arrived I found the CARE administrative camp tent and walked in and introduced myself to Carsten, the sole person in the tent. He looked like a Viking about to attack a British village, and bluntly told me that he had no time for me now, he was rushing to an important meeting and would talk to me later *if* he had time. I asked him what I could do to help. He told me to clean the office which, I found out later, was a product of bad German humor. He noisily gathered paper and left.

I shrugged and began to clean the office by organizing paper, straightening chairs and even sweeping the sand floor. I guess my humility and my willingness to do anything, even as a CARE/U.S.A. senior staff member, made an impression with the CARE team and there were no problems after that. Realistically, I was more worried about being bogged down in office administration at CARE response headquarters in Tirana. I wanted to be in the field helping refugees—not moving paper and writing reports. I became a sort of backup for Carsten and I was very comfortable with his leadership.

And who was the primary enemy skulking along the edges of the camp and hoping to infiltrate it? Not the Serbs, nor the Kosovo Liberation Army (KLA), nor the Kosovar Freedom Fighters, but the Mafia! Rumor had it that when the Italian government cracked down hard on the Mafia in the 1980s, those who could afford it moved to the U.S. or Europe, but the lowest of the low flocked to Albania. There they joined up with the already established Albanian Mafia, which became the de facto government in many areas of Albania. And here we were in the heart of their territory.

It was obvious from the beginning that the Mafia saw a lucrative business in our camp. Women and young girls could be taken and sold into prostitution; children would bring big profits if sold to adoption agencies. Marine guards told me that mafia cars regularly drove by their posts. Men in the cars would make a fake gun with their fingers and point and shoot at the Marines to taunt them and to signify who was really in charge.

US Marine security team deploying.

Twice at night during my stay at Camp Hope, the Marine compound came under automatic weapon fire from the Mafia. Although night vision scopes revealed targets to the Marines, to their credit they did not return fire, avoiding the potential for an international incident. I had no doubt that without my Marine guardian angels, the Mafia would have swooped down, killed the NGO staff—myself included—looted the camp, and absconded with the women and children.

NGO workers were safe as long as we stayed within the Marine perimeter protecting the camp, but we had to get home at night. "Home" was an apartment we had established in the city of Fier, a 40-minute drive away, and our work often kept us in the camp long after dark.

One evening, Carsten and I were called by Marine security just before we were to leave for the day. A baby had stopped breathing. The Marine corpsman was able to get the child breathing again but we could not leave her in the camp. The nearest hospital was 40 minutes away in Fier, the sun had already set, and the Mafia was lurking.

Still, we knew that the child had to go immediately to the hospital for observation. So we filled our 4-wheel drive vehicle with parents, grandparents, extended family and an interpreter, dropped off the baby and family at a safe hospital, then drove back to the camp to bring the interpreter to his home.

The road, which was heavily rutted, was used mostly by horse-drawn farm equipment and light vehicles. For the past month, however, it had been abused by heavy earth-moving equipment that had transformed it into an obstacle course fit for a 4-wheel drive enthusiast. Bridges over irrigation canals were in danger of collapsing. The dust kicked up by traffic settled like thick fog.

Driving this road at night, my military mind saw the potential ambush points. We were carrying more than $5,000 in cash because we had not yet established a bank account. In the back of the vehicle we had computers, a photocopier, and radio equipment. The car was a brand new $40,000 Mitsubishi SUV. This would not have been a bad haul for a Mafia carjacker.

We made it through that night, but I kept thinking how I kept using more of my nine lives. I was also morbidly amused by the irony of the situation. I had lived through two tours in Vietnam, evacuations from Iran, minefields in Cambodia and Angola, refugee camps in Asia and Africa and now my life was threatened by the Mafia. What would my Sicilian ancestors think of that? I thought about scrawling "Hey, paisan!" on the dusty sides of our vehicle.

In a very short amount of time, Camp Hope was filled to capacity in the sections that were complete. Refugees in the north heard of the camp and either paid out of pocket for buses or drove their cars to the camp. One teenage girl told me that she had come to Camp Hope because she knew that the Americans would protect her. She had heard that there had been rapes in the camps to the north.

With the unfinished camp overflowing, CARE appealed for help from the Prefecture of Fier, and the local government graciously made space available in empty warehouses. We supported these satellite camps by providing food, blankets, cooking utensils and lamps to make conditions at least somewhat livable.

French military vehicles delivering refugee families
from train station to Camp Hope.

Meanwhile, construction continued at a feverish pace, even as CARE received a difficult order from the United Nations High Commission for Refugees (UNHCR). Camp Hope was to accept only refugees arriving from the north on specially ordered U.N. trains. These trains were to be escorted to Fier by French troops. French military vehicles would move them from the train station to the camp. We were not to admit any spontaneous arrivals nor were we to take any refugees out of the temporary accommodations in the Fier warehouses.

This turned out to be a catastrophe of the highest order. UNHCR is the agency mandated by the U.N. to take responsibility for the health, welfare and security of refugees worldwide. In other words, they are in charge of all refugee camps. When Carsten told me this, I envisioned some bureaucratic logistician in a small corner office in Geneva or New York thinking that this would be an excellent way to systematize refugee movements, as if refugees were lifeless dolls on a conveyor belt.

But what do you tell a refugee who makes it to your doorstep and is seeking your protection? "Sorry, you are not U.N.-designated?" Or simply, "The U.N. hotel is full"? And what about the Fier government that trusted us and helped by temporarily taking the spillover population of refugees into their warehouses? How would they feel about the logic of the UNHCR orders?

The local UNHCR representative stood his ground. In return, we did what humanitarians always do; we ignored him. I learned this in the military, too: take the direct order, smile, salute and then do what makes sense. Fortunately for us, the U.N. never seemed to be able to live up to its own program goals. The trains of refugees that arrived were never full and as camp construction slowly added more tent space we were able to accommodate refugees arriving by train and car, as well as those housed by the local government.

The next logic-defying UNHCR-issued edict concerned protection. The officer in charge of the Marine guard privately told us that if war broke out in Kosovo, the Marines would be deployed from the camp to the front lines within eight hours. There would be little warning. That would leave the camp completely at the mercy of the Mafia. I felt very close to the captain of the Marine guard and I have always had a warm spot in my heart for the U.S. Marine Corps. Still, they have to obey orders.

The captain and I had several conversations. While he understood my view, the Marines are essentially an assault force and his orders were clear. I knew he was extending me the courtesy of a heads-up in case the war flared again, as everyone expected at the time.

We began to make contingency plans to protect the camp

population and ourselves in case the Marines were pulled out. A privately trained Albanian security force that guarded nearby oil fields was available at reasonable cost and the U.S. government was willing to pay for their service. They could seamlessly replace our Marines if needed. This private force was registered with the Albanian government to carry weapons, and they had been well-trained by ex-British Special Forces personnel.

This group also knew the language, politics and culture of the area. We felt that we had solved our problem—until we presented the plan to UNHCR. It was rejected on the grounds that the U.N. was "responsible for the protection of refugees." We were told that the U.N. was training its own security force that would arrive in three months, or maybe four—or maybe more. They couldn't be sure. Regardless, the UNHCR forbade the use of private security forces. This would infringe on the U.N. security mandate. If the Marines pulled out, we were to leave the camp unprotected.

The U.N. seemed more concerned with making a point than protecting refugees. We decided that if those under our care needed protection, we would ignore the U.N. again.

The events filling a single day at Camp Hope serve as an example of what managing a refugee camp entails. One day, Carsten had to attend a day-long meeting with the local government, which left me in charge of camp management.

The day started with the usual planning session at the Civilian-Military Operations Center. At the meeting, we had talks with the construction crew on the need for firebreaks between the tents, and the rapid construction of schools, health and religious centers. Discussions were held on the latest food ration and the breakdowns in the poorly constructed water system.

At the end of the meeting we were informed that a NATO helicopter would bring 22 refugees down from the northern border area, even though a U.N. refugee train had arrived that morning. Flying refugees into Camp Hope could only mean one thing: the refugees on the helicopter were too sick to be put on the train. The British NGO responsible for the camp medical care was notified and began to prepare for whatever and whomever the helicopter brought.

The morning gained momentum as various NGOs worked on registering and settling in the newly arrived refugees from the train. By noon I was in high gear—and covered head-to-toe with a layer of dust. We kept checking with the military communications unit about the NATO helicopter. No one seemed to know where it was, the status of those on board or if it even was in the air.

Shortly after noon, I received a visit from several representatives from the U.N. World Food Program (WFP) which was responsible for supplying the camp with food. The WFP representatives had been told that the NGO responsible for food distribution was not doing the job properly, and they wanted him replaced. While it was true that this NGO had problems in start-up, as we all did, their food distribution system was now working very well. To release this group from its duties at this point would cause a breakdown. It could also have a serious impact on morale among the other NGOs working in the camp. I was able to convince the WFP representatives that all was well in food distribution and I was able to turn to my next problem.

As the WFP representatives were leaving my office tent, in came several officials from the British government. They were investigating the U.N. management of Camp Hope, but I was not about to get in the middle of a political dispute between the British government and UNHCR. We talked candidly, but I did not have to say much. They could see for themselves there was not a U.N. representative to be found at Camp Hope and that the administrative tent set aside for the U.N., looked like it had never been occupied. I referred them to my higher-ups in Tirana.

It was now 1:30 P.M. and I got a call from the Marine guard. They had a problem at one of their outposts. A mentally ill man, whom they knew was an Albanian citizen, was trying to get into the camp as a Kosovar refugee. I dispatched an interpreter to handle the problem.

The Coca Cola representative for Albania showed up next. Coca Cola is a big sponsor for CARE. Both the national headquarters for CARE U.S.A and for Coca Cola are in Atlanta, Georgia. In Albania, Coca Cola was providing much-needed water and funds for refugees. This man deserved my attention. I gave him a quick briefing on the situation of the camp and arranged for an interpreter to take him on a tour.

At 1:55 P.M., we heard the twin rotor blades of an army CH-47 Chinook helicopter. It was the NATO helicopter. I hurried the Coke rep out of my tent to begin his tour, ran to my vehicle, and headed to the helicopter landing pad. I got there just as the Chinook was lifting off.

By the look on the nurses' faces I knew this was trouble. All of the 22 refugees disembarking were invalids. Most could hardly walk. The camp dispensary was partially built and could handle only the most basic of medical problems. A refugee camp is not a nursing home or a long-term critical care facility. One nurse complained to me that, "They just dropped these people off like pieces of furniture; they didn't even consult with us."

In true military fashion, the NATO helicopter had orders to drop off 22 items (I doubt it mattered if they were people) and they did just that.

Three people in the group could not walk at all. The medical team quickly discerned that some were shell-shocked and tortured former POWs. Several of the refugees had chronic illnesses. The worst case was a 300-pound woman. It took five NATO troops just to carry her off the helicopter. It was obvious she would not fit onto any of the available cots. She would not fit through the door of the latrines. The nurses had to use a wheelbarrow to transport her into the camp. Once there, the only place for her to rest was on a mat on the floor.

The medical team had received no information about any of these arrivals. I looked at the nurse and she looked at me. Nothing was spoken but I knew that she would do what she had to do to get these people through the night. We would work things out in the morning on where and how to relocate the worst of the cases.

I got into my vehicle and headed back to the NGO compound. As I crossed the dirt road near the main gate I noticed six Roman Catholic nuns in gray habits entering the compound in single file. From my Catholic-school past, I wondered if all nuns walked this way. Normally, the Marines stop everyone at the checkpoint entrance unless they had either a refugee identification tag or were carrying either NGO or government ID cards.

"Now what?" I wondered.

We met up at the entrance to my administrative tent. I looked back at the trailing Marine sergeant and said, smiling, "A little lax in security, are we?" The sergeant's only reply, "They're nuns, sir."

Luckily, one young nun was American and, ironically, grew up near my home town in Upstate New York.

This was a Belgian order. Most of them were nurses and health care workers, and they had come to see if they could help. Knowing how busy the medical staff was with the newly arrived refugees, now was not the time to introduce our new volunteers to the medical team. I also did not know if Merlin could accept support from a religious order, since part of Merlin's mission involved reproductive health and family planning—a no-no in the Catholic Church.

I told the nuns that I would arrange for a meeting with the medical team the next morning. This would give everyone time to factor in where their very much needed services could best be used. They also requested a visit inside the camp as they had the names of some friends who were refugees. I arranged another tour.

As the nuns disappeared down the camp road, I became aware of a disturbance somewhere else in the camp. Conflicts often arose among the refugees, generally over food, clothing distribution or living space. Marines were dispatched to deal with the situation.

Moments later, several large trucks pulled into the camp. They were delivering furniture and stoves, much-needed supplies for the newly arriving refugees. Men jumped down from the trucks and began dumping their cargo off on the NGO compound. It was now 2:45 P.M. We shared the compound with French troops who were responsible for moving refugees from the train station. They were an extremely friendly and helpful bunch. I ran to their senior officer, a lieutenant, and asked if we could use his vehicles and soldiers to move the newly arrived supplies to where the newly arrived refugees were being billeted. With a smile that warmed my day, he gladly consented.

It was now 3:00 P.M. Someone called to me, "Sir, are you responsible for camp management?" I considered saying "No." I turned to the man who had spoken. He told me he represented "Clowns Without Borders," and wanted to know if he could help in the camp. I bit my lip. I didn't want to laugh, but at that point in my day, I'd just about had it. Yet it somehow fit. I wanted to ask if he'd like to be my deputy.

"Clowns Without Borders" is probably a good idea and a worthy organization. Helping children and adults too traumatized by war to laugh had immense value. But I couldn't handle it at that moment, nor were the people he needed to talk to available. Save the Children ran the school and social services. They were the logical people for him to coordinate with but they were off-site at a meeting.

I suggested that he return the next day. I could see I was filling up my next day schedule, as I now had returning clowns and nuns and had to figure out where to locate patients we could not medically handle. And, of course, there was the crazy Albanian at the gate trying to impersonate a refugee. I was sure he would be back tomorrow.

Things continued to roll at me for the rest of the day. Before I knew it, it was 7:30 P.M. and the sun had set. Carsten returned from his meetings and the CARE team got together to head back to our apartment in Fier. As always, we traveled cautiously, fearing ambush as we drove through the darkness.

We stopped at a restaurant in the city for a beer and some food. By the time we got to our small apartment, it was 10:00 P.M. All of us were covered in dust and sweat. As usual, there was no running water. We would go to bed dirty and hope that water would be flowing in the morning.

Finally, we began our evening routine. Equipment was put away. Batteries for the handheld radios were placed in their chargers. I crawled into a bed that was inches from the bed of my Kenyan team member and friend, Peter. It was 11:00 P.M., everything hurt on my body and my eyelids scraped with sand underneath them. I could hear my Kenyan friend praying as I began to drift off, knowing that 6:00 A.M. and the start of another workday at Camp Hope would arrive soon enough.

THE GYPSY BOY

Along with the Serbs, the Gypsies would also become an Albanian target for vengeance since they were widely believed to have collaborated with the Serbs and to have looted Albanian homes.

Tim Judah,
—*Kosovo: War and Revenge*

The cherub materialized from the swirl of dust and hot wind that surrounded the refugee camp called Hope. I didn't see him at first, just heard the rumors. "*A gypsy boy was here,*" one of my interpreters mentioned.

If we had a gypsy boy at Camp Hope, we had a problem. Gypsies, by and large, were sympathetic to the Serbs in Kosovo and had helped them in their ethnic cleansing against the Kosovars. The Kosovars hated the gypsies as much as they hated the Serbs.

The gypsies were seen as the people who raped and tortured Kosovo's mothers, wives and daughters and tortured and killed the fathers, sons, and brothers. Those Kosovars who survived the "cleansing" were thrown out of their family homes with only the clothes on their backs. An entire population of 700,000 souls had been cast out into the bone-cold winter, a land riddled with landmines, and vulnerable to Serbian snipers and bombings.

A pale, helmeted face peeked into my office tent through the flap. It was a young soldier from the U.S. Military Civil Affairs unit assigned to help us manage the camp. I could not help but wonder whether I had looked that young and eager some 30 years ago, back in Vietnam.

"Excuse me, sir," he said. I cringed. I hated it when they called me "Sir." "Name's Paul," I responded.

The corporal went on, "Yes, Sir. Sir, there was trouble in the camp last night. There seems to be a little boy here that no one likes."

He added that, "The marine guards are escorting the boy this way down the central camp road."

It was easy to spot the gypsy boy coming toward me. He was small and walked round-shouldered, like a tough guy from the movies. He was bracketed by two well-armed, flak-jacketed, lanky U.S. Marines. They were being followed by a crowd of about fifteen or twenty refugees. When the Marines were about ten feet away from me, I loudly called out to them above the noise of passing trucks and construction: "Do you think you have enough armament to subdue this kid?"

The African-American Marine, who was carrying an over-under combination M-16 and grenade launcher, laughed and replied, "Not sure, sir. We have seen this whirling dervish in action."

I sent for one of the interpreters, a cocky seventeen-year-old Kosovar. The kid was blond, blue-eyed, good-looking, and had an attitude. We took what we could get when it came to interpreters. We approached the gypsy boy, also a good-looking kid between 10 to 12 years of age, just over four feet tall, with jet black hair and black eyes. He showed no signs of starvation, and in fact he carried a bit of muscle. He kept his head down and moved his feet in the gravel as I cautiously walked over to him and tried to put a reassuring hand on his arm.

Pushing it away, he yelled out something in his native tongue. Judging from the expression on my interpreter's face, I had no doubt that what the boy said was profane and probably had something to do with my family lineage. When he moved, I caught a glimpse of cuts, abrasions and bruises on the side of his head and arm.

I asked for a name but got a grunt in return. I asked for an age, and he spit out an answer: 12. Then he told me, through the interpreter, that his father was dead and his mother was missing and possibly in Germany. I knew it was useless to ask for details about her. Probably he knew about as much as I did.

I cursed to myself as we conducted this interrogation in the noonday sun. This was not my job. Where were the United Nations Human Right investigators? The caseworkers? The U.N. had requested an interview tent over a week ago. We had it set up and there it sat a few feet away from me unused. It wasn't just this boy who needed help.

Every day, refugees approached me with claims about relatives living in Germany, France, Britain, Canada and the United

States. They had a U.N.-protected right for family reunification, but I could only tell them that the U.N. would be at the camp "soon"—whatever that meant.

I asked the boy what he wanted to do. He stopped and thought, and I realized he just didn't know. "How did you get here?" I queried, but got nothing from him.

Still, this was a refugee camp, and he had a right to be here. He also had a right to protection—and it looked like he was going to need it.

The crowd began to move closer. Someone said something to the boy that he didn't like. He shouted something back. In seconds, it seemed, rocks started flying. The boy returned fire with his own stones. The scuffle escalated quickly. Four or five Marines from the guard post a few feet away moved in to break up the stoning. As the gypsy boy squatted down for more stones, I grabbed his hand, forcing him to drop his ammunition. God, he was both strong and determined.

Another six or seven Marines came up and dispersed the group. No one appeared to be hurt. I had my hand tightly around the boy's arm, and was hit by the irony of what was happening. This camp was packed with people who had been abused, tortured and humiliated. They all knew what it was like to be on the wrong side of a hateful mob, to be social outcasts. And now they were giving it back in kind to a frightened, angry 12-year-old gypsy boy who should never have been there in the first place.

No one seemed to care that this was just a kid. For all his toughness, he was still a little boy who needed protection, and he had come looking for it in a place called Hope. These people seemed as willing to snuff out his life as they would have been to kill a rattlesnake.

In one incredible thrust of strength, the boy broke my grip and started running toward the crush of Kosovars, who were now being escorted down the central camp road. As the boy ran, he picked up stones and threw them at the crowd. Now that he'd made it into the light of day, he was going to get his tormentors, even if it was going to be his last stand. It might have been, too, except for the fact that ten to twelve Marines swiftly positioned their bodies between him and the crowd. May God or Allah bless the US Marines. I raced to catch up with him.

Things finally settled down again. My interpreter came back from wherever he had been hiding. It was my turn to be furious. I bellowed at the gypsy boy, "Just what the hell do you think you are trying to do? Do you think you can take on the camp and win?" He stood in his defensive position, eyes down, and his worn shoes digging into the dirt.

"I need to get some of my stuff," the boy blurted out through my interpreter. "It's up in the camp in a tent."

I got him to explain, as best he could, the location of his "stuff," and asked a Marine and my interpreter to go on the recovery mission without the boy. If I had sent the boy alone, I am sure it would have become a "search and destroy" mission.

With the Marines' permission, I put the boy in their compound for the day. For most of the time, he sat on the ground while a marine with a gun straddled him. My plan was to move him that night to the NGO compound. We had office tents there with cots and blankets. A detail of French soldiers were also billeted there. I figured that both the soldiers and NGO workers could keep an eye on this little terror.

Later that day I was informed that some U.N. personnel had arrived. I immediately sought them out. The U.N. staffer I met was not a human rights representative or caseworker, but someone responsible for refugee registration. No matter—I quickly told him my story. In order to save the boy's life, the U.N. needed to take the boy out of the camp immediately. I emphasized the word *immediately*. I was told that a U.N. Human Rights case officer would be in the camp early the next morning and the issue would be solved then. Since we had to wait, I pursued my first plan to move the boy into the NGO compound and requested the French troops to put a night guard on the boy.

But the next day came and went without any U.N. personnel showing up. Another day went by, another night. During the day, I would ask the Marines to guard the boy as few staff stayed in the NGO compound. The Marines began to complain to me. The boy was troublesome. It was not their job to babysit a child, especially one so angry and bad-tempered. On several occasions, he tried to escape their compound. If it were up to me, I would have taken the boy to my living quarters in the city, but the team I was with consisted of five men literally sleeping on top of each other in a small rented apartment in Fier, a forty-minute drive away. The road to Fier was rough, insecure roads. Mafia attacks were a real possibility.

Then, one night, the boy did succeed at outwitting his guards and escaping. I did not learn of this until I arrived at the camp at 8:00 the next morning. The Marines and other personnel were scouring the grounds, looking for him. My heart sank. I assumed he was dead.

As I was gathering my thoughts, I heard a commotion on the camp road and ran out of my tent. About 300 feet away were a couple of Marines. They were dragging the gypsy boy, kicking and screaming, behind them. Two other Marines were deployed behind the boy, and a good-sized crowd of Kosovars followed them.

The Marines dragged the kid closer. I noticed how frustrated they looked.

"A tough one, sir," one said to me. "Lucky the kid is alive. Apparently, he has been telling people that his father is—or was—a Serb cop, and that his dad is going to come and get them all."

The boy's face showed new cuts and bruises. How long could this last? The Marines went to work dispersing the angry crowd. We dragged the little gypsy back to the Marine compound. I asked for a nurse to apply first aid, and this time two Marines stood guard over him. I went to see the Marine captain in charge of the guard detachment and asked him to be patient a little longer. I was determined to end the siege.

Later that morning I headed to Tirana, the capital of Albania, for a staff meeting. The trip brought me through Fier City which was where the main U.N. office was located. Generally, I am very diplomatic. That morning I wasn't. I marched into the U.N. office with a purpose and insisted on a meeting.

Within a short time I had a meeting with a Human Rights officer. I told him that the gypsy boy's life was in immediate danger, that his rights were being abused, and that he must be removed from the camp by noon that day, if not sooner. I indicated that I didn't care how this was done. Even if the boy had to sleep in the U.N. office under guard, he had to be taken from the camp.

The head of the U.N. office assured me that he would dispatch a caseworker immediately, and the boy would be taken into protective custody. I left for my meeting in Tirana, relieved that something was finally going to be done.

That evening I was dining out with some friends at a café in Tirana when, by sheer coincidence, I spotted the same U.N. caseworker I had talked to in Fier City entering the café. I rushed over to learn what had been done about the boy. It took a second for him to figure out who I was, but then he grudgingly replied that the boy was still in the camp. The caseworker went on to explain that he had gone all the way out to the camp and questioned the boy, and the boy told him that he wanted to stay at Camp Hope.

"Since when does an abused 12-year-old tell a U.N. protection officer what to do?" I asked.

"What would have been the implications if the boy was seriously hurt or killed and CNN picked up the story?" I asked the UN staffer.

I hated to pull the CNN card, but something had to draw these folks into action. I told this man that I was returning to Camp Hope the following day. If I found that the boy was still in the camp, I would personally take action.

I was unable to sleep that night. I blamed myself. I had not done enough for this child. How could a system designed to protect thousands of human beings fail him? Would I find him dead the next day?

As the sun broke on the horizon, I sped back to Camp Hope. I immediately went to the Marine guard compound and spotted the sergeant who had been guarding the boy. Even before we could exchange salutations, I asked where he was.

"Gone" was the reply. U.N. officers had come into the camp before sunlight and removed him. They said that they had found a safe house in town where the kid could stay until they figured out what to do next.

I never learned what happened to the little gypsy. I told myself that the boy was safe, and that was what counted. His story, like so many others, had an unfinished feeling. That was how it usually was in this type of work.

I would leave Camp Hope after about a month and return to Kate and Kara and CARE headquarters in Atlanta. From CARE headquarters, I followed how Camp Hope was doing. In June 1999, NATO Forces crossed into Kosovo ending the war, followed by a mass spontaneous repatriation of refugees from Albania.

Camp Hope, which was never filled to capacity, would no longer exist, but not before heavy rains would completely flood the camp. Those of us who train others in emergency response and planning, and who knew about Camp Hope, would use it as a training example of how not to build a refugee camp.

THE DAY
THE MUSIC STARTED

Say ye, "We believe in God and the revelation given to us and to Abraham, Ismail, Isaac, Jacob, and the Tribes, and that given to Moses and Jesus, and that given to (all) Prophets from their Lord. We make no distinction between any of them and it is unto Him that we surrender ourselves."

—Quran (2:136)

I had arrived at my office in Atlanta at 6:03 A.M., a glint of sunrise peeking through the window. I lost myself in work as I sent e-mails to CARE offices in Africa and Asia and made phone calls to the CARE International office in Geneva. Just before 9:00 A.M., someone stuck his head in and blurted out that a plane had struck the World Trade Center up in New York. I didn't even turn around as he went on to tell others. I thought to myself, "My God, what a terrible accident."

I remembered reading about an incident in the 1940s or 1950s when a military plane had struck the Empire State Building. There were few casualties then and I wondered how an accident like this could happen now. I thought of my friends in the Red Cross who would be called to assist. Airline crashes are such grisly affairs.

Eventually, though, my curiosity got the best of me, so I walked down to the communications conference room just in time to see the other passenger jet fly into the second building. It was 9:06 A.M. when United Airlines Flight 175 blasted through the upper stories of the World Trade Center like a deadly dart hitting its mark.

September 11, 2001: Time stopped for me and just about everyone in the civilized world. The world as we had known it had just changed, and my emotions caught fire. In a split second I felt anger, hate and a thirst for revenge. This just simply couldn't be! Not in America!

We stared in dull surprise as the newscast on CNN filled airtime with more talk than news. At 9:40 A.M. we heard that American Airlines Flight 77 had struck the Pentagon! For all practical purposes, America was under attack. But from whom? Most around me made the logical leap to Islamic extremists and Osama bin Laden as the most likely perpetrators of these cataclysmic events.

I watched as long as I could before getting back to work. There could be trouble in the Muslim countries where CARE had field offices, and I immediately thought of Afghanistan and Pakistan. Not far behind in my thoughts were Egypt, Sudan, the Philippines and Indonesia. As I started back to my office to check e-mail traffic and call our field offices, I found myself walking alongside CARE's Senior Vice President for External Relations. We said very little, but we both knew some form of American military response would be forthcoming. America would be at war again.

"We're all going to be bloodied by the time this one is over," I told her.

Little did I realize that my statement would be prophetic for myself.

The Twin Towers began to collapse and United Airlines Flight 93 crashed into a field in rural Pennsylvania and we at CARE began our own plans for a response to save the vulnerable who undoubtedly would be affected by this catastrophe.

On Friday, September 21, 2001, I was asked by CARE's senior management to fly to Thailand to support CARE's Regional Management Unit (RMU). It was obvious by then that there was going to be U.S. military action in Afghanistan, where Osama bin Laden was protected by the radical Taliban government in Kabul. CARE wanted to be ready to respond with support, and the Bangkok RMU had direct command and control over the CARE offices in Afghanistan and Pakistan.

In Bangkok, I would meet the acting director of CARE Afghanistan (an Englishwoman named Anne Murphy[74]), the assistant country director (Mohammed Ali[75], a Somalian) and was told that Nicolas Palenque, a French Canadian was in route to join us.

74 Fictitious name
75 Fictitious name

I knew Anne from training. She was a strong woman and an excellent administrator. I had not met Mohammed but if he was Somali, I instinctively knew that he would be topnotch. Somalis are very resourceful and direct, and I have always enjoyed working with them. Nicolas was coming from CARE/Canada. He was an ex-paratrooper and had worked in Afghanistan before. Anne and Mohammed had been evacuated from Pakistan after 9/11.

The four of us, plus the Director of the RMU, quickly commenced contingency planning, a process to develop an emergency response for any disaster scenario. In this case, we were asked to plan for the possibility that up to one million Afghan refugees might cross the border into Pakistan. The thinking was that the U.S. military would initiate massive airstrikes to disrupt the Taliban's command and control capability. The Afghan capital, Kabul, and other large cities would be struck. The civilian population, to escape the bombings, might take the Khyber Pass and other routes to head east for safe haven in Pakistan.

I left for Bangkok on my 53rd birthday. Kara, who was nine years old, was planning a surprise birthday party for me, and she was heartbroken. As I left home for what we both knew could be a dangerous assignment, Kate showed the stoic face she always had, but there was tension as I departed.

Although I was proud that I had been chosen to help plan for CARE's response, my survival instincts flashed a warning. The 9/11 attack had changed the rules, and civilians, especially American civilians, would be a new target for these extremists.

Once I got to Bangkok and met up with the CARE team, it became clear that the situation had settled somewhat in Afghanistan and Pakistan. But it was probably the calm before the storm, as U.S. forces gathered their intelligence, re-positioned military assets and developed a strategy for the upcoming operation. We determined that a team could do better planning for CARE's response and coordinating with the UN and other NGOs in Pakistan. Nicolas had not joined us yet and was being re-routed to Islamabad.

I was no fool—the danger we faced was real. I knew about security, first as a soldier and then as a civilian, but I also knew that we were climbing into a dormant volcano that could blow at any time.

Anne, Mohammed and I left for Karachi on September 28th.

We departed in the middle of the night on Thai Air, one of those red-eye specials so common in Asia and Africa. Almost all of the other passengers on the plane were Pakistani or Afghani men dressed in traditional clothing. I surmised that they were probably returning from a vacation in Bangkok.

With its world-famous red light districts, inexpensive shopping, incredible restaurants and liberal views on life, Bangkok was, and is, a popular destination for males from around the world. For Muslims and Christians, Bangkok allowed visitors the opportunity to leave the Bible or Quran home and partake of what Thailand had to offer.

Mohammed fit right in with the passengers. Anne and I looked like we had luminous signs around our necks that flashed, "*White people, targets of opportunity.*" Still, with this many Muslims on board, I felt that no one was apt to hijack the plane and fly it into something. Once the flight took off and we had our meal, the captain turned off all the lights in the cabin to let people sleep. It was as if we were in a cave.

A number of the Muslim tourists did not want to sleep. Many stood in the aisles chatting loudly in Arabic or Pashtu. Perhaps they were speaking of their experiences in Thailand. They might also have been talking about the impact of 9/11 and the coming war with America. I wondered to myself about these Arabic men. Whose side would they be on?

The three of us were in the center section. I sat in an aisle seat. Anne sat next to me and Mohamed was in the middle of the five seats. From a security point of view this was a foolish arrangement. Mohammed should have been in the aisle, with me next to him and with Anne farthest from the aisle. I kept wondering about the political and religious bias of our fellow passengers and how this might impact our safety. Being a disaster planner, I naturally gravitated to the worst-case scenario.

A group of men next to me was talking loudly. They were so close that one kept bumping into me during their lively conversation. For all I knew, they could be saying "Let's kill the dumb American in the 319 aisle seat."

Paranoia took over. I started to think, in the noise and darkness, how easy it would be to slit my throat. These people could have been Taliban or returning Osama bin Laden operatives. I got little sleep that night. I never discussed my worries with Anne, who slept soundly. I was relieved when we made it to the Karachi airport without incident.

We entered the Karachi air terminal jet-lagged and proceeded to the security screening. I was carrying a satellite phone for emergency communications, which was not legal in Pakistan. True, I was carrying an "official" letter from CARE saying that this equipment was to be used for emergency humanitarian operations, but illegal is illegal. I put the double-locked case that held the "sat phone" on the x-ray belt and it went through the machine without arousing interest. I was relieved but troubled that no one wanted to open the case. With all the wiring it could have been a bomb.

Our next stop was to a booth where we were to pay the entry tax. It looked like a ticket booth for a circus sideshow. The man taking the money was more interested in his cigarette than in the passengers. He put the money into a simple dirty box, and every move he made seemed like an imposition.

Security guards cradling automatic rifles were positioned throughout the terminal. This is not unusual in most Third World airports, but tonight it had an aura of foreboding. While standing in line for baggage someone asked my nationality. I am not sure if it was my jet lag, foolishness or the fact that this person already knew the answer but I told him, "American."

Once we had our baggage, we started out of the terminal to look for a cab to take us to our hotel. In the few hundred yards it took to get clear of the terminal building, I was asked again about my nationality. This time I think I said "Italian." One person actually asked me if I felt safe in Pakistan. I did not. We caught a few hours' sleep in a hotel, returned to the airport, and re-boarded a plane bound for Islamabad, the capital of Pakistan.

What we found was a media circus. Journalists from all the major TV networks and newspapers across the globe were everywhere. Yet while everyone knew that war would be coming to Afghanistan, at that time there was really nothing to print or talk about. America was lining up its allies and setting up logistics operations to deploy troops. Humanitarian aid agencies like CARE were discussing contingency plans with the UN and government representatives from America and Europe to line up funding for relief action once the fighting started in Afghanistan, as it undoubtedly would.

But there was nothing really happening that a photojournalist could photograph for the evening news.

The media was desperate for a story. Anywhere you went you risked having a reporter accost you or thrust a video camera in your face in an attempt to gain some newsworthy blather.

The Sheraton Hotel was renting out its roof so the media could have a single spot to set up cameras. I went up there once out of curiosity. They had taken up more than half of the roof. There were actually tents set up for computer equipment and a tent for commentators who had to report during the heat of the day. The commentators' tent was spotlighted for broadcasting at night. In front of this tent was the largest assortment of video cameras I had ever seen. They looked ominous, almost like weapons. You could actually watch a reporter speaking in the tent, take the elevator down to the lobby, and catch that reporter's broadcast on the BBC, CNN or NBC.

The media had booked all the hotel rooms in Islamabad. The Sheraton had 297 rooms, of which 290 were filled by members of the media. Media staff were sleeping three, four and five to a room. This irony was not missed by the NGO response staff. The media were there to film humanitarian workers coming into Pakistan to help in the response effort, and yet the media had taken the living space away from these workers, who now had to find sleeping accommodations elsewhere. In essence, the media presence was inhibiting the very response action they had come to document. Yet the media wonders why they are often looked on with disdain, even distrust, around the world.

The day after our arrival, Nicolas Palanque arrived. The team was complete and through a local contact, we found a few rooms in a small hotel. We did what coordination had to be done with the government and UN representatives. Soon it became clear that we were not close enough to the action to be effective. We needed to be in Peshawar, near the border with Afghanistan.

CARE had maintained a large office in Peshawar for years. Although CARE did not have development or relief operations in Pakistan, the Peshawar office functioned as a logistics staging area and communications hub for Afghan operations. Peshawar was also a hotbed of terrorist and Taliban activity as well as one of the biggest arms manufacturing and drug trade centers in the world.

The drive to Peshawar from Islamabad takes three hours

over a well-maintained, hard-surfaced road. Anne had arranged for a 4-wheel drive vehicle to pick us up. The journey was pleasant enough. It was a warm sunny day. The conversation in the vehicle was light and sometimes focused on the work ahead. About two hours into the trip our driver pointed out a pro-Bin Laden madrasa, or Muslim school. It could be a potential choke point if trouble started on the border and we needed to evacuate back to Islamabad.

A little further down the road we crossed a bridge that signified the beginning of what the government of Pakistan called "the Tribal Areas[76]." I was told that many in this section believed that Afghanistan actually started once you crossed this bridge. Even in the most peaceful of times the government had a hard time controlling the Tribal Areas. With a U.S.-backed war in Afghanistan imminent, this region was a potential boiling hotbed for anti-U.S. sentiment.

The Tribal Areas was like the Wild West—but instead of six guns, the bad guys were carrying AK-47 rifles and B-40 rocket-propelled grenade launchers. The terrain looked much like parts of our American Southwest. There were rugged hills, mountains and valleys perfect for ambush, as the Russians discovered a decade before on the Afghan side of the border. Warlords controlled sections of this wild territory and had their own well-armed armies to protect them. The people who inhabited this region carried a greater allegiance to Afghanistan, the Taliban and Osama bin Laden than their own government. It was also well known that Osama bin Laden supporters had infiltrated many of the police and security forces. For us there might not be any "good guys with white hats" on the tribal side of the bridge.

Even on this warm sunny day I had no doubt that we had crossed both a physical and political boundary. We had gone from an area that had somewhat of a security problem to an area where extreme violence was common.

CARE's office in Peshawar was a well-established complex. There was a large main building and room to park five or six vehicles. At one time it must have been a huge private home. Now, it housed numerous offices, storage areas, and meeting rooms. The compound was surrounded by a 10 to 12-foot high cement wall, a foot thick, with

---

76   The semi-autonomous tribal lands consist of seven parts called "agencies": Bajaur, Mohmand, Khyber, Orakzai, Kurram, and North and South Waziristan. There are also six smaller zones known as frontier regions in the transitional area between the tribal lands and the North-West Frontier Province to the east.

sharp glass shards embedded along the top. There were guards at the gate. Normally I hate high walls. In Peshawar I learned to love them.

CARE also rented a number of staff houses in secure areas. Nicolas and Anne were billeted in one such house and I was located in another. I wondered whether the reason they split us up was to ensure that all of us would not be kidnapped or killed together. The staff house I stayed in had four bedrooms (each with its own bathroom), a large living room and dining area. There was a guard at the front gate armed with a 12-gauge pump shotgun. We had an excellent cook who had left Afghanistan with his family years ago. He had been working for an American NGO and left his homeland because he fell under suspicion of the Taliban. We could even get cable TV within 24 hours if we knew what palms to grease. The method of hooking cable up was throwing the cable over your compound wall. The streets were literally covered with cable lines. It looked like black spaghetti.

At that time there were several hundred CARE staff members at the Peshawar office or living in Peshawar. CARE had a total local staff of about 500, including those working in Afghanistan; all but five were Afghanis. A number of the Afghan staff and all foreign staff had been evacuated out of Afghanistan after the World Trade Center attack.

The office was extremely well-run. This is a remarkable achievement and typical of all CARE country offices. The majority of CARE country offices are staffed by people from the countries served by that office. I interviewed section leaders in the Peshawar office, almost all of whom spoke English. They seemed to be anticipating my concerns. They had handled the situation so well I started wondering if I was really needed.

It was about a week after my arrival in Peshawar that I noticed the dull pain and stiffness. I found that I had difficulty standing up for more than 45 minutes at a time. I seemed to tire easily. Lifting was a struggle. I assumed this was some form of a strain since I had to carry all of my equipment—computers, sat phones, personal luggage—with me all day in case of evacuation.

When men and women were crossing borders facing death, it is hardly the time to raise your hand and say, "I don't feel well today." I said nothing and just went to work. I would see my doctor on my return home.

My first priority was to coordinate with the United Nations High Commission for Refugees (UNHCR) and other NGOs regarding potential refugee operations on the Pakistan side of the border. I will never forget the first few times that I met with the UN or my NGO colleagues. I felt like the odd man out. There was generally a surprised look at seeing an American. Some actually asked what I was doing in Peshawar. It was a good question. At that time no other international agency would allow staff with American passports into this area. There were international staff from Canada, England, France, Germany, and other European, Middle Eastern and Asian countries but no Americans. As far as I could tell, I was the only American in Peshawar besides the Americans at the U.S. Consular office. And the U.S. Consular office was so heavily fortified that it looked like a World War II bunker system.

The Taliban had an office two short blocks from the CARE office. Bands of Taliban could be seen along the streets. Street vendors had a successful business selling pro-Osama Bin Laden t-shirts. I began to sign my e-mails to CARE headquarters in Atlanta with the salutation, "The Last American in Peshawar."

The UNHCR meetings were key to my CARE/USA assigned mission to develop plans for CARE Pakistan to respond if one million refugees from Afghanistan crossed the border. Jamal, a CARE Afghan senior staff person accompanied me to these meetings. Jamal became a friend, counsel and political strategist. He was about 5' 9" with jet-black beard and hair. He wore glasses and traditional Afghan dress. Although he was younger, he looked stately, like a college professor. We had more similarities than differences. Jamal was a family man. He had deep religious convictions but did not overstate them. He believed in peace, cooperation and helping his fellow man. As always with the Afghan staff, I felt like asking, "Why do you need me?" I soon realized that as a senior American with years of disaster response experience, my strength was that I could open doors that Jamal and others could not, and I could make recommendations that might have been difficult coming from an Afghani.

The daily UNHCR meetings were held at 9:00 A.M, and there must have been 25 or more NGOs attending, including the International Rescue Committee, Doctors Without Borders, Save the Children, and World Vision. Some NGOs were totally Arabic-speaking. Because of the number of attendees, the meetings were held under a large open-sided tent on the shaded lawn within the UNHCR compound.

During the briefings, Pakistani fighter jets from the nearby military airbase streaked overhead. They made hearing almost impossible. Between the noise of the jets taking off and landing, we could hear only snippets of birds chirping in the trees above us, of people talking on the street on the other side of our protective wall, of the occasional call of street merchants and the grind of new four-wheel drive SUVs. These meetings were always an odd blend of war activities mixed with the serenity of daily life.

These meetings were designed to give participants information about refugees along the border and to bring us up to speed on what was happening in the volatile Tribal Areas, where the UN hoped to establish refugee camps. The primary mission was to develop a coordinated response strategy, but the meetings actually accomplished little, as they were poorly organized and tended to ramble, leaving the UN and the rest of us in the dark about anything outside of Peshawar. We were at the mercy of our hosts, the government of Pakistan, and Pakistani officials seemed to be disorganized and reluctant to make decisions. After all, they were in an area they hardly had control of under normal circumstances.

The meetings usually started out with a briefing from one or more Pakistani government officials on the current government position toward refugees and the situation along the Afghan border. Confusion reigned in these briefings. If one Pakistani talked he would often contradict himself during the same briefing. If two spoke they would contradict each other. We heard that Pakistan would not let refugees cross the frontier; then we learned about the plans they were making along the Pakistan side of the border for refugee camps. We were told that we would soon have access to the border. Then we heard access would not be granted. Then we were told we could only send Pakistanis selected by the government of Pakistan to border refugee camp sites. And the NGOs and UN would have to pay the salaries for these selected Pakistanis. Then we were back to complete access for all NGO staff again.

According to the Pakistani government, construction of these camps was going to be done by companies only they could designate. Can you spell "b-o-o-n-d-o-g-g-l-e"? Every day we heard this from Pakistani government officials. And the UN representative seemed to be agreeing with them or made no attempt at definitive clarifying questions.

UNHCR would then brief us on their progress for refugee camp construction and planning. The government of Pakistan identified what land could be used for refugee camps, and UN teams were sent to survey these locations. Then the government told the UN that the locations that had been picked were no longer available. New locations were selected. Different UN teams were sent out. But the teams used different assessment tools, making comparison for site selection impossible. Sometimes, assessment teams did not know what was needed to build a refugee camp. In many cases, vital requirements for camp construction—water for drinking and washing, soil permeability for latrines, proper grade for drainage, road access and other key construction requirements—were simply ignored. The only real criteria in site selection seemed to be any place the government of Pakistan indicated the UN could access.

The most essential and most poorly addressed refugee site problem was security. The Pakistani government wanted to place the refugee camps within a few kilometers of the border. This would put them within artillery range of Afghanistan. Although this violated international law, the UN seemed to consent to this idea, or at least they did not object in front of us.

The major rationale for these meetings, namely the coordination of the relief effort, rapidly deteriorated. Everyone had wanted to avoid the typical NGO-UN-U.S. government feeding frenzy where NGOs pressured for lucrative contracts from the UN, the U.S. government and other donor governments. Money became more important than the work at hand. I had seen this same situation happen in Albania, Bosnia, Rwanda, and Sudan. The morning meetings among the NGOs were intended to allow a strategic distribution of funds according to NGO interests, strengths and capabilities. But the UN let this vital process fall apart. I soon heard that backdoor deals were being cut between UNHCR and individual NGOs for the management of key sites and activities.

To make matters worse, I had been sent into this situation without written terms of reference—"orders" in NGO jargon—on my mission. I had no clear documentation of why I was there or what I was supposed to accomplish. I had been told at CARE headquarters in Atlanta "to prepare for the potential movement of up to one million Afghan refugees into Pakistan." However, without written terms of reference, I was technically under the direct control of CARE Afghanistan. They wanted to concentrate resources on setting up supply lines and maintaining their programs inside Afghanistan, not preparing for one million potential refugees.

I didn't necessarily disagree with prioritizing supply lines and Afghanistan in-country program support over refugee relief, because I had some doubts that we were going to see a large-scale refugee movement across the border. However, a disaster planner must plan for all contingencies. What would CARE do if the exodus did occur? Would we say to the arriving refugees, "Sorry, but we didn't plan for your arrival"? I felt that CARE was large enough to do both. Besides, planning for one set of options did not eliminate planning for another. I was, in effect, between the proverbial rock and a hard place—between what CARE Atlanta verbally told me to do and what CARE Afghanistan was planning for.

Still, I did what I could. I went to Islamabad and met with UN officials. With them I developed a "memorandum of understanding" that CARE would play a significant role in refugee camp management or the delivery of needed food and supplies in the region. I took this document back to Peshawar and persevered until CARE Afghanistan management signed it, thus committing CARE.

With Jamal and the help of others, we lobbied CARE management to rent additional warehouse space and provisioned this space with enough tents, blankets, and cooking material to assist 5,000 families. This stockpile served a dual purpose. Once things heated up, warehouses would be in short supply and the equipment we had purchased could be used on either side of the border.

Then the U.S. bombing began in earnest inside Taliban-controlled Afghanistan. Our security procedures were ratcheted up. We no longer had the luxury of eating at restaurants, shopping, or even walking along the streets. I spent my time in one of three places: the CARE Peshawar office, the CARE guesthouse and the daily UN meeting. The NGO's and the UN set up an emergency warning system using radios and telephones to notify everyone if fighting broke out in Peshawar. There were intense anti-American demonstrations in cities across the country, including Peshawar. Several times we had to evacuate the CARE office when the demonstrations became too turbulent.

I was starting to get that old feeling again. I wouldn't call it a flashback, but it felt like Vietnam: the knotted stomach, the tingling down the neck and back, the feeling of complete vulnerability to outside forces. I knew instinctively that if the Taliban wanted to kill me there was little I could do to prevent it. I could change my driving routes and times to the office or UN meetings but the bad guys knew that I had to go to the CARE office to work and the CARE guesthouse to rest. By simply positioning one or two men at both points and waiting, it would be simple to eliminate my driver and me.

The night the bombing began, we were sitting on the front porch of the guesthouse after dinner. CNN told us everything we needed to know. Then our sat phone rang. It was my headquarters in Atlanta. For some reason they did not know that I was in Peshawar, although I did not doubt that I had relayed that information to them. I was to leave for Islamabad immediately. It was dark, and under normal daylight circumstances, the three-hour road trip to Islamabad was dangerous because of traffic accidents and bandits. And there was a pro- Osama bin Laden school between the capital and us. I was safer where I was. As we got off the phone, at my residence my guard with the shotgun was joined by two men carrying automatic weapons. My security had been increased.

CARE quickly sent an American security expert to Peshawar. Lynn Thomas was a former U.S. Navy SEAL and an expert in complex emergencies. Lynn stayed in the staff house in which I was billeted. Once Lynn was in place, our guard with the 12-gauge pump shotgun stayed but the men with the automatic weapons no longer showed up. The government of Pakistan had begun cracking down on the Taliban. Everyone felt that security was fragile but improving.

I took little comfort from the guard. I knew he must have a wife and family. What could he really do to protect us? Lynn and I discussed escape plans in case the house was attacked at night. Plan "A" was to go over the back wall, carrying money, passports, CARE ID and travel permits and lay low somewhere until the sun came up. We had no Plan "B." As I had in other hot spots, I started sleeping with my escape clothes folded on my bed and my passport, money and other important papers ready to grab and go. However, there were times I thought about eating my American passport and try to claim I was another nationality if I were to be kidnapped.

The normally volatile border tribal regions had begun to percolate. We heard reports of a government helicopter being shot down, government buildings attacked and burned to the ground, government vehicles fired upon. It was dangerous. Still we focused on our mission. Then came an announcement at the UN briefing. The UN had declared the border a Class IV security area. This was bad. It meant that the UN would have no security for operations along the Afghan/Pakistan border region and that they were on orders from their headquarters that UN staff could not enter the area.

Despite the UN orders and a lack of security the UN officer leading the meeting wanted a show of hands from the audience indicating those NGOs that would be willing to work within this area with no security. Obviously the ones who raised their hands would get the lucrative contracts for work in border refugee camps. I thought the noise of the jets had distorted the words. Someone in the crowd asked for clarification. The UN representative repeated the message.

"God," I whispered to Jamal, "I wish I had a recording of that statement." We looked at each other in disbelief. Jamal shook his head and looked to the ground in thought or prayer. Sadly, the smaller, poorer NGO groups in the audience put their hands up while all the major NGOs took a giant step backwards.

Although the larger NGOs protested this UN decision, events would eliminate the potential for refugee camps inside Pakistan. The bombing began but there was no surge of refugees across the border. Instead, people scattered inside Afghanistan, moving back to their home villages, taking to the hills or heading for the traditional hiding places that had been used throughout hundreds of years of tribal warfare.

Because the Afghans did not leave their country they were not considered refugees under the formal definition of the term, but Internally Displaced People (IDP). Still, their status in life, their needs and the dangers they faced, were no different from those faced by refugees. The focus within the CARE offices soon shifted entirely to operations inside Afghanistan. This was a good thing, too. If the projected one million refugees, or even one quarter of that number, had crossed into Pakistan, with the indecisiveness and lack of control shown by the government of Pakistan and UNHCR, the results would have been catastrophic.

The bombings stimulated the Taliban to lash out at the world, and its leaders let it be known that anyone contacting the outside world from inside Afghanistan would be immediately shot as spies or traitors. CARE and other agencies needed information about IDPs and their immediate needs. CARE staff in Afghanistan understood the situation and acted heroically. Using satellite phones, couriers, and even public telephones, they got the information about IDP numbers and locations and the security situation to the Peshawar office. It was the type of unselfish heroism our military would acknowledge with medals in time of war.

CARE also began to probe the border to see if there were routes to bring supplies into the country. For one thing, the organization had good contacts among the commercial trucking companies. As in the Sudan operation in 1985, I have always been impressed that no matter what conflict area I have been in around the world, private trucking companies always seem to have the skill and daring to get the product through to the customers.

I began attending intensive planning and strategy meetings at the CARE offices aimed at expediting the movement of material and relief personnel across the border. These planning sessions were difficult for me. The CARE staff being asked to go back across the border to risk their lives were people with whom I ate and shared office space. It felt like the life-threatening tasks we were giving them rolled off our tongues too easily. Yet it did not seem to trouble my Afghan counterparts. They never hesitated or complained. I wondered about that. It troubled me and it showed.

The Afghan security officer, a stout man with a long gray beard who wore magnificent turbans and looked as if he had walked out of a Rudyard Kipling novel, summed up their bravery and my doubt succinctly.

"These are our people," he said, "and it is our responsibility to help them, not yours."

This war against the Taliban belonged to the Afghans. The exiled Afghanis in that CARE office did not avoid the responsibility toward their country.

After a particularly turbulent meeting, I walked with Jamal out of the CARE offices. I was still troubled with the fact that my friends so effortlessly accepted tasks that could get them killed. Jamal took my arm, stopped me and looked straight into my eyes. "You know, Paul," he said, "we all pray to the same God."

It was an amazing statement to me. In America, anti-Muslim

feelings were brewing as if all Muslims were responsible for what terrorist thugs had done. Were there not innocent Muslim civilians also
killed in the 9/11 attacks? Here I was on the rim of a war zone, watching Muslim men and women preparing to put themselves in harm's
way to fight our common enemy. These were men and women who
would risk their own lives to protect me. I thought how wonderful it
was that my Muslim friend would draw my attention to the God to
whom we all prayed.

The war to topple the Taliban government in Afghanistan
was relatively quick and successful. Afghan society opened up. Music
could be heard again in the streets of Kabul. Men could walk the
streets clean-shaven. Women returned to school. Kites flew freely
in the clear blue sky. While the American bombs and troops got the
press, I knew that much of the credit belonged to the Afghans themselves, Afghans I worked with in Peshawar. They carried a heavy load
for a long time in their fight against the Taliban.

I returned to the U.S. and an immediate operation in a hospital. It turned out the pain I had been walking around Pakistan
with for over a month was a double hernia. My recovery was slow. I
also changed jobs and accepted a position as a consultant with the
Center for Disease Control[77], to research and study the implications
of disaster response and planning from a public health and hospital
perspective.

My initial area of study would be the U.S. jurisdictions in the
South Pacific, an opportunity that I could hardly have imagined, a
disaster planner's dream come true. But sometimes dreams can turn
into nightmares.

---

77   The Centers for Disease Control and Prevention (CDC) is the leading national public health
     institute of the United States. The CDC is a federal agency under the Department of Health
     and Human Services that focuses national attention on developing and applying disease
     control and prevention. It especially focuses its attention on infectious disease, food borne
     pathogens, environmental health, occupational safety and health, health promotion, injury
     prevention and educational activities designed to improve the health of United States citi-
     zens.

HOI BINH AT LAST

During the life of any heart, this line keeps changing places; sometimes it is squeezed one way by exuberant evil and sometimes it shifts to allow enough space for good to flourish. One and the same human being is, at various ages, under various circumstances, a totally different human being. At times he is close to being a devil, at times to sainthood. But his name doesn't change, and to that name we ascribe the whole lot, good and evil.

—Aleksander Solzhenitsyn,
The Gulag Archipelago

Some of the most enjoyable and enlightening moments of my life were when I sat on Kara's bed reading stories to her when she was a child. She was at her most relaxed and animated then. This was when her insights and innermost thoughts came out in extraordinary ways.

As I read to her one night when she was about six years old, she asked me this: "Daddy, were you ever in a war?"

Yes, I told her, I was. I knew she had seen old pictures of me in uniform.

"Who did you fight, Daddy?" I told her I fought an army that was called the Viet Cong.

"Did you win, Daddy?"

"No," I answered, "we lost." Her head went down as if disappointed her daddy would lose at anything. She thought for a few more minutes and asked, "Then why are you still alive?"

I almost fell off the bed laughing. At the end of a war not everyone dies. But certainly no one walks away untouched or wound-free.

In May 2002 I joined three friends on a hajj of sorts. It was a journey other Nam vets had taken, returning to the land where some lost their friends, some lost their limbs, some their souls and all had lost their youth and innocence. Others had found themselves. Our story was probably not unique, but it was ours.

Our group met in Saigon. All of us were born in Upstate New York. All of us came from middle-class, Catholic families. After the war, with the usual crazy readjustments, we each went on to our own successful careers. Two of us hailed from the same hometown and knew each other before the war. Three of us served in the same platoon.

David, who was then 55, served as a Marine radio operator with the 11th Marine Regiment, 1st Marine Division. He returned to the hometown we shared and worked for the City of Auburn as an assistant civil engineer until he retired.

Pat, also 55, had been an interpreter with the 29th Civil Affairs Company in Hue City and taught school in Vietnam. He worked as a communications and marketing manager for the National Transportation and Safety Board Academy in Washington, D.C. until his retirement.

Steve, 57, had been a medic with the 29th Civil Affairs Company in Hue with Pat and me and was now a retired U.S. Navy doctor and public health consultant. He married his sweetheart from Vietnam, a Vietnamese school teacher, and they lived in Silver Spring, Maryland.

I was 53. I had also been a medic and had done two tours with the 29th. My first tour was spent in Hoi An, where David had seen action with the Marines. My second was in Hue with Steve and Pat. I worked in Atlanta as a consultant researching emergency preparedness and response in public health until my retirement in 2014. I now live in Hillsborough, NC. I was the linchpin of the group.

Pat, Steve and I had talked about returning to Vietnam for years. When I mentioned to David that a few friends and I were planning a trip there, he asked if he could come along for the ride. And so our team was formed. I jokingly labeled our trip the "They Didn't Kill Us the First Time Tour—2002."

Our journeys in Vietnam, both 30 years ago and in the summer of 2002, began with our arrival at Tan Son Nhut Airport. Unlike my first arrival, the plane came in low and slow this time rather than the abrupt wartime entrance of drop and stop. Although we had arrived at different times during the war, both Steve and I recall having flown in just after rocket attacks. The heat was the same, but now we entered a modern air-conditioned terminal. No sergeants yelled at us to hurry and get in line with all the flowery expletives they would use to make us feel at home. No departing battle-scarred "grunts" jeered at us or called us "cherry[78]."

On our first trip after arrival we had been transported on an old U.S. Army olive drab bus with wire mesh over the windows to repel hand grenades. This time we were picked up by a new air-conditioned minivan from the Windsor Hotel.

Ho Chi Minh City, or Saigon as it is still commonly called, remains the noisy, bustling metropolis it was during our war, but now modern buildings and hotels are changing the skyline. We spent our one afternoon there rediscovering the city. We sought out the aging buildings that held the history of our war, like the Continental Hotel where correspondents and writers stayed; the Rex Hotel, where officers were billeted; Le Loi Street, the turf of bar girls and street hustlers.

The building that was once the American Embassy still stood. It was here where our flag came down and evacuation helicopters circled on the day of final defeat and humiliation. The image is forever etched in every Vietnam veteran's mind.

Mr. Huong[79] arrived at the hotel as planned at 7:30 A.M. the day after our arrival. Mr. Huong was to be our tour guide. He was a friend, and had been Steve's counterpart during the war.

Unlike other GIs, civil affairs advisors like Steve, Pat and I worked directly with the civilian population. As such, we were assigned civilian counterparts to develop projects. Steve and I had an office in the Thua Thien Provincial Health Service on Le Loi Street in Hue. Steve was Huong's counterpart for the construction of the Tu Aui Maternity Infirmary Dispensary near the old U.S. airbase and 101st Airborne Division headquarters at Phu Bai.

Mr. Huong had been a district medicine chief. He was trained as a male nurse with advanced training in family planning. He was now in his late 50s—short and stocky, built like a guard or tackle on an American football team. Like many former workers in the "puppet" regime, he had been barred from working in his profession.

---

78   Cherry is military jargon for someone who has not seen combat.

79   This is a fictitious name to protect his identity.

His children were not allowed to attend school. He earned about $50 a month teaching English. This was the untold price for having been on the losing side of the war. Mr. Huong jumped at the chance to be our tour guide as he would see Steve and me again and pick up some extra money.

Saigon always was a noisy city and I did not care to stay. It was not where my story was and I yearned to go to where my life had been so dramatically altered. We also wanted to enjoy the countryside. The first leg of our travels brought us to the scenic mountain resort of Da Lat, then the seaside resort of Nha Trang. Both places are beautiful in their own right. We enjoyed the mountain air in Da Lat. There we visited the summer home of the last emperor of Vietnam, Bao Dai. The art deco style of architecture of the emperor's home seemed out of place in this Asian land—but then again, Bao Dai was out of place, also.

Nha Trang brought us the calm of the South China Sea. We took a half-day boat ride to an island resort, ate seafood that we picked out for our dinner live from fishing nets, and wondered at the striking contrast between Da Lat and Nha Trang.

Then we headed north, up the infamous and scenic Highway 1. During our war, ambushes along this route were common. The Viet Cong were the toll collectors after dusk, and they exacted a heavy price in American and Vietnamese lives. In 2002, Highway 1 was scenic but still miserable, in a state of continuous repair and disrepair. Small sections of the road are smooth and drivable while larger sections, mile after mile, are under construction. All the labor was being done by hand.

The morning was clear, sunny and pleasantly warm. Soon we would be overtaken by the intense heat of the day. We drove north along the coast, enjoying dramatic views of the cliffs, the South China Sea and the bright blue sky. It was hard to imagine the sheer terror produced on this same strip of asphalt so many years before. It was hard for me to picture the war in my mind, but the images came eventually: the long military convoys raising clouds of dust in the air, the constant whump, whump, whump of the rotor blades of our guardian helicopters overhead, the occasional whine of artillery, the clatter of small-arms fire. You would often spot jets streaking in from aircraft carriers off the coast with their heavy bomb loads heading for some inland targets.

The peacefulness of our ride and the postcard-perfect scenery was almost disconcerting. Vietnam had been just as scenic back then, too. But during the war we looked at the landscape through a different lens. We watched for possible ambush sites and the movement of the people for anything suspicious. We'd scour the road for signs of land mines and booby traps. Though we traveled the same roads in 2002, I saw beauty, not fear and destruction.

This was something we needed to witness, that life goes on, that people can transcend the horrors of war. Vietnam had seen some hard times after our war. The country had invaded and occupied Cambodia and had been attacked by China. It had suffered from drought and floods, initially from poor development policies. While living under the communist regime could not have been easy for many people, America did everything it could through economic embargo and propaganda to make the Hanoi regime look like the biggest threat to world peace since Hitler or Stalin. But for most of the population, the American War, as the Vietnam War was called by locals, was behind them. Most of the population were not even born when the war ended. What was currently in vogue politically did not matter much. The people farmed, fished and lived life as they had for centuries. And they were at peace, or Hoa Binh.

I had my own opinions as to whether or not Vietnam was better or worse off after the fall of Saigon, but these opinions seemed trivial in the van that day. I did not see good or bad; black or white. I saw only the continuum of life. A man plowing his rice field wearing only shorts and a rice hat, women trotting along the roads barefoot wearing red and green sari style dress and chewing betel nuts with heavy stacks of vegetables on each shoulder, lorries loaded with commodities to be sold in the next town and huge black and grey water buffalo basking in tropical green and blue ponds with Vietnamese children lying or standing on their backs. The conversation in the van was light. There was little talk of the war and how we had experienced it. We talked a great deal on the Vietnamese concept of road construction. Mostly, though, we stared and commented on the view of this vibrant country that had drawn us all back.

We were anxious to get back to what the military would call our areas of operation (AO). We thought we could make Hoi An in a day but we were wrong. The road was not in good shape and the distance was longer than we had anticipated. We spent the night in

Quang Ngai and proceeded the next day to Hoi An.

Just before reaching Hoi An, we stopped at a Champa ruin near My Son[80], a UNESCO Heritage site, in Quang Nam Province. The young girl who acted as our tour guide at the site spoke excellent English and provided a thorough explanation of the Kingdom of Champa. She was also able to give us a fairly technical description of the ordnance and explosives that had been dropped on the site by American planes. There was something about her Western dress that caught my eye. She was wearing a bright orange sun hat. The name on the brim read "Curley's Restaurant."

I pointed this out to David, and we both had a good laugh. Curley's Restaurant was—and is—one of Auburn, New York's favorite watering holes. Where she got the hat or if it came from "our" Curley's we will never know, but seeing the name signified to us how small this world is that we inhabit.

South of Hoi An is the area where David had been stationed at a fire base. Finding the location was a great deal more difficult than finding where Pat, Steve and I had been billeted. We lived and worked in the cities of Hue and Hoi An. We knew the exact streets of our base and offices. David's firebase was situated in a remote area. Fire bases were generally sited on hills with good fields of fire but away from major roads and villages. All we knew was that David had been based south of Hoi An.

He had a few grainy photographs that showed hills and a few mountain peaks but little else to go on. We searched the area where David thought his base might have been. We were able to piece together an approximate location by looking at several different photos and triangulating our position. But the best we could do was an approximation. We did not even know if there still would be a road to a long-gone, isolated firebase. Thirty years brings a great deal of change.

David seemed satisfied with what we were able to locate, yet I was disappointed that we could not give him more.

David was the most energetic about engaging with the Vietnamese people. He had never had the chance to mingle with many civilians when he was a soldier. He reflected what I observed as a

---

80 Mỹ Sơn is a Hindu temple complex built by the Champa, a united kingdom of various tribes of the Cham ethnic group. The Champa ruled South and Central Vietnam from the 3rd century until 1832. Upon their succession, Champa kings would build temple complexes at Mỹ Sơn.

civil affairs advisor during the war, that the grunts only saw the camp
followers and not the real citizens of Vietnam. Steve, Pat and I had
worked with the Vietnamese during our tours of duty. This type of
contact was all new for David and he reveled in the interactions.

It was a wonder to watch David discovering the people and
culture of Vietnam. When the rest of us took an afternoon siesta, he
would continue on with his own individual tour. After a big evening
meal of Vietnamese fare and "333" beer we would head off to bed
but David would charge out again to explore, to engage people, and
move in a land that was once most unfriendly to him and had now
embraced us in peace.

David's enthusiasm was contagious. It brought new light to
what Vietnam had become for us.

Hoi An[81] is considered one of the oldest cities in Vietnam.
According to the Lonely Planet's Vietnam guide book, Hoi An was a
"bustling seaport" during the Champa Dynasty from the 2nd through
the 10th centuries. There are records of Persian and Arab merchants
sailing into Hoi An to barter and trade. This city was my personal
lonely planet. It was here I learned the meaning of terror, what fear
felt like deep in my gut. My first mortar attacks, the deadly night of
evacuating the half-soldier, the torture at the Hoi An political prison,
happened on the ground where I stood today.

Hoi An in 1969 was the beginning of my metamorphosis. It
was my greatest real-world education, a living classroom of torture
and terror that was mixed with camaraderie, enculturation and my
own hope to do better. And now it had turned into a quaint tourist
destination.

We arrived in Hoi An late in the day. The hotel Mr. Huong
had booked for us looked very familiar to me as I walked in the front
entrance. It was of French colonial style and had obviously been
recently refurbished. The rooms were pleasant, clean and spacious,
and there was a swimming pool to cool off in during the day.

We went to our rooms early. I woke before dawn, anxious
to explore the city that had drastically changed me. I think my soul
imploded in Hoi An. It was where I lost my ability to cry. The emo-

---

81   Once a major Southeast Asian trading post in the 16th and 17th centuries, the seaside town
     Hoi An is basically a living museum featuring a unique mixture of East and West in the
     form of its old-town architecture. Hoi An has been successful in preserving and restoring its
     charming roots and was declared a UNESCO World Heritage site in December 1999. Read
     more at: http://www.vietnam-guide.com/hoi-an/hoi-an-old-town.htm?cid=ch:OTH:oo1

tions that I first experienced in Hoi An would become magnified during my second tour in Hue. Those emotions were intense. My traveling companion, Steve, has often said that "after war you spend the rest of your life trying to match the intensity of it."

I walked out of the hotel early that morning. I went alone, not wanting to share my personal Vietnam rapprochement. None of the others had been in my compound. The experience of finding it would mean nothing to them.

After pausing, I went through the hotel's front gate. I walked across the busy street, turned and faced the hotel. It had been a long time and I tried to orient myself. To my left was the road out of town. Behind me was the port. I looked back across the street, through the bustling morning traffic, at my hotel. This felt familiar. Flashes of old photographs passed through my mind. Vietnamese men in traditional dress carrying colorful banners, another one of the many "fake" pro-government rallies staged in 1969. In the backdrop I could see the Quang Nam province headquarters building. As I stood there, my mind came back to the present. The same building stood before me: our hotel.

Quang Nam Provincial Headquarters Hoi An, 1969.

This realization was a shock. The new regime had turned the old province headquarters into a tourist hotel. It meant that I was very near my old compound. I looked to my left again. My headquarters and where I slept, MAC/V Team 3, would have been on the corner abutting the Province Headquarters. I looked but saw nothing.

I slowly walked to my left, crossing the street again. As I approached the corner I saw that a park now stood on the site of my compound. It was verdant and peaceful, filled with students studying, people exercising and reading, children playing. This place was the base of my nightmares. The place from where I ventured out to care for the blown apart half-soldier, the tortured children, the starving refugees was now a park, a place of life and laughter.

Former Quang Nam Provincial Headquarters, Hoi An
now a government hotel, 2002.

I entered, half-expecting to feel the rumble of military vehicles and hear the squawking of radios from the tactical operations center (TOC), the sound of rock n roll from an enlisted men's hooch, and feel the dust, sweat and fear. But there was nothing but peace in that place.

A children's ride caught my eye. It consisted of American-style military vehicles going around and around on a metal track. Metal tanks, planes and helicopters pursued one another on a ride to nowhere. It was somehow so fitting. It's the ride we'd been on over 30 years ago, only some of us had never gotten off.

I did not share much of this experience with my friends. There was not much to say; or maybe too much to say. I had returned to confront the past but the past was now a place where children congregated before going to school. The past had moved on.

Children's' playground at the former site of the MAC/V compound in Hoi An.

The next stop on our hajj was to be the ancient imperial capital of Hue, in Thua Thien Province. Pat, Steve and I had met there in 1970 and developed a friendship that is hard to explain to someone who is not a veteran. That bonding can surpass family ties. Possibly we would not have given each other the time of day in the "real world." But thrown together in the life-and-death intensity of war does something to forge a bond that can be strong and lasting. You accept people as they are in those circumstances; you understand a person's weaknesses and what makes him different from you, but you concentrate on his strengths and enjoy his differences. If you are smart you realize that each individual in your platoon has something to offer. In your desire for self and group survival you embrace those strengths.

On the way to Hue we drove through Da Nang a few hours to the north. Mr. Huong suggested we stop in Da Nang for the night but we were anxious to continue on to Hue. So, we continued up Highway 1 and across the Hai Van Pass. Hai van means "sea clouds" in Vietnamese. The pass goes through the Trung Son Mountain range that noses out into the South China Sea. It is truly a breathtaking ride. The road winds through a mountain pass along sheer drop-off cliffs with views of the sea and pristine deserted beaches.

In 1970 this pass was both beautiful and frightening. Viet Cong would often conduct ambushes from the high peaks along the pass. There was not much that could be done if you were caught in an ambush except to keep driving through the attack and hope you didn't get hit or go over the cliffs. Today there was no such fear about getting shot at. As we drove I spotted a small cove down on the shore where a German NGO had operated a hospital for lepers. At the peak of the pass there still stood a series of massive French bunkers, relics from the First Indochina War. As we cleared the pass, we could see the long white sand beach that runs toward Hue. On the northern end of the pass sits the village of Long Co[82] a picturesque village on a small barrier island. The steeple of a Catholic church rises from the center of the village.

In an hour we were on the outskirts of Hue. As we approached the city, the huge Notre Dame Cathedral greeted us. A large statue of Jesus Christ still stood in the foreground of the church, his hands outstretched, and welcoming visitors. If Hoi An was where my soul descended into darkness, Hue was the site of my rebirth. It was here I reached my zenith. In 1970, I was 22 years old and I felt unbeatable.

In Hue, during the war, those of us in my platoon spent our days trying to help the Vietnamese and our nights engaged in serious conversations about war, politics and life after Nam. It was the movie M*A*S*H personified but on steroids: a small group of cocky Americans fighting a war within a war. As America bombed and strafed for democracy, we also fought to improve the lives of civilians and refugees.

To locate the old MAC/V compound where Steve, Pat and I were housed would be fairly easy. Steve and I had been back to Hue since 1970 and had visited the compound. It was across the river from the Citadel and a few blocks behind Le Loi Street near the Provincial Health offices. Steve and I worked in those offices in 1970. But we were in for some surprises.

---

82   This scenic village is a good stop over place for a lunch or even a day with a beautiful beach to swim at or the village houses and the church to explore Vietnamese lifestyle.

Former Doezema MAC/V compound, 1992.

Former Doezema MAC/V compound 2002.

Mr. Huong brought us first to the government-run hotel where we would be staying. Again, the area looked vaguely familiar. It was getting late as we checked in. The place was clean but Spartan. The staff spoke English and was extremely helpful and polite. We settled into our rooms and agreed to meet once we freshened up.

Leaving the hotel with the others I first found it difficult to get my bearings. I had last been in Hue in 1991. It was amazing how much things had changed in the interim. Within a few minutes, though, Steve and I knew we were close to MAC/V. We simply had to walk out of our hotel, turn right, walk one block and there it was. Our hotel actually butted up against the back of the old MAC/V compound.

The MAC/V Team 18 compound in Hue had formerly been a French hotel. At the corner there used to be a huge bunker that covered both streets. We entered the compound from a side street. There was another bunker at the gated entrance where 30 years earlier an MP would direct us to clear our weapons. As we went through the gate, there stood the two-story L-shaped hotel.

In 1970, the hotel housed the officers' quarters and mess hall. Behind the hotel were two rows of what we called hooch's, semi-permanent screened–in barracks made of cement and wood that housed the enlisted ranks. The compound also had a small PX where we could buy toiletries, canned goods and beer. There was a basketball court, an enlisted men's, NCO and officers bar, a chapel and a dispensary.

The compound we were now facing had seen better days. The last coat of paint was probably pre-1975. The cement was riddled with cracks and the compound was dirty. There was no one to stop us at the main gate. Mr. Huong was not with us so we simply walked in, stopping to take pictures. There were some Vietnamese nearby who seemed to be a little perturbed by our visit. We passed the officers' billets and went directly to where hooch #19, the Civil Affairs hooch, would have been. We came instead to a fence and found ourselves staring at the back wall of our hotel.

We looked at each other and laughed at the irony. Our hotel was placed directly over where the enlisted men's hooch's used to be. We were sleeping in the same spot that we had slept in more than 30 years ago. The next day we learned that the compound itself was now the billet of the North Vietnamese military. The billets now held soldiers wearing different uniforms but ironically the compound continued in the same function. I was amazed we were not arrested, considering that we had strolled through a military area taking pictures. We had inadvertently infiltrated a North Vietnamese installation!

Having located the old MAC/V compound, we began our

quest to see some of the other sites we wanted to focus on in our short time in Hue. For any traveler, Hue City is another tourist delight. It straddles the Perfume River. It is a lush green emerald with French-style architecture and broad tree-lined boulevards. Hue University in Vietnam had the same reputation as the University of California at Berkeley had in the U.S. Both were known for high-quality education but they were also known for graduating free thinkers and outspoken radicals. Hue University had graduated some of the best and brightest of the military and political intellectuals who would end up fighting on both sides of our war.

We made full use of the time we had in Hue. We visited the six-tiered Thien Mu Pagoda on the Perfume River. We toured the tombs of the ancient emperors outside the city. In 1970, several of the tombs were under control of the VC and NVA and could not be visited.

A trip to Hue would not be complete without a visit to the famous Citadel that once housed the Imperial Court of Vietnam. The citadel had been constructed in 1804 by Emperor Gia Long. It houses an incredible array of Mandarin-style architecture and history.

During the Tet Offensive in 1968 the Citadel was the site of some of the most intense hand-to-hand urban combat of the war. As many as 10,000 NVA and VC troops took Hue City[83]. They held the Citadel for more than 3½ weeks and flew their flag on the 37-meter high Flag Tower to show the world that they were in charge of the area. It was only through direct frontal assault that U.S. Marine and Army units, supported by air strikes, tanks and artillery, retook the Citadel.

I arrived in Hue as a civil affairs advisor two years after that horrific battle. At that time, much of the Citadel remained in ruins. Indeed, much of Hue still showed the bullet and fragmentation scars of battle. Our forces were still uncovering mass graves of civilian casualties. In 1970, few people went to the Citadel. But I used to drive over there when I was having a bad "war day." I would find a place to park my three-quarter-ton Army truck, and walk the gardens and narrow streets. There was a calmness and serenity there, a place where I could find solace from a war about which I had come to have major doubts.

Following our visit to the Citadel we sought out the high

---

83   For an excellent account of the fighting in Hue City during the 1968 Tet offensive read Mark Bowden's account "*Hue 1968: A Turning Point of the American War in Vietnam*"

school where Pat had taught English. It was a French style, gated, red brick school on Le Loi Street along the Perfume River. Because we had dropped off Mr. Huong for the afternoon, we did not have anyone who spoke Vietnamese. Classes were not in session and the guard would not let us onto the grounds. His reluctance was not due to any anti-American sentiment but because of regulations. How many schools in the U.S. would allow strange men to walk around on their property after hours? Pat had to settle with looking at his former school from outside. It was enough.

Pat, Steve and I had no real battlegrounds to visit. At least there were no battlegrounds in the classic sense. My daily battle, and that of many in my platoon, was to save or improve the lives of the Vietnamese.

While my enemies included the Viet Cong and the NVA, they were not the ones highest on the list. For me the real killers were those who betrayed the trust of the Vietnamese people, the war profiteers and those who were hypocritical to our own principles. The VC and NVA were trying to kill me but the hypocrites and those making money off the lucrative government contracts had set us all up for a grand fall.

The war was personal for most of us. We worked, laughed and cried with the Vietnamese. Many soldiers used terms like "gooks," "dinks," "zipper heads" and "slopes" in order to de-humanize the enemy. It made killing easier. For civil affairs advisors it was different. Respect and cultural sensitivity was the mandate for our work. It is an easy mandate, for this is what all humans should do.

We worked alongside the Vietnamese. They were friends, colleagues and associates. We knew their families and their joys and hardships. It was the gift and the curse of the double-edged sword I had first became aware of as a young army advisor. I would often have dreams that I was a child looking in the window of my family home, a family I would never be totally part of again. My strength and my Achilles' heel was that I saw the war and life through the eyes of the Vietnamese and, during the war, I did not like very much of what I saw.

Over the course of a long dinner, we looked at the American effort in Vietnam through the eyes of our guide, Mr. Huong, and Mr. Keim, who had been the number two person at Provincial Health when Steve and I were advisors there. He had an effervescent smile that lit up a room and an advanced degree in public health from a university in Europe. He, like the director of public health in Thua Thien Province, Dr. Do Van Minh, never believed that America would desert Vietnam. Now here we sat on a hot evening in Hue City in his small apartment with him and his wife.

Both Mr. Keim and his wife had aged a great deal. He had major health problems. He was not permitted to work in public health after the fall of Saigon. His dedication to public health and the people of Vietnam was forgotten in the new political order. He lived and would die in poverty, yet he did not talk with anger or hatred of the new regime. In fact he did not mention it at all. We reminisced about the old times. We shared photographs and stories. We talked about Dennis Barker, my civilian boss, who had died in 1991, and Dr. Minh, who went insane under captivity.

We hear a great deal about how Americans suffered during the Vietnam War—our dead, our POWs, our mentally and physically wounded. Little is mentioned about what the Vietnamese, Cambodians and Laotians lost. Like Mr. Keim, many Vietnamese went along with the corrupt South Vietnamese regime because they believed that America, the land of freedom and opportunity, would never leave them. We could be trusted. But we had left our fairness and democracy at home. In Vietnam, we were not trustworthy. America paid the price in wasted and lost lives. But the loss of Vietnamese, Cambodian and Laotian lives, homeland and culture dwarfs our sacrifices.

It was bittersweet seeing our two counterparts. How I loved seeing them again. These were the men who helped mold my life and guide me through Vietnamese culture and public health planning. To show our honor we brought them treats and some money but this hardly compensates for how America ruined these men, their careers and their families' lives.

The evening ended quietly. We departed from Mr. Keim knowing that we would probably never see this kind man again.

The next day David and Pat had to catch a plane to Saigon, so Steve and I said our goodbyes. I sometimes think that Vietnam is mostly about goodbyes. Steve and I continued on with Mr. Huong to the last stops in our journey to the past.

Steve and I had been responsible for the construction of two public health dispensaries while we worked in Hue. They were actually called Maternity-Infirmary Dispensaries or MIDs. Their function was to provide public health services to a number of villages or to isolated areas. I was responsible for the An Duong village MID. Steve helped build the Tu Aui clinic on the road to Phu Bai, near the old 101st airborne base.

Original An Duong MID in 2002.

We went to my village first. I had been there in 1991 and I felt confident we could find it quickly. The trip to An Duong took us east of Hue toward the coast. In 1970, I would drive to the Tam My port and go across to the barrier island on converted US Navy landing craft. In 2002 a bridge had been built to connect the narrow island to the mainland.

As Steve, Mr. Huong and I drove over the bridge, the landscape looked barren. The bridge had brought progress and progress had overcome this barrier island and the quaint little fishing villages along its dunes were gone. The road was no longer sand but asphalt. This sandy strip of land now housed ship-building yards, oil storage tanks and areas where small seagoing ships were berthed. It was difficult to find a familiar landmark or a village but I did spot a large ornate graveyard on a dune that I seemed to recognize.

Then we passed the An Duong Dispensary. I almost missed it

because it was in such disrepair and the village that surrounded it was all but gone. The MID was a long one-story building with fading pink paint. I remembered calling the facility "the Bowling Alley" because it was so big. It was apparent that it had not been used in some time. I recalled that Mr. Keim had told me at dinner that the MID had been damaged by a typhoon several years before and had not been used since.

The MID was testimony to the unstoppable march of nature and time. The typhoon had washed sand deep inside the building. The walls were falling apart. The ceiling had collapsed. The only utility the building served now was as shelter for animals.

A little girl who stopped to look at us told us there was a new dispensary down the road. We went to investigate. This dispensary was being run by a young Vietnamese doctor who greeted us at the door. Here was a man who projected the energy and future of Vietnam. He seemed very engaged in his work and about caring for the people in the surrounding hamlets.

This doctor verified what I knew about the dispensary I helped build in 1970. The dispensary transcended the war. It was used as a dispensary until 1985. It then became a community center, and for a time was a training center used by a United Nations agency. I did not feel so bad that it took a typhoon to finally end what I had started with a group of Vietnamese villagers.

We bid adieu to the doctor and headed for the MID that Steve had helped build. Tu Aui was on the road south of Hue back towards the Hai Van Pass. It took us a while to locate it. The march of time and development compacted the area where the MID was located in a maze of old and new construction. Through the help of Mr. Huong we finally found the building.

It was now being used as a dormitory for nurses. As we stood staring at the building, unsure what to do next, a woman approached. She questioned Mr. Huong about who we were and what we were doing. She thought she recognized Steve. Fate was kind to us. The woman had been a midwife when the Tu Aui dispensary was a working facility. She left us for a short time, returning with a woman in her mid-20s. The older midwife said that this young woman had been born at the MID Steve helped build. We could not have asked for a greater reward to mark the end of our journey.

Former Tui Ai midwife standing with woman born at the MID.

The MIDs at An Duong and Tu Aui transcended the war in Vietnam. Both were glowing embers in a black universe of misguided foreign policy and government corruption. For me, it was humbling to re-visit them. It was not a reflection of what "I" did but rather a reflection of what a group of people from different cultures did for the health and welfare of a community. I knew that my initial development model still rang true, well after the guns were silenced: that people from divergent cultures and backgrounds could and should come together as partners for the common good.

These sites proved to me what I have believed from the very start: public health should never be used as a political tool. Relief and humanitarian programs should never be managed by those who use them for political gain. But when public health and humanitarian efforts are pursued purely and with the support of the people they serve, then the projects will thrive, often beyond their original intent.

I had returned to Vietnam with my brothers-in-arms searching for something—resolution, perhaps, or closure, or forgiveness. As a soldier, there was certainly much I had lost, including my naiveté and my blind trust in our government. There was much that had haunted me and perhaps needed to be exorcised: the ghosts of a half-soldier, tortured civilians, starving refugees. But I found that what I had lost

I could do without, and what I needed to exorcise was there but lingering on the periphery of my life, not as threatening. Perhaps I rediscovered a country and a people who had moved forward after our war, more so than most Americans had.

I could leave Vietnam with an internal peace, my own Hoa Binh. In my life since the Vietnam War, I have tried to help others and tried my best to keep faith with my inner self. I have been an educated voter. I have always supported our troops, no matter what quagmire our government puts them in. I have learned so much from some very powerful individuals.

Like the Vietnamese rice farmer who talked with me about the limits of American politics. In Sudan, a Belgian nurse taught me about compassion and going the extra mile to save a child. In Pakistan, I learned about God from a Muslim.

Looking back on my life there is little I would change. My wife and daughter give me my heart, soul and reason to live. I have wonderful friendships, people who are compassionate, funny, and who sometimes even laugh at my jokes, who are from diverse political and religious beliefs and cultures and who always seem to be there when I need them. I hope my daughter, in the course of her life, will be able to say the same thing on the paths she will take.

EPILOGUE:
TAPESTRY OF MY LIFE

My life has been a tapestry of rich and royal hue
An everlasting vision of the ever-changing view.
A wondrous, woven magic in bits of blue and gold
A tapestry to feel and see, impossible to hold.

—Carole King,
Tapestry

My tapestry of life is so rich, vibrant and fascinating to me that it's hard to believe I was fortunate enough to have lived it.

Its brightness comes not just from the exotic places I've visited, but the people I encountered along the way, many of them valiantly and silently fighting for daily survival while maintaining their human dignity. They were my human luminous light houses in my journey through the dark, cold frightening places in my life's journey. They kept me focused and true to the human spirit.

I see on the tapestry images of a four-year-old child battling all night against cholera in the Kassala refugee camp in Eastern Sudan and winning; my An Duong village clinic construction committee making a two-hour journey over a dangerous road during the Vietnam War to give me going-away presents; my best Iranian friend in Iran risking arrest by the new Islamic government after the fall of the Shah to air freight my personal possessions to me in America.

Then there was the doctor with the Thai Ministry of Public Health who always introduced me at every meeting as his "mentor;" the copper bracelet received for marking a mine field for a village's safety in South Sudan during the civil war; the African-American I met in West Africa who has returned to his home country in Liberia under threat of death to help his motherland in its fight for democracy and freedom; the little Kosovar girl who came to the Camp Hope refugee camp in southern Albania during the Kosovo war, knowing she was safe from being raped "because the Americans were there."

And what provides the richness and texture of this fabric are the men and woman I have worked with in the field. These deep threads include host country government leadership; local and international NGO field staff who put cross-cultural development above ego and power, at the risk of their own lives; the highly qualified local men and women who supported the United Nations and local and international NGOs. They are underpaid, overworked and do their duty in the worst and sometimes most dangerous conditions. They arrive home at airports unnoticed for their heroism.

These are the ground troops and unsung heroes in the continuous fight to save people's lives, the battle for human rights and the dignity of the human race, epitomized by a Muslim colleague who comforted me after seeing me upset about staff decisions that would put our staff in "harm's way" by telling me "we all pray to the same God;" a supervisor who was brave enough to send a cable to a US president telling him the truth of the US Indochinese Refugee Program only to be fired for honesty; my USAID mentor counseling me when I begin to realize the ugly truth about the Vietnam War; a Belgian WHO doctor telling me during the Vietnam War that my sole duty as a public health advisor is to save only one life, knowing I would save more.

The tapestry is strengthened by the way it is made. The tight knots in the stitching are formed by my work ethics and love of country given me by my blue collar family, the support and encouragement provided me by my wife and daughter, my friends from elementary school, high school, college and Vietnam provided me with a sense of unity and bonding. SUNY Brockport and the University of Michigan gave me the analytical and programmatic tools to contribute to my profession.

The people of Vietnam and other "developing world" locations gave me the sensitivity and humility to care for my fellow human beings, the endurance to persevere during the worst circumstances, the structure to listen, learn and the strength of honest friendships.

Yes, there are some dark places in the tapestry, representing the ghosts of sad and sometimes horrific events. And there are stains that remind me of hate, ego and betrayal. None of them can be washed away, nor should they be. They too are learning experiences, sometimes more so than the good times in my life. These marks exemplify hard-fought experience—and in the name of public duty, they can't be forgotten. The dark places and ugly stains mark the cloth like military medals, and without them the journey and learning experiences would be far less than I have received.

The first stain came in Vietnam when a senior US government official, finding out I was heading home to attend college, told me to "demonstrate for the war instead of against it," since he had grown rich because of it.

But it was my last ten years of service at CDC and CARE that truly serve as a microcosm for the marks that stain body and soul. In the late 1990s CARE established what amounted to a discrimination policy against white males and females, and I was one of its victims. At the time I had been Deputy Director of the CARE/USA Emergency Group for five years. My boss, the director of the Emergency Group, was retiring. I applied for this position just after the 9/11 terrorist attacks and before departing for Pakistan but upon my return CARE refused to even interview me. It was a move that shocked a lot of staff, since over my five years at CARE I had been "acting" director almost 40% of the time due to the travels of my boss. The person hired as the Director of the CARE Emergency Group had no emergency response or training and his previous job was that of a car salesman in Atlanta. The successful reverse discrimination law suit I filed in US District Court Northern District of Georgia; Atlanta Division (Civil Action File No 1:03-CV-0061) more than proved my case.

Many former and current staff members supported what I did. When Paul Barker, my supervisor in Pakistan, found out that my yearly evaluation did not include work on the Pakistan/Afghan border, he wrote to my new boss: "First of all I would like to give Paul Giannone credit for bravery. For any American to get on a plane so soon after 9/11 and fly to, of all places, Peshawar, Pakistan, requires a high level of bravery and commitment." He later went on to state "Paul G. regularly attend UNHCR meetings. He drafted a document which would have laid the ground work for CARE collaboration with UNHCR in the event of a major refugee influx. And he did all of these things while suffering a double hernia."

This information was never put in my yearly evaluation to upgrade it.

There is still hope for CARE. I still tell people that CARE field staff are some of the best in the world. CARE had major problems with senior staff, especially at the director level. On April 19, 2015 Michelle Nunn was selected as the President of CARE. This is a person I totally respect and have politically voted for when she ran for the US Senate. I pray she can bring the humanity, trust and compassion back to the headquarters staff.

At CDC, my education on the realities of the politics of humanitarian work continued. A doctor known for abusive behavior toward staff members (including myself) triggered several letters of protest to upper management. Despite that, he was promoted.

A CDC staff person took a weapon into a CDC facility which is against federal law, and later threatened suicide and suggested a willingness to take other staff along. This individual was not fired, disregarding the rights and the protection of those working near his cube.

During the height of the Ebola crisis CDC was desperate for qualified staff to deploy to West Africa. I was asked to deploy immediately because of my emergency response experience in Sierra Leone and Guinea and a long history of emergency work in Africa but the request was rescinded when it was recalled I was on the CDC "naughty list" for asking difficult non-status quo questions. Other qualified staff were not deployed for the same reason. Against HHS deployment policies, many of the CDC staff who were sent to West Africa had no experience in Africa, let alone West Africa. Later a CDC senior staff apologized in the media for the cross-cultural mistakes made by these novices. People in Africa and other international locations have their lives put at risk when CDC deploys unqualified staff. Retrospectively, CDC has documented that West Africans were contaminated with Ebola because those sent to help them had no knowledge or burial customs[84]. Ironically CDC was able to publish papers on this issue without truly acknowledging their potential contribution to the death by deploying unqualified staff.

In my last two years at CDC I witnessed a microcosm that I had documented in my 40 year career. It was the answer to the questions our citizens often ask "Why does US foreign policy often fail?" It was the pattern of US foreign policy failure based on ego, power and

---

84   Curran KG, Gibson, JJ, et al. "Cluster of Ebola Virus Disease Linked to a Single Funeral — Moyamba District, Sierra Leone, 2014." *MMWR Morb Mortal Wkly Rep 2016;65:202–205.* Centers for Disease Control and Prevention, 2016.

money that I had first seen in Vietnam and witnessed again in Iran and numerous other countries. The deployment of unqualified staff. The fabrication of American "success" stories to please the budget process of a US Congress. The designation of unqualified staff as leaders who disdained any recommendations from junior staff. The multiple CDC lab accidents and staff complaints of safety. My whistleblower disclosure had over 31 external references of staff pleading for help or scientific professionals sounding a word of caution because they felt CDC staff and the citizens near CDC facilities were in danger. A quote from CDC employee Pam Gilbertz (AJC 3/27/2015) and head of the CDC union said it best: "How are we supposed to protect the public, if we can't even protect ourselves? Once you're identified as a troublemaker, your career is shot at CDC."

Two other anonymous quotes published in the Lancet Medical Journal (3/3/2012) state: "CDC is no longer a science based organization.... Skills, training and experience are secondary when making important decisions" and "An object evaluation of this center and its activities are long overdue, in fact, an in-depth congressional investigation might be in order."

And then, the ultimate betrayal of the whistleblower process concerning my disclosure (OSC File No: DI-14-3809)—the Office of Inspector General at the US Department of Health and Human Services determined that CDC could investigate itself. Not surprisingly, the accused found themselves "not guilty," while staff and citizens lives remained endangered.

Forty years of emotion came back to me at that news. Once again, I could see myself pleading and on the edge of tears in a Saigon hotel room in 1970 with my friend and mentor Dennis Baker over the death of US Marines not far away, while the rich government officials dined in protected luxury realizing that the policies based on lies and treachery would not end with that conflict. The Vietnam foreign policy experience would be "exported" to other countries and imbedded in our federal agencies. And then it happened again in Singapore as the US administration twisted history to make the North Vietnamese the sole creator of all the suffering of the "boat people," and when I saw a US consular officer fail to report facts to the US Embassy in Tehran to protect his career. Yes the American government *is* capable of pursuing policies that were not only harmful to the citizens of this world but threaten the lives of American citizens.

My stories of the move of refugees in Vietnam, the Iran debacle and the boat people stand as well documented statements on what the American government has become. Can we be surprised at the fiascos of Afghanistan and Iraq? Can we be surprised at the type of egocentric leadership we have today in the White House?

At the end of my life's journey I am fulfilled with what I have personally accomplished in my profession but I would not be true to my own spirit if I did not admit there is some disappointment in the trek. The vision I had as I came out of the rice fields in May 1971; my personal "Holy Grail" of a changed and humanitarian US foreign policy based on our Constitution and Bill of Rights, has not been realized. The US government does not learn from its mistakes. With President Trump, America has voted the country back into the prejudice and saber rattling years of the 40s, 50s and 60s.

There is a glimmer of hope. I still believe Americans are stronger than this. The answers are still there, documented in books and the press. Books like "The Pentagon Papers;" "Winners and Losers;" "Fiasco;" "Fire in the Lake: The Vietnamese and the Americans in Vietnam;" "Reclaiming Democracy" and "Drift." All give insights on why our democracy and policies fail and what to do to correct them.

In the last chapter of her book "Drift," Rachel Maddow's provides ideas on how to change. But I fear those in power in America will do nothing about it. In the end I will cling to my truth and continue to support the humanitarians and military personnel who do the good work, risk their lives and save lives at field level.

So there sits my proud tapestry of life. It is the yin and yang of 40 years of public health and emergency response work. In the end I believe the good will outweigh the bad, and those who do good work will win out. But the road ahead will be dangerous and difficult and it can only be accomplished if Americans get off their couches and get involved to save the country.

There are beacons of hope off in the distance rising from the soil. The "Me Too" movement, the "March for Our Lives," "Black Lives Matter," and the heroic thumbs down vote to stop the repeal of Obama Care by the late senator and war hero John McCain are hopeful signs of America reawakening to the realities of our political and social world.

In the waning light of a wonderful career and life's journey I know now that it is time to pass the baton. I pass this baton of hope and service to my daughter Kara, a public health graduate student at Emory, and any other young or old students of public health and emergency response and the grass roots movements mentioned who believe in the American democracy, are willing to open their hearts and minds, ask the hard questions, learn and take action.

It is their turn to create their own tapestry and become the doers and teachers for our democracy and those in need.

"You who are on the road
Must have a code that you can live by
And so become yourself
Because the past is just a good-bye.

Teach your children well,
Their father's hell did slowly go by,
And feed them on your dreams
The one they picks, the one you'll know by.

Don't you ever ask them why,
if they told you, you will cry,
So just look at them and sigh
And know they love you.

And you, of tender years,
Can't know the fears that your elders grew by,
And so please help them with your youth,
They seek the truth before they can die.

—Graham Nash,
Teach Your Children

THE AUTHOR

Paul J. Giannone retired from the Centers for Disease Control on September 24, 2014, having worked in international and domestic public health and emergency response for over 40 years, covering more than 35 countries. In 2017 Paul and his wife, Kate, fulfilled a dream by moving back to Hillsborough, North Carolina. Their daughter, Kara, is attending Emory University and, like her dad, will receive a Masters of Public Health (MPH) degree in May 2019.

The Giannones enjoy the small-town atmosphere of Hillsborough as well as the cultural and recreational events in nearby Durham, Chapel Hill, and Raleigh. They also enjoy golfing, gourmet cooking, the North Carolina beaches, travel, and reading. What Paul cherishes most is being with Kate, Kara and the many friends he has collected throughout the world. He is famous for saying "I never give up on my friends."

Paul looks forward to organizing the 20,000 slides he took over 40 years, continuing to write and being publically active.

Connect with the author at:
www.paulgiannone.com

9 781611 533347